THE ATLANTIC ENLIGHTENMENT

Ashgate Series in Nineteenth-Century Transatlantic Studies

Series Editors: Kevin Hutchings and Julia M. Wright

Focusing on the long nineteenth century (ca. 1750–1900), this series offers a forum for the publication of scholarly work investigating the literary, historical, artistic, and philosophical foundations of transatlantic culture. A new and burgeoning field of interdisciplinary investigation, transatlantic scholarship contextualizes its objects of study in relation to exchanges, interactions, and negotiations that occurred between and among authors and other artists hailing from both sides of the Atlantic. As a result, transatlantic research calls into question established disciplinary boundaries that have long functioned to segregate various national or cultural literatures and art forms, challenging as well the traditional academic emphasis upon periodization and canonization. By examining representations dealing with such topics as travel and exploration, migration and diaspora, slavery, aboriginal culture, revolution, colonialism and anti-colonial resistance, the series will offer new insights into the hybrid or intercultural basis of transatlantic identity, politics, and aesthetics.

The editors invite English language studies focusing on any area of the long nineteenth century, including (but not limited to) innovative works spanning transatlantic Romantic and Victorian contexts. Manuscripts focusing on European, African, US American, Canadian, Caribbean, Central and South American, and Indigenous literature, art, and culture are welcome. We will consider proposals for monographs, collaborative books, and edited collections.

The Atlantic Enlightenment

Edited by

SUSAN MANNING
and
FRANCIS D. COGLIANO
University of Edinburgh, UK

ASHGATE

Published by
Ashgate Publishing Limited
Gower House
Croft Road
Aldershot
Hampshire GU11 3HR
England

Ashgate Publishing Company
Suite 420
101 Cherry Street
Burlington, VT 05401-4405
USA

Ashgate website: http://www.ashgate.com

British Library Cataloguing in Publication Data
The Atlantic Enlightenment. – (Ashgate series in nineteenth-century transatlantic studies)
   1. Enlightenment 2. Europe – Intellectual life – 18th century 3. United States – Intellectual life – 18th century
I. Manning, Susan II. Cogliano, Francis D.
940.2'5

Library of Congress Cataloging-in-Publication Data
The Atlantic Enlightenment/edited by Susan Manning and Francis D. Cogliano.
   p. cm. — (Ashgate series in nineteenth-century transatlantic studies)
   Includes bibliographical references.
   ISBN 978-0-7546-6040-8 (alk. paper)
   1. Enlightenment—Atlantic Ocean Region. 2. Atlantic Ocean Region—Intellectual life—18th century. 3. Atlantic Ocean Region—Intellectual life—19th century. I. Manning, Susan. II. Cogliano, Francis D.

   B802.A819 2008
   909'.0982107—dc22

                                                                              2007007392

ISBN 978-0-7546-6040-8

Printed and bound in Great Britain by TJ International Ltd, Padstow, Cornwall

Contents

List of Figures

Acknowledgements

We would like to thank the College of Humanities and Social Science at the University of Edinburgh and its predecessor, the Faculty of Arts. As Dean of the Faculty, Dr Frances Dow gave this project encouragement and financial support for which we are grateful. The Institute for Advanced Studies in the Humanities at Edinburgh gave us an institutional home and we are grateful to Anthea Taylor, its administrator.

Notes on Contributors

Thomas Ahnert is Lecturer in Early Modern Intellectual History at the University of Edinburgh. He has published a monograph on the German Enlightenment jurist and philosopher Christian Thomasius, as well as several articles on German and British intellectual history in the period from *c*.1670 to *c*.1820.

James K. Chandler is Barbara E. and Richard J. Franke Professor in the Department of English Language and Literature at the University of Chicago, where he also serves as Director of the Franke Institute for the Humanities. His publications include *England in 1819: the Politics of Literary Culture and the Case of Romantic Historicism* (1998) and *Wordsworth's Second Nature: A Study of the Poetry and Politics* (1984). He is currently working on the *Cambridge History of British Romantic Literature* and a book about the history of the sentimental mode in literature and cinema.

Francis D. Cogliano is Professor of American History at the University of Edinburgh. A specialist in American eighteenth- and nineteenth century history, his most recent work is *Thomas Jefferson: Reputation and Legacy* (2006).

Paul Giles is Professor of American Literature and Director of the Rothermere American Institute at the University of Oxford. Among his books are *Atlantic Republic: The American Tradition in English Literature* (2006); *Virtual Americas: Transnational Fictions and the Transatlantic Imaginary* (2002); and *Transatlantic Insurrections: British Culture and the Formation of American Literature* (2001).

Paul A. Gilje is Professor of History at the University of Oklahoma and studies United States history, 1750 to 1850. He is author of *The Making of the American Republic, 1763–1815* (2006); *Liberty on the Waterfront: American Maritime Society and Culture in the Age of Revolution, 1750–1850* (2004); *Rioting in America* (1996); *The Road to Mobocracy: Popular Disorder in New York City, 1763 to 1834* (1987). He has edited or co-edited six other books and written over twenty articles and essays.

Daniel Walker Howe is Rhodes Professor of American History Emeritus at Oxford University and Professor of History Emeritus at UCLA. His writings include *The Unitarian Conscience: Harvard Moral Philosophy, 1805–1861*; *Making the American Self: Jonathan Edwards to Abraham Lincoln*; and *What Hath God Wrought: The Transformation of America, 1815–1848*.

Susan Manning is Grierson Professor of English Literature, and Director of the Institute for Advanced Studies in the Humanities at the University of Edinburgh. She works on the Scottish Enlightenment and on Scottish-American literary relations and convenes the STAR (Scotland's Transatlantic Relations) Project; her most recent transatlantic study is *Fragments of Union* (2002).

Peter S. Onuf is the Thomas Jefferson Foundation Professor of History at the University of Virginia. Onuf is the author of numerous works on the history of the early American republic, including two books co-authored with his brother, international relations theorist Nicholas G. Onuf: *Federal Union, Modern World: The Law of Nations in an Age of Revolutions, 1776–1814* (1993) and *Nations, Markets, and War: Modern History and the American Civil War* (2006).

Emma Rothschild is Director of the Centre for History and Economics at King's College, University of Cambridge, and Visiting Professor of History at Harvard University. She is the author of *Economic Sentiments: Adam Smith, Condorcet and the Enlightenment* (2001) and of *The Inner Life of Empires*, 2006 Tanner Lectures at Princeton University.

Charles W. J. Withers is Professor of Historical Geography at the University of Edinburgh and a fellow of the British Academy. Recent co-edited publications include *Science and Medicine in the Scottish Enlightenment*, with Paul Wood (2002), *Georgian Geographies: Essays on Space, Place and Landscape in the Eighteenth Century*, with Miles Ogborn (2004), and *Geography and Revolution*, with David Livingstone (2005). The author of *Placing the Enlightenment: Thinking Geographically about the Age of Reason* (2007), he has research interests in the geographies of science and the Enlightenment, and on memory, biography, commemoration and the history of geography.

Sarah F. Wood has degrees from Cambridge and University College London and held a Leverhulme Fellowship at the University of Sussex from 2004–2005. Her *Quixotic Fictions of the USA, 1792–1815* was published by Oxford University Press in 2005. She is currently writing a novel set in 1790s Philadelphia.

Foreword

This volume began with a question about two apparently contradictory tendencies in current scholarship: that is the relationship between, on the one hand, an extensive body of scholarship supporting the idea of a unified Atlantic world of cosmopolitan exchange, and, on the other, a plurality of Enlightenments characterised intellectually by disparate local manifestations. To address this issue we invited a number of leading scholars from different disciplines to the University of Edinburgh to address issues arising from consideration of the broad question: was there an Atlantic Enlightenment? We began holding seminars on the Atlantic Enlightenment in January 2002. The series culminated in a day-long colloquium held on a beautiful spring day in May of that year which brought together more than thirty scholars from several countries who considered the conceptual issues and examples, illuminating the study of the Enlightenment from an Atlantic perspective. The evidence, and the arguments, advanced were impressive. We subsequently invited several of the participants to write essays for this volume: the latest thinking of leading scholars at the end of a process begun by the seminar series. In commissioning the essays we additionally sought contributions from scholars from multiple disciplines—intellectual, cultural and social historians and literary specialists, as well as an historical geographer and a political economist. We have also attempted to balance the volume by presenting the thoughts of well-established scholars and the work of younger researchers. In consequence this volume seeks to continue and share the colloquy on the eighteenth-century Atlantic which we began in 2002. Our conclusion at the end of this process is to believe that the connections between the two terms are so intrinsic and so far-reaching that the Enlightenment cannot be understood apart from its Atlantic context.

Susan Manning
and Francis D. Cogliano

Introduction
The Enlightenment and the Atlantic

Susan Manning and Francis D. Cogliano

Our starting point is that there was no Enlightenment without the Atlantic. From jurisprudential definitions to the depths of spiritual desolation, the principles of Enlightenment were cast in consciously global and comparative terms. Discussing the principles of 'Property' in his *Second Treatise of Civil Government* (1690), for example, John Locke wrote 'In the beginning, all the world was America'; while at the other end of the emotional spectrum William Cowper's 'Castaway' found the nadir of despair amidst the roar of 'Atlantic billows'.[1] In structural terms, Samuel Johnson's magisterial statement that 'All judgement is comparative' announces a habit of mind that is constitutive of Enlightened discourse.[2] Johnson was referring to the moral education of the fictional prince Rasselas, but his critical procedure—knowing 'here' in relation to 'there'; weighing one thing against another; general principles derived from particular examples; objectivity, measurement, analysis arrived at by experience tested through mediation—suggests some of the reasons why Enlightenment principles were so frequently articulated in Atlantic contexts, and how the empirical exchanges of eighteenth-century trade, colonisation and political experiment are embedded in discussions ostensibly far removed from 'Atlantic' topics.

Malcolm Bradbury, Stephen Greenblatt and others have shown how ideas of America helped to shape Renaissance culture and discussions of profit and colonisation, adventure and humanist endeavour.[3] The present volume is concerned less with the ideals and projections that dominated sixteenth- and seventeenth-century discussions, and more with the exchanges and circulations—commercial, material, spiritual, intellectual and imaginative—that characterise encounters and transformations in the eighteenth century. There are always two—and sometimes more—*points d'appui*. As the essays in this book cumulatively demonstrate, the Atlantic Enlightenment is not a compound product of modern scholarship, but a framework intrinsic to the articulation of the modern world as it was perceived and described by the major figures of that eighteenth-century world. The Atlantic was embodied and traversed in the trade and colonisation, the discoveries and debates, the discourses and concepts that together became known as Enlightenment.

---

1   William Cowper, 'The Cast-away', in eds. John D. Baird and Charles Ryskamp, *The Poems of William Cowper* (3 vols, Oxford, 1980–1995), vol. 3, p. 214.

2   Samuel Johnson, *Rasselas and Other Tales*, ed. Gwin J. Kolb (New Haven, 1990).

3   Malcolm Bradbury, *Dangerous Pilgrimages: Trans-Atlantic Mythologies and the Novel* (London, 1995); Hugh Honour, *The New Golden Land: European Images of America from the Discoveries to the Present Time* (New York, 1976); Stephen Greenblatt, *Marvellous Possessions: The Wonder of the New World* (Oxford, 1991).

One of the aims of this book, then, is to contribute to the recent re-centring of Enlightenment discussion on the Atlantic. These essays move away from static, essentialist definitions of Enlightenment exemplified in the foundational works of Ernst Cassirer, Paul Hazard, Peter Gay, and others which identified typifying 'characteristics' of Enlightenment such as rational empiricism or religious scepticism.[4] The study of the Enlightenment, by contrast, has become increasingly fragmented. Whether this multiplicity is understood in regional, disciplinary or conceptual terms, not all scholars now speak of 'the' Enlightenment, or, if they do, it is not always to talk of the same thing. Rather, they often see multiple Enlightenments and they rightly give as much attention to the social and political contexts in which ideas were generated as to the intellectual movements regarded in isolation. In addition to the possibilities for re-orientation offered by comparative study, the field has been revolutionised by increasingly sophisticated social, cultural and intellectual research into local and regional Enlightenments.[5]

While the study of the Enlightenment has become increasingly fragmented over the past two generations, the Atlantic has emerged as a subject of study that has united disparate scholars during the same period of time.[6] This has to date primarily been the province of historians; although the potential of 'Atlantic' Enlightenments has engaged individual scholars across the disciplinary spectrum, their discussions have not, until now, been in dialogue. A further aim of this collection is to explore points of connection, disjunction and mutual enrichment that emerge when a range of approaches and scholarly methods is directed towards a series of linked and cognate topics. In this way we hope to complement and to extend the important conversations that have emerged from the institutional centre for the study of the early modern Atlantic during the past decade, namely Bernard Bailyn's International Seminar on the History of Atlantic World at Harvard University. *The British Atlantic World, 1500–1800* (2002), edited by David Armitage and Michael J. Braddick, emerged from this Seminar and reflects the range, quality and intellectual breadth as historians of its participants.[7] The evolution on both sides of the Atlantic of broad

---

4   The 'classical' literature of the European Enlightenment is enormous. See, for example, Cassirer, *The Philosophy of the Enlightenment* (Boston, 1955); Hazard, *The European Mind: The Critical Years 1690–1715* (London, 1953) and *European Thought in the Eighteenth Century* (London, 1954); Gay, *The Enlightenment: An Interpretation* (2 vols. New York, 1967–69); Alfred Cobban, ed., *The Eighteenth Century: Europe in the Age of Enlightenment* (New York, 1969).

5   Roy Porter and Mikuláš Teich, eds., *The Enlightenment in National Context* (Cambridge, 1981); Roy Porter, *Enlightenment: Britain and the Creation of the Modern World* (London, 2000).

6   See Paul Butel, *The Atlantic*, trans. Iain Hamilton Grant (London, 1999). Notable transatlantic studies include R.R. Palmer, *The Age of Democratic Revolution: A Political History of Europe and America, 1760–1800*, (2 vols., Princeton, 1959–1964); David Brion Davis, *The Problem of Slavery in the Age of Revolution* (New York, 1975); Ralph Davis, *The Rise of the Atlantic Economies* (London, 1973); and Philip D. Curtin, *The Rise and Fall of the Plantation Complex: Essays in Atlantic History* (Cambridge, 1990).

7   For recent developments in Atlantic history see, Bernard Bailyn, *Atlantic History: Concept and Contours* (Cambridge, MA, 2006); David Armitage, 'Three Concepts of Atlantic

themes such as trade, slavery, and revolution have become major subjects of study. More recently social historians have focused on the 'red' Atlantic, arguing that the working men and women of the early modern Atlantic vigorously defined and defended their rights in a manner which anticipated the class tensions characteristic of nineteenth-century industrialisation. Still others, students of race and the African diasporic experience, have described a 'black' Atlantic in which Africans were not only victims of the Atlantic slave trade but played a central role in shaping the development of an Atlantic culture.[8] Intellectual and cultural historians have demonstrated that ideas crossed the ocean along with commodities and people. This is a major theme of this volume. What each of these interpretations share is an assumption that the Atlantic is a dynamic context that brings together disparate peoples, ideas and commodities.

The emergence of the Atlantic as an important conceptual paradigm, and a renewed scholarly interest in the Enlightenment understood less as a magisterial agglomeration of grand narratives and scientific confidence and more as a network of actively contested discourses and experimental possibilities, have established contexts for the essays in this volume. The Altanticist perspective is also able to move beyond regional exceptionalist narratives (either contemporary or retrospectively imposed), to consider how much the modern world was created by the interaction of people, ideas, and commodities from Europe, Africa, and the Americas during the seventeenth and eighteenth centuries. The Atlantic was a crucial space that allowed for exchange, mutual influence and conflict between the peoples of four continents; its crossing needs to be understood as both a literal action whose material conditions require elucidation and analysis, and a culturally dense symbolic experience in

---

History', in eds. David Armitage and Michael J. Braddick, *The British Atlantic World, 1500–1800* (London, 2002), pp. 11–27; Linda Colley, 'The Sea Around Us', *The New York Review of Books*, 53:11, June 22, 2006; J.H. Elliott, 'Atlantic History: A Circumnavigation', in Armitage and Braddick, *The British Atlantic World, 1500–1800*, pp. 233–34; Peter A. Coclanis, '*Drang nach Osten*: Bernard Bailyn, the World-Island, and the Idea of Atlantic History', *Journal of World History*, 13 (2002): 169–82; and Nicholas Canny, 'Atlantic History: What and Why?', *European Review*, 9 (2001): 399–411; 'The Nature of Atlantic History', *Itinerario*, 23 (1999); 'Forum: The New British History in Atlantic Perspective', *American Historical Review*, 104 (1999): 426–500; Nicholas Canny, 'Writing Atlantic History, or, Reconfiguring the History of Colonial British America', *Journal of American History*, 86 (1999): 1093–114; Bernard Bailyn, 'The Idea of Atlantic History', *Intinerario*, 20 (1996): 19–44. We are grateful to Emma Rothschild for sharing her paper, 'The Atlantic and Other Oceans' presented at the 10th Anniversary Conference of the International Seminar on the History of the Atlantic World at Harvard University on August 9 2005. It will be published in 2008 in Bernard Bailyn, ed., *Atlantic Soundings*. It provides a brief overview of the history of the seminar and assesses its scholarly contribution.

8   For the 'red' Atlantic see Jesse Lemisch, 'Jack Tar in the Streets: Merchant Seamen in the Politics of Revolutionary America', *William and Mary Quarterly*, 25 (1968): 371–407; Marcus Rediker, *Between the Devil and the Deep Blue Sea: Merchant Seamen, Pirates, and the Anglo-American Maritime World* (Cambridge, 1987); Marcus Rediker and Peter Linebaugh, *The Many-Headed Hydra: Sailors, Slaves, Commoners and the Hidden History of the Revolutionary Atlantic* (Boston, 2000). For the 'black' Atlantic see: Paul Gilroy, *The Black Atlantic* (Cambridge, Ma., 1995); and John Thornton, *Africa and Africans and the Making of the Atlantic World, 1400–1800* (Cambridge, 1998).

which ideas, beliefs, and consciousness itself were transformed. Taking forward some recent debates, these essays collectively offer a strong demonstration of the ways in which the Atlantic context put the Enlightenment, in Paul Gilje's phrase, literally and metaphorically 'at sea'.

Another version of 'Enlightenment' that no longer sustains unconditional assent is that arising from the conveniencies of historical and literary periodisation. J. C. D. Clark identifies the first use of 'Enlightenment' to specify a discrete historical period occurring in 1865—a year which to contemporaries itself seemed to mark the end of an era, which spawned a wave of epochally-structured thinking around defining moments of inception and conclusion.[9] In this frame, 'the' Enlightenment began, variously, with the 'Glorious Revolution' of 1688–89 or the publication of Locke's *Essay Concerning Human Understanding* in 1689; or Hume's *A Treatise of Human Nature* (1739–40), or perhaps Newton's *Principia* .... One thing which for a long time seemed agreed, and unshakeable, however, was that 'the' Enlightenment ended on 14 July 1789, ushered violently off-stage by the French Revolution which itself provided a hinge into the next 'period', Romanticism. This caricature, of course, by no means does justice to the subtlety and reflectiveness of such period-defined studies as Carl Becker's *Heavenly City of the Eighteenth-Century Philosophers* (1932), Paul Fussell's *Rhetorical World of Augustan Humanism* (1965), or Roy Porter's *Enlightenment* (2000), but it does perhaps point out the arbitrariness of the criteria which tend to circumscribe Enlightenment defined by dated event, whether in print or in popular consciousness. Several of our contributors make compelling cases for a flexible definition of 'Enlightenment' able to accommodate events and discussions occurring well into the nineteenth century. By pointing out the multifarious inflections of 'Enlightened' principles in local contexts and individual expressions, the work of Porter, Teich and others has broken up the universalising tendencies of earlier analysis, but it carries the danger of more parochial forms of essentialism: arguments from national exceptionalism increasingly seem both historically untenable and ethically unacceptable in a world of international trade, moving peoples and shifting boundaries. Modern Atlantic studies, initially focused on the Renaissance, have encouraged students to consider the common experiences which link the Old and New Worlds during the early modern period. And the contributors to this volume demonstrate the limited viability of nation-based analyses that discover 'French, 'German', 'Scottish', or British' Enlightenments with their own particular characteristics.[10]

A defining factor of Enlightenment as an Atlantic phenomenon was the use of the spatial as a device for opening up both temporal and ethical assumptions. The transatlantic, spatial dimension of the Enlightenment is so important partly because it prompts questions about the evolution of societies over time, and about the development or degeneracy of the natural environment in time and space. Both issues were prominent subjects of enlightened debate with powerful political consequences. Transatlantic travellers and commentators found the past of Europe (via the four-stage theory of Scottish conjectural historians such as William

---

9   See Paul Giles's essay, below, for further discussion on this point.
10   See Porter and Teich, *op. cit.*

Robertson) and its future inscribed on the American landscape and in its native inhabitants. At one level, geographical exploration and surveying were activities practised by transatlantic reporters as different as William Byrd II of Virginia, Peter Jefferson, the Swedish naturalist Peter Kalm, and the soldier, diplomat, farmer and possible double agent Hector St John de Crèvecoeur who named his eldest daughter América-Francès in honour of the alliance that sustained his activities and almost cost him his life. Crèvecoeur corresponded with Peter Jefferson's son, the more famous Thomas, on the appropriateness of the physiocratic theory of the French *philosophes* to the American environment. In one of the earliest recorded uses of the term 'transatlantic', in 1782, Jefferson expressed his 'doubt'—the Revolutionary war which would establish the separate existence of America still ongoing, and its outcome uncertain—'whether nature has enlisted herself as a cis- or trans-Atlantic partisan'.[11] 'Nature' here is not the inert abstraction identified by classical studies of Enlightenment, but a transitive *force* whose ultimate alignment will, he hopes, record a decisive shift in the balance of inter-continental power. Jefferson's 'doubt' embeds the Enlightened political and moral questions surrounding the patriot case within a much older rhetorical formula: the classical trope of *translatio studii et imperii*, which held that virtues flee a decadent civilisation for a simpler, regenerate one. Norman kings invoked the *translatio imperii* trope to underwrite the transfer of power from the Classical civilisations to the French, and thence to England. Conjoining progress with authority, they devised the foundational myth of King Brutus of Troy, who instituted the kingdom of 'Britain' (Jefferson collected references to this story when he sought an appropriate name and official Seal for the new nation which, in a new phase of the *translatio*, was to inherit British imperial grandeur).[12] Other eighteenth-century observers of shifting relationships between Europe and her transatlantic colonies renewed the assumption of the *translatio* that civilisation consistently migrates from East to West. Its most celebrated eighteenth-century expression is George Berkeley's poem 'On the Prospect of Planting Arts and Learning in America', which transposes time and space, projecting the rise and fall of empires onto the movement of European migration:

> The Muse, disgusted at an age and clime
> Barren of every glorious theme,
> In distant lands now waits a better time,
> Producing subjects worthy fame …

> There shall be sung another golden age,
> The rise of empire and of arts,
> The good and great inspiring epic rage,
> The wisest heads and noblest hearts.

---

11   This is the first citation offered for the term by the Oxford English Dictionary.

12   See *Thomas Jefferson's Literary Commonplace Book*, ed. Douglas L. Wilson (Princeton, NJ, 1989). Information on the translation trope is drawn from http://cla.calpoly.edu/~dschwart/engl513/courtly/ translat.htm, copyright Debora B. Schwartz.

Not such as Europe breeds in her decay; ...
    Westward the course of empire takes its way;
The four first acts already past,
A fifth shall close the drama with the day;
Time's noblest offspring is the last.[13]

The transforming nature of the 'space between'—the Atlantic voyage, the 3000 miles' separation, the time taken between writing a letter and having it read—is an ever-present feature of Atlantic Enlightenment consciousness. At least from the time of the early seventeenth-century Puritan conversion narratives, traversing the Atlantic, whether on a boat or in the mind, was an extraordinarily powerful agent and image of defamiliarisation, setting Enlightened minds 'at sea' in the uncertainties of an existence become irremediably comparative and relative. The writers considered in this book were aware that their environment and their identity were partly comprehended in that transatlantic 'other', be it the botanical specimens that might prove the New World to be a degenerating or an appreciating sphere in relation to Europe, or the evidence of different racial or cultural communities that enabled them to describe their own. Amongst our contributors, Charles Withers in particular considers the Atlantic as a subject for Enlightenment inquiry as a space over which ideas and practices moved and as a site in which the Enlightenment was made and tested, while Paul Gilje studies the penetration of the Enlightenment into the world of the men who worked the ships which traversed the Atlantic—transporting people, ideas, and commodities across the ocean. Assembling the extensive 'oceanic' connections of even the sedentary self-avowedly indolent philosopher David Hume, Emma Rothschild's essay demonstrates the extent to which the intellectual history of the Enlightenment on such formative issues as commerce, empire and public credit was inflected by Atlantic thinking. Other essays—such as those of Thomas Ahnert, Sarah Wood and Peter Onuf—consider the impact of the transmission of Enlightenment ideas on intellectual communities on both sides of the Atlantic. Read together the last three essays remind us that the transatlantic traffic in ideas moved from west to east as well as east to west, and in circulatory patterns that complicate vectors of transmission. In this as in other respects, *The Atlantic Enlightenment* re-conceptualizes the influence-led binaries of earlier studies such as Richard B. Sher and Jeffrey Smitten's distinguished collection *Scotland and America in the Age of the Enlightenment* (1990). For our contributors, the Atlantic itself becomes a transformative third term in the equation. Attending to the realities and fantasies of distance and passage, and interrogating the grounds for comparison, we hope to open new perspectives on previously documented connections.

    Atlantic discourse generates a politics, and a poetics, of both distance and sympathy. Awareness that knowledge and expression are relative, contingent and timebound

---

13   (wr. 1726, publ. 1752). Text taken from Roger Lonsdale, ed., *The New Oxford Book of Eighteenth-Century Verse* (Oxford, 1984), p. 175. Edward Said has pointed out the irremediably cultural nature of geography: 'space acquires emotional and even rational sense by a kind of poetic process, whereby the vacant or anonymous reaches of distance are converted into meaning'. Edward Said, *Orientalism* (London, 1995), 55.

does not lead us, or our contributors, to the extreme endpoints of linguistic scepticism. Even the supposed arch-sceptic David Hume was—whatever the tendencies of his epistemological theories—a devotee of 'intelligence' and thoroughly engaged in the politics of Atlantic discourse, corresponding with Benjamin Franklin, and (as he put it), 'an American in [his] principles'.[14] As a figure of the 'American' Enlightenment, on the other hand, Jonathan Edwards usually appears in biography and intellectual history as the true heir of Founding Fathers who articulated their sense of the special destiny of American settlement in millenarian terms derived from Old Testament Judaic rhetoric. Edwards's first American biographer, Samuel Hopkins, described his subject's sense of the slippery slope of doctrinal latitude: 'For if these [Calvinist] doctrines, in the whole length and breadth of them were relinquished, he did not see, where a man could set his foot down with consistency and safety, short of Deism, or even Atheism itself; or rather universal Skepticism.'[15] The rigorous consistency of this position begins to blur at the edges when we set Edwards's New Light Calvinism in the context of his transatlantic correspondence with Nisbet on doctrinal issues and his *Treatise Concerning Religious Affections* (1746), which develops a sensationist psychology every bit as subtle as that of Hume or Adam Smith; it metamorphoses entirely when his theological enquires are read as part of an intellectual profile that included an early and lifelong engagement with the writing of Locke, and a full awareness of its sceptical possibilities. Perry Miller stressed this affiliation many years ago, but Edwards has never made it into the canon of great writers of the (Eurocentric) Enlightenment, and his evangelical views make him an uneasy term in an American intellectual lineage that comfortably conjures with the names of Franklin, Jefferson and Adams.[16] An Enlightenment reconfigured 'Atlantically', so to speak, would, on the other hand, accommodate Edwards's Lockean insistence on the primacy of experience equally in the political, scientific and spiritual spheres as part of a comparative configuration that would also include Joseph Priestley (another American in his principles), and Thomas Paine. Properly transatlantic accounts of these three exemplars of Enlightenment remain to be written; in this volume, Daniel Howe's essay on John Witherspoon in Scotland and America represents a dissenting, evangelising version of Enlightenment that expressed itself fully in a transatlantic context. James Chandler's essay on the fortunes of the Scottish Enlightenment's ethical and aesthetic theory of sympathy in early American fiction offers a context in which the elastic perception enabled by comparison may enlarge understanding and refine self-definition without succumbing to 'universal Skepticism'. The kind of reflexive consciousness that Henry James would develop in his 'international

---

14 *Letters of David Hume*, ed. J.Y.T Greig (2 vols, Oxford 1969), vol. 2, p. 302. Emma Rothschild's essay in this volume considers the Atlantic dimensions of Hume's Enlightenment.

15 *The Life and Character of Reverend Mr Jonathan Edwards* (1765), in ed. David Levin, *Jonathan Edwards: A Profile* (New York, 1969), p. 52.

16 Perry Miller, *Jonathan Edwards* (New York, 1949); for a more orthodox view of the 'great figures' of American Enlightenment, see (for example) Carl Van Doren, *Benjamin Franklin* (New York, 1938); Charles L. Sanford, ed., *Benjamin Franklin and the American Character* (Boston, 1955), Merrill D. Peterson, *Adam and Jefferson: A Revolutionary Dialogue* (Athens, Ga., 1976).

novels' of transatlantic encounter in the late nineteenth century has both experiential and theoretical origins in transatlantic Enlightenment.

The manner in which Enlightenment ideas moved and the relationship between their production and reception in different intellectual, social and geographic milieux is the major theme of Paul Giles's overview of recent Enlightenment scholarship, which looks further into our argument that viewed from an Atlantic perspective the shared characteristics and mutual engagements of the various national and regional Enlightenments become apparent. The obstacles to such exchanges also emerge. For example, while colonial exchanges broadened the horizons of European thinking, assumptions about race and its implications for societal progress in the conjectural historiography of the Scottish Enlightenment exemplified in William Robertson's widely acclaimed *History of America* (1777), had the effect, as Emma Rothschild shows, of severely limiting the circulation of ideas within the Atlantic world. Warfare, endemic in this world during the eighteenth century, was a further obstacle to the circulation of trade and people—a phenomenon analysed with some urgency by Adam Smith in his *An Inquiry into the Nature and Causes of the Wealth of Nations* (1776).

Here we should note the broad disciplinary ethos that informs this volume as a collective contribution to Enlightenment and Atlantic Studies. The degree to which the individual authors draw on multiple disciplinary perspectives within their essays is striking, and suggests that the multi-layeredness of the subject requires of its students a similar flexibility with respect to the parameters and methodologies of traditional disciplines. Paul Giles, a literary specialist, provides an historiographical overview of the Enlightenment. Sarah Wood's closer textual approach to literary study is informed by the political history of the early American Republic. Taking examples and contexts from intellectual history, geographer Charles Withers considers how eighteenth-century natural scientists came to understand the Gulf Stream. Emma Rothschild, a political economist, presents an analysis heavily inflected by the philosophical debates of the Scottish Enlightenment. The intellectual historian Peter Onuf presents an analysis of Adam Smith's reception in the antebellum United States that recruits the study of political economy to its argument. Social historian Paul Gilje draws evidence and insights from literature in order to recreate the mental world of mariners during the 'Age of Sail'. This navigation within and across disciplinary lines presses hard at the limitations of established approaches to the study of Enlightenment.

The essays in this volume show, that is, how the Atlantic perspective renders Enlightenment boundaries of all kinds fluid and permeable. It problematises assumptions not only about the categorisation of knowledge, but also of perception and articulation. If the Enlightenment (as Michel Foucault has argued influentially) is defined by its taxonomic imperatives, Enlightenment viewed through the prism of the Atlantic insists that we recognise the constantly contested and renegotiated features of these taxonomies in the context of the comparative data collection referred to above.[17] Jefferson's *Notes on the State of Virginia* is in part a powerful

---

17 See, in particular, Foucault's *Les mots et les choses* (1966), translated as *The Order of Things: An Archaeology of the Human Sciences* (London, 1970).

engagement—not to say refutation—of the degenerationist theories of Buffon and the Abbé Raynal, and a comparative demonstration of the available classification systems of Linnaeus, Catesby, Buffon and 'popular names'. From early in the eighteenth century, antiquarians and collectors exchanged skulls, word lists, botanical specimens, rocks and myths across the Atlantic, in a co-operative effort to expand and characterise the field of knowledge in a global rather than Eurocentric frame.[18]

Methodological flexibility also seems key to further progress in mapping the multiplicity of Atlantic Enlightenment connections. While these essays share an interest in interdisciplinary opportunities, they explore very different angles of approach to the overarching question. Paul Giles's essay, for instance, adopts a conceptual approach in order to consider plural Enlightenments, as he attempts to determine (and question) the common characteristics of 'the' Atlantic Enlightenment as an historicised subject of study. Daniel Howe, on the other hand, focuses on the life, work, and cares of John Witherspoon, reading an individual biography as an exemplification of a particular version of the transformation wrought by Atlantic crossing on Enlightenment ideas. Howe argues for a specifically Protestant Enlightenment as the prevailing version imbibed in late colonial and early revolutionary America; taking Witherspoon as his exemplar of this 'mode' he charts precisely how the Scottish evangelical theologian's emigration across the Atlantic affected his thinking. Howe's demonstration compares the 'Scottish' and 'American' writings of Witherspoon to suggest the natural evolution from Calvinist theologian to Revolutionary theorist. Calvinism and Revolution are parameters which help to define Howe's version of the Atlantic Enlightenment. His reading is indicative; it makes a convincing case for Witherspoon as an unjustly neglected central figure in the picture of an Atlantic Enlightenment which should—more than it has hitherto been—be viewed from a specifically Scottish point of origin.

At this point, a particular bias and unique contribution of the Atlantic Enlightenment described by this volume should be made explicit. Ours is, by design, a *North* Atlantic Enlightenment primarily protestant in denomination, and anglophone in orientation. This is both a practical consequence of our particular interests as Americanists living and working in Edinburgh, and a deliberate decision to focus attention within a field of enquiry potentially so large as to overwhelm attention. South American and Caribbean Atlantic circulations are beginning to be explored by historians, literary scholars and political scientists in the wake of pioneering work by Anthony Pagden and Edmundo O'Gorman; more recently, Felipe Fernandez-Armesto's synoptic study *The Americas: The History of a Hemisphere* (2003) has argued for a pan-American approach that recognises a common history of colonisation and north-south circulation within the Americas. 'Latinization', as he sees it, is 'the vital counterpart of Americanization'; there is a hispanic, Catholic

---

18 'Popular names' was one of Jefferson's classificatory categories in his comparison of Old and New World flora and fauna, in the *Notes on the State of Virginia* (1787), ed. William H. Peden (Chapel Hill, 1955). On taxonomies of language, in particular, see Edward G. Gray, *New World Babel: Languages and Nations in Early America* (Princeton, 1999); on transatlantic taxonomies, see Susan Manning, *Fragments of Union: Making Connections in Scottish and American Writing* (Basingstoke, 2002), especially chapter 5.

transatlanticism whose history should not be forgotten because it was not primarily active in the eighteenth century.[19] Aspects of the Transatlantic Enlightenment oriented towards South America have recently been opened up by Mary Louise Pratt in *Imperial Eyes: Travel Writing and Transculturation*, and Nigel Leask in his studies of the travels of Alexander von Humboldt and Frances Calderón de la Barca's *Life in Mexico* (1843). Similarly, transatlantic circulation focused on the Caribbean has been a rapidly expanding field of study in the last twenty years.[20]

Reflecting the location of the discussions which gave rise to this volume, the Atlantic Enlightenment presented here has then its axis unashamedly tilted towards Scotland. Daniel Howe's Witherspoon is exemplary in his Presbyterianism, and Emma Rothschild's essay puts Hume in an original relation to Atlantic Enlightenment discourse. For Chandler, Adam Smith's *Theory of Moral Sentiments* (1759) is a foundational text. Smith's *Wealth of Nations* is the starting point for Peter Onuf's analysis of antebellum American political economy. Sarah Wood marks out continuities between the writings of Benjamin Franklin and Tobias Smollett. Yet these essays equally demonstrate that there is nothing provincial about the Atlantic Enlightenment seen from a Scottish perspective. A straightforwardly nation-based reading of productive influences and of their passive reception—as indicated above— is not something to which any of our contributors would subscribe. Scotland's Enlightenment was itself a multifarious and fractured set of possibilities, exemplified equally by the Presbyterian Witherspoon and the skeptical Hume, as also by Smith in both his ethical and economic writing. Scottish intellectual movements were themselves intimately interwoven with the Enlightenments of France, Germany, and other European countries, and these essays reveal some of these networks in operation. Even as our authors look across the Atlantic, Gilje points us towards Voltaire, Diderot and Rousseau as contexts for his maritime exemplars of the Enlightenment 'at sea', Wood's 'Transatlantic Cervantics' offers a 'hispanised' transatlantic exchange which also draws on the Anglo-Irish Edmund Burke and the discourse of sentiment, an English perspective is voiced in Giles's and Ahnert's essays by Samuel Johnson's writing, and Emma Rothschild's Hume is deeply European in his sensibilities.

---

19   *The Americas: The History of a Hemisphere* (London, 2003), p. 141. Also see Edmundo O'Gorman, *The Invention of America: an Inquiry Into the Historical Nature of the New World and the Meaning of Its History* (Bloomington, IN, 1961), Anthony Pagden, *European Encounters With the New World: From Renaissance to Romanticism* (New Haven, 1993), Lester D. Langley, *The Americas in the Age of Revolution* (New Haven, 1997) and Lester D. Langley, *The Americas in the Modern Age* (New Haven, 2003) for other examples of hemispheric history.

20   *Imperial Eyes: Travel Writing and Transculturation* (London, 1992); Nigel Leask, *Curiosity and the Aesthetics of Travel Writing 1770–1840* (Oxford, 2002); Nigel Leask, 'The Ghost in Catapultepec: Fanny Calderón de la Barca, William Prescott and 19th Century Mexican Travel Accounts', in Jas Elsner and Joan-Pau Rubiés, eds., *Voyages and Visions* (London, 1999). On the Caribbean and the Atlantic world, see, for example Jerald T. Milanich and Susan Milbrath, eds., *First Encounters: Spanish Explorations in the Caribbean and the United States, 1492–1570* (Gainesville, FL., 1989), and David Barry Gaspar and David Patrick Geggus, eds., *A Turbulent Time: The French Revolution and the Greater Caribbean* (Bloomington, IN, 1997).

And Scotland, of course, is not the only point of origin from which to view even a North Atlantic Enlightenment. Study of the Atlantic Enlightenment to date has unaccountably neglected German contributions to its counter-currents. In this volume we begin to address this lack. Giles opens his analysis of 'Enlightenments' with Kant's famous formulation, and Hegel's conceptual historicisation. The importance of Goethe's *Sorrows of Young Werther* (1774) to the transatlantic economy of sentiment in William Hill Brown's *Power of Sympathy* (1789) is noted by Chandler. German responses to the American Revolution are the particular subject of Thomas Ahnert's essay. Ahnert brings to bear a set of jurisprudential considerations derived from the work of John Pocock; he situates German reactions in the context of European Enlightenment debates about natural law, civil law and the *ius gentium* or law of nations, and reminds us of the intense theoretical scrutiny to which the Americans' actions in declaring independence from Britain were subject across Europe. Ahnert's emphasis on the extent to which religio-political *Schwärmerei*, or enthusiasts, were also part of the intellectual world of the Atlantic Enlightenment offers a counterpart to Howe's Presbyterian Enlightenment. The contradiction, if so it appears, *is* only apparent: reformed religious practice is fundamental to both cases, and Howe's and Ahnert's essays between them exemplify the polyvalency of Atlantic Enlightenments. More specifically they make it clear (as, in different ways, do Chandler's and Gilje's literary readings) that the Atlantic Enlightenment should not only be read as a space for the influential exchange of abstractly conceived ideas about governance and justice, but as an intense emotional and spiritual battleground in which, in the ultimate analysis, nothing less than the soul's salvation might be at stake.

Giles offers an illuminating analysis of how the concept of an Atlantic Enlightenment has been formulated in recent scholarship. Starting from the general question of how 'Enlightenment' historically been located and described, he moves in to focus on how specific eighteenth-century commentators such as Samuel Johnson and Richard Price who, unlike John Witherspoon, did not themselves undertake the physical crossing of the Atlantic, but nonetheless found it figuring largely on their ideological horizons. The now-obvious limitations of their interpretations should, Giles argues, be instructive to us as we attempt to read Atlanticism back into the Enlightenment. James Chandler's essay on the 'first American novel' locates the Atlanticism of the Enlightenment at the level of precise inter-textual analysis. Chandler shares with Howe the sense that the Scottish intellectual background offered something particularly conducive to Atlantic export—in this case, the ethics of sympathy developed by Hume and Adam Smith which, in its aesthetic aspect, manifested itself in the sentimental novel. Chandler reminds us that Jefferson's favourite fictional and poetic reading was the novels of Sterne and James Macpherson's translations of Ossian. One of the major contributions of this essay is its consideration of 'the meaning of a "transatlantic idea"' (to adapt a phrase from Lionel Trilling) in the context of the prevailing and eminently transportable literary discourse of sensibility.[21]

---

21 Lionel Trilling, 'The Meaning of a Literary Idea', *The Liberal Imagination: Essays on Literature and Society* (New York, 1940; rpt., 1976).

As the Atlantic is bounded by the Americas, Europe, Africa and the Antarctic and Arctic, Enlightenment thinking is bounded by the limits of race, status and gender. Paul Gilje's essay delineates the degree to which Enlightenment thinking transcended both disciplinary and social boundaries. His discussion of the conjunction of economics, politics and sentiment that informed contemporary views of sailors and the seafaring life reminds us that the Enlightenment was not confined to a social elite, and that its theoretical ideas were intimately bound to practice. There are echoes here of Thomas Munck's pioneering exploration of the meaning of the Enlightenment for partially educated social groups.[22] While Munck considers the degree to which Enlightenment ideas transcended class and educational boundaries in three western European cities—London, Paris and Hamburg—Gilje demonstrates that sailors were themselves well-versed in Enlightenment discourse and, by the nature of their peripatetic employment, helped to circulate those ideas around the Atlantic world. Seen from the perspective of the lower decks of the ships which plied its waves, the Atlantic was not a barrier to be surmounted but a vast pool which facilitated the diffusion of ideas (as well as people and goods) across space and social boundaries. Nonetheless, as Gilje's discussion of Thomas Paine shows, restrictions on education and opportunity made it inevitable that most of the perspectives available to us now on the Atlantic Enlightenment come from writers of middle- or upper-class backgrounds. These essays are at least able to indicate how the non-written experience of working men, women and slaves were subjects of active interest and importance to the Atlantic discourse of the Enlightenment.

For women whose livelihoods depended on the Atlantic, life could be precarious. Nonetheless the fluidity of life at sea and on the waterfront offered women opportunity as well as uncertainty. During the eighteenth century, women in maritime communities, especially seaports (as well as the smaller number who went to sea) enjoyed more opportunities to amass wealth and achieve social and economic autonomy than their counterparts in inland communities.[23] As the sea broadened women's horizons economically and socially, Enlightenment offered some women a degree of intellectual and cultural opportunity. The sentimental novel as described here by Chandler gave a growing number of female readers entertainment and an entrée into the Enlightenment. Moreover the late eighteenth century saw the substantial presence of published female authors as well as readers on both sides of the Atlantic. Chandler's enquiry into the conjunction of 'sympathy' with 'power' suggests that we look carefully at transatlantic intertextualities not as simple instances of 'influences' on a juvenile and derivative culture from a more established and authoritative source.

22　Thomas Munck, *The Enlightenment: A Comparative Social History, 1721–1794* (London, 2000).

23　Paul A. Gilje, *Liberty on the Waterfront: American Maritime Culture in the Age of Revolution* (Philadelphia, 2004), ch. 2; David Cordingly, *Women Sailors and Sailors' Women: An Untold Maritime History* (New York, 2001); Elaine Forman Crane, *Ebb Tide in New England: Women, Seaports and Social Change, 1630–1800* (Boston, 1998); Lisa Norling, *Captain Ahab Had a Wife: New England Women and the Whalefishery, 1720–1870* (Chapel Hill, 2000); Margaret S. Creighton and Lisa Norling, eds., *Iron Men, Wooden Women: Gender and Seafaring in the Atlantic World, 1700–1920* (Baltimore: Johns Hopkins University Press, 1996); Suzanne J. Stark, *Women Aboard Ship in the Age of Sail* (Annapolis, 1996).

We need in addition to be alert to the challenging revisions produced by the repositioning of apparently familiar and uncontentious ideas in frameworks that put pressure on their illusion of 'naturalness'. Such a perception allows us to return to the canonical works of British sensibility, such as Sterne's *Sentimental Journey* (1767) or Henry Mackenzie's *Man of Feeling* (1771), with renewed awareness of their aesthetic sophistication—apparent to Hill Brown as a transatlantic reader and adaptor, but too readily naturalised by British audiences who took their fictions for ethical instruction. Some women writers such Susanna Rowson, Frances Wright, Maria Graham or Frances Calderòn de la Barca (née Inglis) were themselves transatlantic figures who wrote on transatlantic themes and subjects. From the standpoint of gender the Enlightenment remained male dominated, but—as Abigail Adams famously reminded her husband—it was in no sense an exclusively male domain.[24] By the late eighteenth century the gender boundary of the Enlightenment was somewhat like the 'boundary' of the Atlantic Ocean at Tierra del Fuego, or in the polar regions—shifting, imprecise and sometimes stormy.

Charles Withers demonstrates that coastal west Africa, integral to the Atlantic economy, did not figure in the thoughts of most of those who contributed to Enlightenment discourse about the geography of the Atlantic world.[25] As a consequence, Africa and Africans are not central to the essays in this book, despite the fact that the transatlantic economy which so concerned thinkers from Hume to Jefferson depended on the transatlantic slave trade and the commodities produced by African slaves in the New World. Nonetheless, as Emma Rothschild demonstrates in her analysis of Hume's infamous footnote on Africans, assumptions about race brought severe pressure to bear on Enlightenment discourse. Her essay shows, in a different way from Paul Giles's, how the imaginative sympathy (and its failures) that underpinned discourse of the Atlantic inflected the writing of major Enlightenment figures who never made the crossing for themselves, and their understanding of evidence brought back by travellers, traders and those others who did. Hume's comments on race need to be understood not only in the light of the empirical observations of those who encountered Africans in enslaved conditions in the Americas, but in relation to the theories of government and the theoretical historiography of universal societal development being worked out so notably in Enlightenment Scotland. This was articulated in the fourth book of Hume's friend Robertson's *History of America*, where—in a central and influential case of that comparative social evolutionism opened up by the Atlantic perspective—the primary examples of the 'primitive' stages of society are Native Americans and Scottish Highlanders.

Neither Hume nor Robertson had direct experience of New World slavery when they made their assertions about the inferiority of Africans. The same cannot be said of Jefferson, who articulated some of the noblest aspirations of the Enlightenment,

---

24   Abigail Adams to John Adams, March 31, 1776, in L. H. Butterfield *et al.* eds., *The Adams Family Correspondence*, 7 vols to date (Cambridge, Mass,1963–), vol 1, p. 370.

25   For example T. Carlos Jacques, 'From Savages and Barbarians to Primitives: Africa, Social Typologies, and History in Eighteenth-Century French Philosophy', *History and Theory*, 36 (1997): 190–215.

and both as philosopher and politician was an active reader of the major figures of the Scottish Enlightenment, and also embodied many of its limitations and contradictions. Despite some well-intentioned denunciations of slavery, he took no steps towards abolition in Virginia. By contrast in his most extensive publication, *Notes on the State of Virginia*, Jefferson offered, 'as a suspicion only, that the blacks, whether originally a distinct race, or made distinct by time and circumstances, are inferior to whites in the endowments of body and mind'. Unlike Hume, Jefferson based his claim of supposed African inferiority on empirical observation and comparison with Europeans:

> Comparing them by their faculties of memory, reason, and imagination it appears to me that in memory they are equal to the white; in reason much inferior, as I think one could scarcely be found capable of tracing and comprehending the investigations of Euclid; and that in the imagination they are dull, tasteless and anomalous. It would be unfair to follow them to Africa for this investigation. We will compare them here, on the same stage with the whites, and where the facts are not apocryphal on which a judgment is to be formed.

He dismissed the notion that the environment—that is slavery—produced the inferior characteristics he described. 'It is not their condition then,' he concluded, 'but nature which has produced the distinction.'[26]

Jefferson's racial comparisons were not confined to Europeans and Africans. In the *Notes on the State of Virginia* he compared Native Americans favourably to Africans.

> Some [African slaves] have been liberally educated, and all lived in countries where the arts and sciences are cultivated to a considerable degree, and have had before their eyes samples of the best works from abroad. The Indians, with no advantages of this kind, will often carve figures on their pipes not destitute of design and merit. … They astonish you with strokes of the most sublime oratory; such as prove their reason and sentiment strong, their imagination glowing and elevated. But never yet could I find a black that had uttered a thought above the level of plain narration; never see even an elementary trait of painting or sculpture.[27]

Whereas Africans were inferior by nature, Jefferson claimed that circumstances alone accounted for the seeming differences between whites and Native Americans. If the circumstances of Native American life changed, then Native Americans could achieve equality with European Americans, a status which Africans could never achieve. As expressed here, Jefferson's views on race suggest a common outlook in Edinburgh and Monticello. Notwithstanding his intimate knowledge of slavery and Africans—including, of course, his own children by his mixed-race slave, Sally Hemings—his racial attitudes are reminiscent of Hume. Like Hume, though perhaps for different reasons, Jefferson contended that Africans (unlike Native Americans) were incapable of the intellectual development necessary to participate in civil society.

---

26   Jefferson, *Notes on the State of Virginia*, ed. Peden, quotations, 143, 139, 141–2. The best analysis of Jefferson's writings on race in the *Notes* is Winthrop D. Jordan's *White Over Black: American Attitudes toward the Negro, 1550–1812* (Chapel Hill, 1968), ch. 12.

27   Jefferson, *Notes on the State of Virginia*, ed., Peden, 140.

Jefferson's racial thinking owed other debts to Scottish Enlightenment thought. Although he felt that blacks were intellectually inferior to whites, the races were equal in their common, or 'moral sense'. Jefferson, who derived his thinking on the subject from the writings of the Scottish common sense philosophers, believed that the moral sense was distinct from the intellect. 'State a moral case to a ploughman and a professor,' he wrote in 1787, 'the former will decide it as well, and often better than the latter, because he has not been led astray by artificial rules.' Like the ploughman, the African slave was the equal to his white master in determining right from wrong.[28] Similarly Jefferson's enthusiasm for the primitive potential of Native Americans—reminiscent of William Robertson—particularly the tragic oratory of Chief Logan, may be derived from his enthusiasm for Ossian.[29]

The more general point here might be the mutually constitutive interaction of empirical data, system, and imaginative exploration in the cross-currents of Atlantic Enlightenment discourse: if the evidence gained in observing Native Americans and slaves helped European writers to construct universal conjectural histories of mankind—and subsequently seemed to confirm these theories—the examples offered by the early Roman republic and the evidence of the contemporary abuses of the French *ancien régime* were formative in American revolutionary thinking. Equally formative, as Chandler's and Sarah Wood's essays remind us, were the literary structures of sentiment and satire. At this point it becomes possible to see the underlying relationships between the symbolic structures they explore, and the more empirically-based accounts of movement on and across the Atlantic presented by Withers and Gilje.

Indeed, it is one of the strengths of the interdisciplinary approach of this collection to reveal how 'literary' the Atlantic Enlightenment was, in the sense of being articulated, debated and contested in contexts ranging from taxonomy and political philosophy to historiography, psychology and fiction. The generic or disciplinary boundaries between these kinds of writing are revealed as matters of convention and convenience: as Chandler demonstrates, the transatlantic sentimental novel opens up additional ways to understand the sensationist psychology of Hume, Smith, and Edwards, while Wood's essay shows how the established European genre of quixotic

---

28   Thomas Jefferson to Peter Carr, August 10, 1787, in Julian P. Boyd, *et al.* eds., *The Papers of Thomas Jefferson* (33 vols to date, Princeton, 1950–), vol. 12, p. 15. For Jefferson's views on race and the common sense philosophy see: Jordan, *White Over Black*, 439–40 and Garry Wills, *Inventing America: Jefferson's Declaration of Independence* (New York, 1978), chs. 14–15. Wills made a strong case for the Scottish Enlightenment as a source many of Jefferson's ideas. Hostile reviews, notably by Ronald Hamowy in the *William and Mary Quarterly*, (36 [1979]: 503–23), pointed out the many anachronisms and factual errors in Wills's argument, but his fundamental thesis was both sound and surprisingly revolutionary within an American historiography very slow to recognise the substantial intellectual cross-currents between Scotland and pre-Revolutionary America. On the controversy and its implications, see Andrew Hook, 'The Scottish Invention of the USA', *From Goosecreek to Gandercleugh: Studies in Scottish-American Literary and Cultural History* (East Linton, 1999), pp. 8–24 and Francis D. Cogliano, *Thomas Jefferson: Reputation and Legacy* (Edinburgh, 2006), pp. 138–47.

29   Manning, *Fragments of Union* , 182–90.

romance was a ready vehicle for discussion of contemporary politics in a transatlantic context. In addition, it would be possible to find issues of race and slavery explored in the transatlantic novels of, for example, Henry Mackenzie (*The Man of the World* [1773] and *Julia de Roubigné* [1777]) and Robert Bage (*Hermsprong; or Man as He is Not* [1796]); or Smithian theory of Atlantic economic exchange implied in Jane Austen's *Mansfield Park* (1814); or comparative topographies and social analysis in Frances Brooke's *Emily Montague* (1769) or Susanna Rowson's *Americans in England* (1796). What imaginative fiction can do that political philosophy, empirical psychology and comparative historiography may not permit themselves, is to explore at length the poetic and metaphoric implications of certain kinds of 'thought experiment' regarding the effects of personal and cultural displacement.

Walter Scott—Tory, anti-Reform, very much heir to the Loyalist elements in Scottish Enlightenment thought that do not feature largely in this volume—is not readily associated with the kind of experience and ideological imperatives that make travel writers, political theorists, theologians and sailors, obvious starting points for articulating an Atlantic Enlightenment. Yet Scott, who never visited America nor wrote a transatlantic novel, and who has been retrospectively identified with some of the most anti-democratic, 'anti-Enlightened' episodes in American history, nonetheless played a part in the continuing imaginative transatlantic dialogues of the nineteenth century, a part that—precisely because of its *unlikeliness*—suggests that we shall indeed benefit from acknowledging the pervasiveness of Atlantic discourse in the formation of concerns far removed from the self-styled revolutionaries of the Enlightenment.[30] Though his 'American' fiction remained unachieved, Scott recognised its possibilities in his fascination with the story of the regicide Goff, who took refuge in Virginia following the execution of Charles I. More material, perhaps, was his delight in a text discussed below by Sarah Wood, the 'most excellently jocose' *History of New York* sent to him unsolicited during the Anglo-American conflict of 1812–14 by its author Washington Irving, whose publication and career prospects in Britain Scott thereafter untiringly championed.[31] Praising the spoof *History* to the publisher John Murray, he wrote of his intention to write an article on the book; in the event, at Scott's instigation, his prospective son-in-law John Wilson Lockhart reviewed Irving's work extensively in *Blackwood's Edinburgh Magazine*, while Murray was sufficiently persuaded to undertake the first British publication of Irving's transatlantic *Sketches of Geoffrey Crayon, Gent.* in 1820. Irving's writing (central to Sarah Wood's argument about the multiply mediated figure of the Quixote in transatlantic writing that hovers between satire and sentiment) makes it clear that just as the Enlightenment receives new conceptual richness and extent

---

30 See, most notoriously, Mark Twain's indictment that Scott was responsible for the American Civil War, in *Life on the Mississippi* (1883), ed. James M. Cox (Harmondsworth, 1986), p. 327. See also Andrew Hook, 'Scott and America', in *From Goosecreek to Gandercleugh*, and Susan Manning, 'Did Mark Twain bring down the temple on Scott's shoulders?' in Janet Beer and Bridget Bennett, eds., *Special Relationships: Anglo-American Affinities and Antagonisms, 1854–1936* (Manchester, 2002), pp. 8–27.

31 H. J .C. Grierson, ed., *The Letters of Sir Walter Scott* (12 vols, London, 1932–33), vol. 3, p. 259.

when considered in its transatlantic dimensions, so too may Romanticism. Indeed, the Atlantic view brings the usefulness of such 'period' compartments once more into question.

As the most successful novelist of his generation (perhaps, depending on one's measure, of the nineteenth century) writing in English, Scott was both a model for, and an enormous challenge to, American writers as they construed a literature that would articulate specifically 'American' experience within the conventions of immensely powerful British literary traditions. Scott's work, which is frequently invoked in terms of 'Romantic nationalism', in fact exemplifies the futility of the kinds of periodisation and localisation in relation to literature that we argued against at the beginning of this introduction. Its thematic, geographical, socio-political and historical amplitude militates against narrow categories of analysis; a more fruitful way of reading the 'Waverley Novels' would be to see them as the fullest imaginative exposition of the kinds of Enlightened enquiry also exemplified in the Atlantic contexts explored in this volume. Progress achieved through resolution of conflict between racial and cultural groups; territorial disputes and their social and psychological consequences; a geographically- and topographically-based understanding of the political world; economic development and its societal consequences; the power of local allegiances and the equally powerful emotional consequences of displacement, dispersal and exile: these were some of the themes that exemplify the Enlightened foundation of the Waverley series of novels. Played into an Atlantic perspective, they presented inescapable—if ideologically troublesome—models for the fictional experiments of James Fenimore Cooper, Nathaniel Hawthorne, Mark Twain and innumerable less celebrated nineteenth-century American writers.[32]

Coleridge and Southey fantasising about a pantisocratic community on the banks of the Susquehanna; the 1802 reprinting of *The Lyrical Ballads* in Philadelphia as a seditious act; the excitement of an unexpected meeting of minds in the first encounter and subsequent correspondence of Emerson and Thomas Carlyle, leading to the literary-historical oddity of the first book publication of the latter's highly Germanic *Sartor Resartus* in America, not England: all are part of the continuing story of Atlantic exchanges whose Enlightenment contours are described, interrogated, complicated and clarified in this volume of essays. We seek here to move beyond a reductive, essentialist, conception of Enlightenment as a fixed set of ideas confined to certain geographic locales or as a period defined by 'turning points' at its beginning and end. Rather we see the Enlightenment as an integral part of transatlantic networks of exchange—of ideas, people, and commodities.

Equally, though, we seek to move discussion of Atlantic worlds beyond the disciplinary framework of historical studies towards a flexible range of methodologies and approaches that will, we hope, encourage future discussion across boundaries, and the opening up of new types of exchanges, networks, dialogues and transformations.

---

32 See, for example, George Dekker, *The American Historical Romance* (Cambridge, 1987), Richard Brodhead, *Hawthorne, Melville and the Novel* (Chicago, 1976; rpt 1977); Susan Manning, 'Scott and Hawthorne: The Making of a National Literary Tradition,' in David Hewitt and J. H. Alexander, eds. *Scott and His Influence* (Aberdeen, 1983); Manning, 'Did Mark Twain bring down the temple'.

Such networks were constitutive of the Atlantic Enlightenment pluralistically conceived: the Atlantic was not just the space in which debates and circulation took place, but, as these essays show, shaped the contours of debate and informed the 'enlightened' profile of the (northern, Protestant) Atlantic world. What we offer here is a more open Enlightenment or Enlightenments viewed through the refracting lens of Atlanticism: a world of exchanges and relationships, whose political and cultural events cannot be understood apart from the dynamic physical and geographical environments in which they were determined.

Chapter 1

Enlightenment Historiography and Cultural Civil Wars

*Paul Giles**

The word 'enlightenment' was used descriptively in writing of the late-eighteenth and early-nineteenth centuries to refer to certain kinds of mental processes. Immanuel Kant, in his 1784 essay 'What is Enlightenment', associated the term with a 'reform in ways of thinking', while G. W. F. Hegel, in *Phenomenology of Spirit* (1807), discussed what he called the 'struggle of enlightenment with superstition'.[1] However, as J. C. D. Clark has pointed out, the first use of the word 'Enlightenment' to specify a particular historical period did not occur until much later, until 1865; certainly nobody in the eighteenth century itself would have used the word in that way.[2] In this sense, 'Enlightenment' can be seen as a term rather like 'Romanticism', another retrospective category quite unknown to figures such as William Wordsworth and Samuel Taylor Coleridge who were subsequently nominated as its chief protagonists. The idea of Enlightenment as a discrete historical phenomenon was projected back onto early-nineteenth-century culture from a theoretical vantage point some sixty or seventy years later.

This is not, of course, to suggest that all academic labels and categories are superfluous or that they may not serve useful and pragmatic ends, but one of the abiding hazards of this kind of cultural history is that scholars often begin intellectually to imitate, consciously or unconsciously, the distant phenomenon they are writing about. Thus, for example, F. O. Matthiessen's classic work, *American Renaissance*, published in 1941, reproduces formally the idealist, synthesising styles of the Transcendentalist writers under his critical scrutiny, just as F. R. Leavis, in *The Great Tradition* (1948), postulates the kind of organic cohesiveness between past and present that he attributes romantically to the novelists whom he installs at the centre of English literature. In the same way, the so-called Enlightenment era has attracted many intellectual historians who have attempted to explain this particular era in terms of various kinds of grand narratives. Classic examples of this might be J. G. A. Pocock's argument about republican fears of corruption and

* The second half of this essay draws on material previously published in *Atlantic Republic: The American Tradition in English Literature* (Oxford University Press, 2006), and is reproduced here by permission of OUP.

1   Immanuel Kant, 'What is Enlightenment?', in *The Portable Age of Reason Reader*, ed. Crane Brinton (New York, 1956), p. 300; G. W. F. Hegel, *The Phenomenology of Mind*, trans. J. B. Baillie, 2nd ed. (London, 1931), p. 561.

2   J. C. D. Clark, *The Language of Liberty, 1660–1832: Political Discourse and Social Dynamism in the Anglo-American World* (Cambridge, 1994), p. 14.

the flight from capitalism, or Joyce Appleby's assessment of the period in terms of the rise of liberalism; but the same principle applies also to more recent work: Michael Warner's thesis about the predominance of print culture in *Letters of the Republic*, or Christopher Looby's account of the persistence of oral culture in *Voicing America*, or Robert Ferguson's explanation of Enlightenment thinking in terms of the rights of property and independence of mind, with his concomitant emphasis on reason, science and experience.[3] All of these are valuable, even some of them magisterial works, but each has a tendency towards what I would describe as reading Enlightenment on its own programmatic terms, interpreting the Enlightenment according to Enlightenment norms of abstraction.

Such synthetic norms have also tended to structure the ways in which we approach individual texts, which tend consequently to be flattened out in an attempt to make them synecdochic of the intellectual controversies of this era. Colin Wells's *The Devil & Doctor Dwight*, published by the Omohundro Institute for Early American History and Culture, offers a fascinating contextual explanation of Timothy Dwight's 1788 poem, *The Triumph of Infidelity*, examining it in relation to the Universalist theological controversy addressed by Charles Chauncy and others in the second half of the eighteenth century: the question of whether such a thing as universal salvation was plausible or even desirable. But the problem with Wells's interpretation is that he offers this intellectual matrix as a full explanatory framework for Dwight's poem, rather than seeking also to interrogate some of the failures of continuity between Dwight's theological theory and his poetic practice; *The Triumph of Infidelity* is, in other words, eviscerated artistically in Wells's account, as if it were purely an exposition of arcane theological ideas in verse form. It seems to me in general that there is more room for discussions of discordances, discontinuities and incoherences within eighteenth-century Atlantic culture, and that a greater recognition of incompatible forces or contradictory pressures could help to focus more attention on the contested and often inchoate nature of this material, rather than seeing it merely as raw data to be subsumed under yet another grand Enlightenment metanarrative. Dwight's poem, for example, mentions the prevalence of dream states, the paintings of William Hogarth, and various grotesque details linked to notions of caricature and excess—a divine with 'cheeks of port', 'lips of turtle green', and so on—all of which introduce into the poem a comic, slightly manic temper which cannot be safely regularised within the intellectual history of the Universalist controversy.[4]

It would also be true to say that over the past half century the conceptualisation of an American Enlightenment, in particular, has been complicated by a traditional,

---

3   J. G. A. Pocock, *The Machiavellian Moment: Florentine Political Thought and the Atlantic Republican Tradition* (Princeton, 1975); Joyce Appleby, *Capitalism and the New Social Order: The Republican Vision of the 1790s* (New York, 1984); Michael Warner, *The Letters of the Republic: Publication and the Public Sphere in Eighteenth-Century America* (Cambridge, Mass., 1990); Christopher Looby, *Voicing America: Language, Literary Form, and the Origins of the United States* (Chicago, 1996); Robert A. Ferguson, *The American Enlightenment, 1750–1820* (Cambridge, Mass., 1997).

4   Colin Wells, *The Devil & Doctor Dwight: Satire and Theology in the Early American Republic* (Chapel Hill, 2002), p. 202.

sometimes even hidebound resistance to what are sometimes thought of as inappropriately foreign theoretical categorisations. When Henry F. May wrote his essay 'The Problem of the American Enlightenment' in 1970, he was consciously reacting against the assumptions of nationalist historians of a previous generation such as Daniel Boorstin, who had argued that the very idea of an American Enlightenment was simply a misnomer, an idea mistakenly imposed on the radically different conditions of American life by scholars working with preconceptions drawn from the European academy.[5] This is, of course, the old myth of American exceptionalism, the belief that the qualities of the American soil are inherently unique and that anterior theorisations are rendered redundant by the providential, unassimilable nature of its new reality. May was clearly right, I think, to point out the limitations, even at times the anti-intellectualism, of Boorstin's approach; but his own reaction to this in the form of a heavily systematised Enlightenment grid—he talks about the 'moderate Enlightenment' between 1688 and 1787, the 'skeptical enlightenment' between 1750 and 1789, and then a 'revolutionary enlightenment', 1776–1800—all this seems to me, in its own way, equally misleading. May's conceptual position tends to eliminate contradictions from his narrative teleologies and, since his line of argument is that the tone of the American Enlightenment was generally cautious and compromising, he has difficulty accommodating Hume and the more heterodox French thinkers into his essentially nationalist matrix. (He calls French thinkers like Diderot 'too divided and too complex' to fit within this eighteenth-century American milieu). Indeed, May's emphasis on the absence of what he calls 'damaging extremes' in the American cultural enlightenment actually mirrors, in an odd way, the Boorstin thesis of mythic exceptionalism; whereas Boorstin asserted that America was exempt from the more abstract theoretical systems of the Enlightenment, May claims by contrast the country was so suffused by pragmatic forms of rationalism that no 'damaging' counternarratives could take root in American soil.[6] Each, in their different ways, imagined America as a protected space, a land whose distinctive qualities impelled it towards a mythic homogeneity.

Gordon Wood in his illuminating study, *The Radicalism of the American Revolution* (1992), is generally more hospitable to the idea of division, but towards the end of that book he again concludes: 'When even a once radical skeptic like Joel Barlow lamely came to insist that he had not really abandoned Christianity after all, then we knew that the Enlightenment was over.'[7] Again, one problem with this formulation is that Wood seems to be working with an *a priori* conception of Enlightenment and what it signifies, a conception that he uses ultimately as a standard against which to judge Barlow. My response to this would be to suggest that contradiction was always an integral part of eighteenth-century culture, that Barlow's poems—*The Hasty Pudding*, *The Columbiad*, and others—are actually radical and conservative both at the same time, and that it is this kind of edgy, fractured quality that effectively

---

5   Henry F. May, 'The Problem of the American Enlightenment', *New Literary History*, 1 (1970): 201–14; Daniel J. Boorstin, *The Americans: The Colonial Experience* (New York, 1958).

6   Henry F. May, *The Enlightenment in America* (New York, 1976), pp. 1, 103, 151, 109; May, 'The Problem of the American Enlightenment', 214.

7   Gordon S. Wood, *The Radicalism of the American Revolution* (New York, 1992), p. 330.

contributes to much of their elusive power, their capacity to evoke conditions of pastoral nostalgia and rationalist radicalism simultaneously. This is, in fact, one area where poetry such as Barlow's, or indeed imaginative literature in general, can work as a corrective to some of the larger theories about the Enlightenment, because such fictions often entertain—indeed, often embrace—a mixed-up, irrational world, evoking a confused or anarchic state of affairs which political or religious polemicists, then as now, have tried to systematise away. Our perhaps rather austere view of the Enlightenment today is, I think, one of the unfortunate by-products of the fact that over the last twenty-five years there have been relatively few literary critics working on the eighteenth century, especially in its American context, as opposed to intellectual historians, who have of course been plentiful. I would also want to challenge the sequential emphasis which is implied by the narrative trajectory of Gordon Wood's argument, his notion that Enlightenment ideals were betrayed as the secular radicalism of the late-eighteenth century came to be superseded by the evangelical revivals of the early nineteenth. It seems more likely that many of these sources of contradiction and potential forms of incoherence—Christianity versus secularism, oral versus written cultures, aristocracy versus democracy, and so on—existed simultaneously within the eighteenth-century Atlantic world, so that the works of writers like Benjamin Franklin and Thomas Jefferson should be understood not in a positivistic but in a chameleonic light. The task of a cultural historian, then, might be to trace these areas of conflict, tension and crossover, rather than to extrapolate any particular aspect of this complex scene into a more abstract model of Enlightenment thought.

My final point about what might be called the cultural historiography of the Enlightenment relates to the common tendency in recent scholarship to think of it in presentist terms. Particularly in the 1950s and early 1960s, as Giles Gunn and others have pointed out, there was a tendency more or less to ignore the eighteenth century in discussions of American culture, to move swiftly from New England Puritanism through to the nineteenth-century Transcendentalists, thus foregrounding an idiom of individualism and spiritual self-reliance that was thought to be synonymous with the American national spirit itself. For instance, in his 1955 essay 'The Romantic Dilemma in American Nationalism and the Concept of Nature', Perry Miller brought together Calvinist typologies and Emerson's interest in reading nature hieroglyphically, thus effectively marginalising an eighteenth-century climate of rationalism which he saw as inhospitable to the progressive ethos of American romanticism.[8] Of course, this tendency to bypass the American eighteenth century on ideological grounds has been successfully challenged in recent years: one thinks of anthologies such as Myra Jehlen's and Michael Warner's anthology *The English Literatures of America, 1500–1800* (1997), which has brought back into circulation a wide range of previously obscure literary texts, or of what David Shields has called the 'archival turn', by which he means a more general intellectual curiosity about

---

8   Giles Gunn, *Thinking Across The American Grain: Ideology, Intellect, and the New Pragmatism* (Chicago, 1992), pp. 119–51; Perry Miller, 'The Romantic Dilemma in American Nationalism and the Concept of Nature', in Perry Miller, *Nature's Nation* (Cambridge, Mass., 1967), pp. 197–207.

rediscovering and opening up the archives of eighteenth-century culture, so that we move away from the five or six best-known writers and begin to find interesting things that we are not specifically looking for. In his 2001 presidential address to the Society for Early Americanists, Shields mentioned as an example of this the poems of Susanna Wright, who was born in England in 1697 and who came to Pennsylvania in her teens, works which were discovered at Haverford College only in 1995.[9] Contrary to popular legend, then, the eighteenth century is decidedly not a period of literary scarcity in America, any more than it is in England, and a diversification of the primary material which we study might usefully complicate the hypothetical assumptions and theoretical frameworks that we customarily bring to this period.

Conversely, the traditional method of representing eighteenth-century culture by just a few texts, Benjamin Franklin's *Autobiography* and one or two others, has resulted in its multifarious nature being more easily telescoped into a scheme of Enlightenment that is made to anticipate present-day concerns. For example, Peter Gay's admirable two volume work on the Enlightenment, published in 1966 and 1969, was clearly impelled by an implicit thesis that it was the cosmopolitan, scientific-minded intellectuals of the Enlightenment that were the true forerunners of what Gay called the exponents of 'modern paganism' in the 1960s.[10] Gay chose, in other words, primarily to focus upon the iconoclastic tone of eighteenth-century culture as a kind of extended prelude to the climate of the 1960s, the era of John F. Kennedy, scientific technocracy, enlightened liberalism and sexual freedom, so that he was effectively appropriating a particular version of Enlightenment thought as a precursor to his own political concerns. More recently, Gillian Brown, in *The Consent of the Governed* (2001), looks back to the influence of John Locke in early American culture, which Brown again sees as anticipating directly the multicultural politics of the contemporary United States. There are various barbed references in Brown's book to William Bennett, the former US Secretary for Education under Reagan, but what perturbs me here is not her intellectual agenda in itself, which I sympathise with, but the fact that she is attempting to essentialise or reify a particular version of the American Enlightenment as a kind of founding myth of origins, a guarantee of the institutionalised nature of American liberal culture. Brown writes at the beginning of her book of how it 'goes back to some of the basics', and of how Lockean liberalism 'crucially helped generate American national identity'.[11] Phrases such as 'American national identity' would seem to be problematic anyway, and just as Perry Miller inscribed a version of cultural nationalism running through Winthrop and Jonathan Edwards to Emerson, so Brown appears to be following an

---

9   Myra Jehlen and Michael Warner, eds, *The English Literatures of America, 1500–1800* (New York, 1997); David S. Shields, 'Presidential Address', Society of Early Americanists conference, Norfolk, Virginia, 8 March 2001.

10   Peter Gay, *The Enlightenment: An Interpretation. The Rise of Modern Paganism* (New York, 1966), and *The Enlightenment: An Interpretation. The Science of Freedom* (New York, 1969).

11   Gillian Brown, *The Consent of the Governed: The Lockean Legacy in Early American Culture* (Cambridge, Mass., 2001), pp. 3–4.

analogous if alternative pattern by trying to establish a different genealogy from the Enlightenment through to Postmodernism and multiculturalism.

There have also been various studies recently from economic historians such as Emma Rothschild, suggesting that the eighteenth-century world of intellectual cosmopolitanism and free enterprise might be said to anticipate the twenty-first-century conditions of globalisation, where national boundaries are less secure and where economic liberalism takes on a transnational impetus. Writing before the events of 9/11 put a damper on this kind of free market triumphalism, Rothschild makes her ahistorical analogy quite explicitly. 'The new prospects of the early twenty-first-century have something of this vastness, this sense of an unbounded future,' she writes: 'We may also have some sympathy, in our societies of universal commerce, for the endless uncertainty, the unquiet imagination, which were believed, in the late eighteenth century, to be the consequence of commercial freedom.'[12] In this sense, one might say that the old mythic triumvirate of Winthrop—Edwards—Emerson, adumbrating a supposedly characteristic national form of self-reliance, has been supplanted by a new genealogy of Enlightenment—Postmodernism—Globalisation, through which Adam Smith and his acolytes stand as precursors to the contemporary interest in a borderless world, a world predicated upon the international circulation of capital and free trade. This is not to deny, of course, that in the final analysis all cultural interpretations must have elements of presentism and partiality inherent within them. What is worth considering, though, is whether an excessively rapid allegorisation of cultural formations and crosscurrents into grand schematic narratives might not have the effect of drastically oversimplifying our view of the past in one way or another. One of my concerns here is to look back particularly to the time of the American Revolution and to demythologise some of the apparatus and iconography surrounding it, so as to recover some sense of how it was a conflicted and messy event, whose outcome owed as much to chance as to providence. In this sense, I prefer to use as an explanatory matrix the historical period of the eighteenth century rather than the more abstract conception of an Enlightenment, since part of my argument is that cultural history generally fails to coincide in any very precise way with these larger theoretical systems.

Pauline Maier, in her recent book *American Scripture*, described how the tombs of the Founding Fathers have been surrounded since the early-nineteenth century with a reverential hagiography of all kinds, and of course the American Revolution itself has now achieved retrospectively the status of a 'sacred' event in the annals of US history, an original point of reference and form of mythic definition for the nation.[13] However, the extent to which this War of Independence actually took its impetus not so much from secessionist or nonconformist ideals as from an idealised conception of traditional British political liberties is a complicated question. J. G. A. Pocock wrote of the 'profoundly important sense in which the American Revolution can only be understood ... as one of a series of crises occasioned by the growth

---

12   Emma Rothschild, *Economic Sentiments: Adam Smith, Condorcet, and the Enlightenment* (Cambridge, Mass., 2001), p. 6.

13   Pauline Maier, *American Scripture: Making the Declaration of Independence* (New York, 1997), p. 197.

and change of English political institutions', and he goes on to describe 1776 as the last in a sequence of 'three British revolutions' after 1641 and 1688, thereby aligning the English Civil War and Glorious Revolution as direct precursors in a broad Anglocentric movement for civil liberties.[14] John Locke is often thought of as the crucial link between the revolutions of 1688 and 1776, though Pocock's larger concern is with demystifying early American history, with seeing it as a 'dialectical process' engaged in a difficult political quest for constitutional liberty; consequently, he takes issue with the popular view that the birth of the American nation was a mythic advent of freedom brought about by 'the attempt to escape history and then regenerate it'.[15] However, Pocock's view of the Revolution as turning upon a transatlantic debate about virtue and corruption has been challenged by American scholars such as Ruth Bloch, who has emphasised how the millennial images associated with ideas of a new birth of freedom helped to galvanise the spirit of revolution among large sections of the American population. Rather than seeing this conflict as impelled by abstruse Augustan debates about the nature of liberty, Bloch focuses upon how ideas of apocalypse taken from evangelical Christianity came to be disseminated throughout the popular culture of the time, so that George Washington himself came to be cast in Biblical terms as, in Ezra Stiles's phrase, the 'American Joshua' leading his people to victory.[16]

Whether the American Revolution had a more legalistic or religious impetus, the point I wish to emphasise here is how suddenly it happened. There was not, as in most colonial situations, a protracted period of dissent and resentment against imperial masters; few in America dreamt of independence in the 1750s, while in 1763 John Adams was still describing the English constitution as 'the most perfect combination of human powers in society which finite wisdom has yet contrived and reduced to practice for the preservation of liberty and the production of happiness'.[17] To talk of the English constitution as designed specifically to ensure 'the production of happiness' might now seem strange, particularly in view of how the Declaration of Independence only thirteen years later, in condemning England, sought to requisition this idea of 'the pursuit of happiness' for itself. What such a sudden turnaround does suggest, though, is the dramatically foreshortened perspective within which the events of the American Revolution took place: one moment the colonists were looking back gratefully to Britain as the guarantor of their political heritage, the next they found they had delivered themselves into a perhaps unexpected condition of independence.

---

14   J. G. A. Pocock, '1776: The Revolution Against Parliament', in J. G. A. Pocock,, *Three British Revolutions: 1641, 1688, 1776* (Princeton, 1980), p. 266.

15   Pocock, *The Machiavellian Moment*, pp. 503, 545.

16   Ruth H. Bloch, *Visionary Republic: Millennial Themes in American Thought, 1756–1800* (Cambridge, 1985); Catherine L. Albanese, *Sons of the Fathers: The Civil Religion of the American Revolution* (Philadelphia, 1976), p. 154.

17   Bernard Bailyn, *The Ideological Origins of the American Revolution* (Cambridge, Mass., 1967), p. 67.

Virtual history is always a meretricious exercise, the province in truth of God rather than man, since its possibilities are quite literally infinite.[18] Suppose, however, that the British forces had displayed a modicum of military competence at the Battle of Bunker Hill in 1775, so that this American uprising was remembered today as a minor skirmish. What would presumably have happened then is that the birth of American cultural nationalism would not have been contemporaneous with the romantic movement at the beginning of the nineteenth century, which worked intellectually to naturalise a people's relationship to their native land. Rather than emerging, like postrevolutionary France, out of this great era of nation-building, America would have been positioned more like Ireland, as a western colony of Great Britain, so that pressure for Home Rule would probably have built up in America over the course of the nineteenth century, as indeed it did in Ireland. This would have meant that the gestation period for American political and cultural independence would have been longer, and that nineteenth-century American literature, in particular, would have been seen as involved in a more explicit dialogue with British imperial power. There is an important sense in which writers like Margaret Fuller and Henry David Thoreau are still driven implicitly by a politics of Anglophobic resistance, but this idiom of postcolonial struggle would have been much more obvious if historical events had taken a different turn. Writing of nineteenth-century Irish literature, from Lady Sydney Morgan to Oscar Wilde, Terry Eagleton saw it as engaged with an intertextual demystification of English hierarchical order: the parallel, sometimes parodic structures of Irish writing tended to create for their English overlords, argued Eagleton, an 'unthinkable conundrum of difference and identity, in which the British can never decide whether the Irish are their antithesis or mirror image, partner or parasite, abortive offspring or sympathetic sibling'.[19] The same thing is true, albeit less overtly, of relations between English and American literature in this modern period, since the formal legalisation of US independence could not altogether alleviate the dynamics of antagonism and oppression, reflecting transatlantic power struggles which continued to reverberate in late-eighteenth-century British culture.

In the wake of their sudden loss of America, a loss which took the English ruling classes largely by surprise, there was a determination in England at the end of the eighteenth century not to make the same mistake twice. Linda Colley has described the American War as being for Britain like the Vietnam War was for the United States two centuries later: a David versus Goliath conflict which divided and demoralised the great power in question and which led, by way of reaction, to a sharp political swing towards the right. Consequently, when a general rebellion broke out in Ireland in 1798, it was crushed harshly by British forces; George III strongly opposed any concessions to the Irish Catholics, and the Act of Union, passed in 1800, proclaimed

---

18   For examples of this hypothetical method, see Niall Ferguson, ed., *Virtual History: Alternatives and Counterfactuals* (London, 1997).

19   Terry Eagleton, *Heathcliff and the Great Hunger: Studies in Irish Culture* (London, 1995), p. 127.

that Ireland was henceforth to be tied indissolubly to Great Britain.[20] There was even a link between these American and Irish uprisings in terms of British military personnel, since General Charles Cornwallis, who had been forced to surrender to George Washington at Yorktown in 1781, had been appointed Lord Lieutenant of Ireland in June 1798, and on hearing of the imminent arrival of French reinforcements to supplement the Irish insurgents he promptly assumed personal command of British forces in the field. Cornwallis was subsequently instrumental in constructing the political Act of Union, working under the 'conviction', as he put it in 1799, 'that an Union is absolutely necessary for the safety of the British Empire'.[21]

What all this indicates is that Britain was not altogether indifferent to the loss of America, as has sometimes been suggested, but was, rather, wary of the emergence of the United States as a significant presence on the world stage. Some of the more far-sighted public figures at the end of the eighteenth century expressed anxiety at how the American Revolution might eventually affect the global balance of power. In 1782, Prime Minister Shelburne was moved publicly to voice his concern in Parliament: 'The sun of Great Britain will set whenever she acknowledges the independence of America,' he said, and he admitted his apprehension that the 'independence of America would end in the ruin of England'. Simon Linguet, a French supporter of strong centralised monarchy who in 1777 started the journal *Annales politiques* from exile in London, similarly feared that the United States, by taking advantage of its rich natural resources, might grow and prosper to such an extent that it could put itself in a position to dominate world trade and to control the destiny of Europe.[22]

The first British responses to the prospect of the new United States, then, were worked out not so much on the level of philosophical abstraction or debates about environmentalism or enlightenment but in terms of brute political power. As Bernard Bailyn has observed, many pamphlets supporting the American patriot cause in the late-eighteenth century argued from the premises of an Enlightenment reason that regarded liberty as indivisible and that tried to rise deliberately above the partiality of local sentiments. Advocates of the British cause, by contrast, tended to favour the more aggressive method of satire, which might be described as an attempt to exercise power in discursive form through its method of seeking not so much to address as to belittle or humiliate its object.[23] This suggests that the very idea of Enlightenment,

---

20   Linda Colley, *Britons: Forging the Nation, 1707–1837* (New Haven, 1992), pp. 144–5; Jacques Godechot, *France and the Atlantic Revolutions of the Eighteenth Century, 1770–1799*, trans. Herbert H. Rowen (New York, 1965), p. 225.

21   Franklin and Mary Wickwire, *Cornwallis: The Imperial Years* (Chapel Hill, 1980), p. 244. It should be noted that Cornwallis favoured Catholic Emancipation as a measure to stabilise and strengthen the Union, arguing that 'some mode must be adopted to soften the hatred of the Catholics to our government'. However, this spirit of compromise was staunchly opposed by George III and Pitt's government.

22   John Keane, *Tom Paine: A Political Life* (London, 1995), p. 233; Durand Echeverria, *Mirage in the West: A History of the French Image of American Society to 1815* (Princeton, 1957), pp. 62–4.

23   Bailyn, *Ideological Origins*, pp. 18–19. On the conflict between Enlightenment radicalism and English nationalism, see also David Simpson, *Romanticism, Nationalism, and the Revolt against Theory* (Chicago, 1993), p. 181.

with its hypothesis of universal reason, was itself an object of political dispute, rather than comprising the overall conceptual context within which such disputes occurred. The English writer charged by Lord North's ministry with producing a quasi-official reply to the Declaration of Rights by the first session of the American Continental Congress was none other than Samuel Johnson, who in his 1759 novel, *Rasselas*, had mocked the human search for rationalist perfectibility, with all of the self-delusions such dreams of the 'happy valley' entail. In 1774, Johnson turned his satirical disposition to political account in his pamphlet *The Patriot*, where he mocks 'the ridiculous claims of American usurpation' against 'natural and lawful authority'.[24] One year later, in response to Sir Grey Cooper, the Secretary of the Treasury who acted as intermediary between Johnson and the North government, he produced *Taxation No Tyranny: An Answer to the Resolution and Address of the American Congress*.

Taxation No Tyranny is in many ways a predictable enough document, which seeks to validate the position of the British government according to what Johnson calls 'the standing order of Nature', and which justifies taxation legally, as 'a payment exacted by authority from part of the community for the benefit of the whole'.[25] There is, of course, an imperial logic at work here, whereby Britain is said to enjoy a 'natural' authority over America: 'A colony,' writes Johnson, 'is to the mother-country as a member to the body, deriving its action and its strength from the general principle of vitality' (425). Johnson accordingly ridicules the republican idea of freedom, seeing it as a 'delirious dream' (428) running contrary to the principles of centralised order and hierarchical subordination upon which his view of the world is predicated. One curious facet of this pamphlet is the intransigence of its rhetoric: the author ends up by advocating harsh punishments for the rebels, saying that 'erroneous clemency' in this case would be 'noxious to society' (453), and recommending that when the Americans 'are reduced to obedience ... that obedience be secured by stricter laws and stronger obligations' (452). The thunderous tone of this pamphlet suggests the intensity of hatred in British conservative circles of this time for the very idea of insubordination which the American Revolution brought into view: James Boswell in 1778 reported that Johnson used to dismiss Americans as 'a race of convicts', saying he would like to 'burn and destroy them'.[26] While the apparently hyperbolic nature of this antipathy might be seen as the reaction of an elderly man raging against a world that would no longer defer to his conception of it—Johnson died in 1784—it should also be understood more generally as indicative of the British government's anxieties about what kind of destabilising properties might be unleashed if this open revolt against the legitimate order were to go unchecked, and it suggests also how the spectre of this American conflict helped to shape English writing towards the end of the eighteenth century. The North government watered down some of Johnson's

---

24   Samuel Johnson, *The Patriot*, in Samuel Johnson, *Political Writings*, ed., Donald J. Greene (New Haven, 1977), p. 396.

25   Johnson, 'Taxation No Tyranny', in Johnson, *Poiltical Writings*, pp. 412, 417. Subsequent page references to this essay are cited in parenthesis in the text.

26   James Boswell, *The Life of Samuel Johnson LLD.*, ed. Christopher Hibbert (Harmondsworth, 1979), pp. 176, 247.

most vitriolic language in *Taxation No Tyranny*, just as the American Congress in 1776 diplomatically toned down some of the purple passages in Thomas Jefferson's Declaration of Independence, but it is not difficult to see how these intellectual arguments over the meaning of liberty and authority at this time touched some raw nerves on both sides.

Another revealing aspect of *Taxation No Tyranny* is its geographic perspective, the way Johnson holds implicitly to an idea of London as the natural centre of the world with America a subordinate territory on the margins, a 'parish in the kingdom' as he puts it (436). In fact, the author mocks the idea of American independence by suggesting it would be as absurd as if Cornwall were to secede by claiming for itself a separate history and language from the rest of Britain (445). It is interesting that Johnson attempts to bolster the power of the centre by testing it against what is most remote from that centre, and this sense of inherent friction, of a social order pushing itself up against physical extremities, may help to explain some of the tortuous, excessive style of Johnson's pamphlets, whose vision of order turns more upon a struggle to force some kind of control upon a chaotic world than upon any polite assumptions about Augustan decorum. Just as Cornwall, on the southwest tip of England, brings America to Johnson's mind, so he constantly compares America to the barren landscapes of the far north of Britain in his *Journey to the Western Islands of Scotland*, which also appeared in 1775, the same year as *Taxation No Tyranny*. Based upon a trip taken with Boswell in the autumn of 1773, and published at the very time when the British dispute with her American colonies was about to issue in war, Johnson's *Journey* can be understood retrospectively in an elegiac light, as an intimation of the loss of that national coherence and administrative control after which his political pamphlets hanker. The narrator continually associates the 'uniformity of barrenness' he finds in Scotland with the 'deserts' and 'wastes of America', mocking this distant landscape as 'merely pastoral' and as altogether lacking in the commodious comforts of the metropolis.[27] Rather than acknowledging Scotland or America as locations with their own distinctive culture, as a nineteenth-century racialist might have done, Johnson simply chastises them as deficient in the properties of universal reason.[28] At the same time, he inveighs against what he calls 'the mischiefs of emigration' (95), insisting that the loss of population weakens a country's defences, and he talks of how the owners of these islands deliberately spread stories of hardships in America in a vain attempt to keep the people content at home. Emigration, indeed, is a recurring theme in this narrative: Johnson writes of how those who fall for 'American seducements' become

> as subjects lost to the British crown; for a nation scattered in the boundless regions of America resembles rays diverging from a focus. All the rays remain, but the heat is gone. Their power consisted in their concentration: when they are dispersed, they have no effect.

---

27 Samuel Johnson, *A Journey to the Western Islands of Scotland*, ed. Mary Lascelles (New Haven, 1971), pp. 40–41, 84, 37. Subsequent page references to this edition are cited in parenthesis in the text.

28 See Clement Hawes, 'Johnson and Imperialism', in *The Cambridge Companion to Samuel Johnson*, ed. Greg Clingham (Cambridge, 1997), pp. 114–15.

It may be thought that they are happier by the change; but they are not happy as a nation, for they are a nation no longer. (131)

The metaphor of decentring and dissemination is especially apt here. Nostalgic and even at times maniacally desperate for the image of an authoritarian centre, Johnson also appears strangely compelled by these rituals of depopulation. (Boswell's *Journal* of the same expedition records how a dance on the Island of Skye was called 'America' after this pattern of communal emigration; the dance, he wrote, 'seems intended to show how emigration catches, till a whole neighbourhood is set afloat').[29]

The colonising mentality in Johnson's *Journey* is obvious enough. As Katie Trumpener has observed, he altogether ignores the intellectual renaissance in Edinburgh at this time and stereotypes the Scottish natural and cultural wilderness as a negative polarity to English civilised values.[30] This is also the basis for his analogies between Scotland and America as provincial territories, analogies which, as Robert Crawford and others have pointed out, were not uncommon in nationalist thinking around this time.[31] What makes Johnson's response unusual, though, is the darker, melancholic streak through which he seems at some level to recognise the demise of empire as fated. Politically, he advocates the kind of centralised authority of which Augustus Caesar would have been proud: 'As government advances towards perfection,' he writes, 'provincial judicature is perhaps in every empire gradually abolished' (46). This is why Ian Baucom is not quite right to suggest that for Johnson the spectre of empire is inevitably a corrupting influence since it imprints 'spots of barbarism' in the native language, thereby undermining the integrity of English culture.[32] It would be true to say, though, that Johnson is always aware of the frustrating discrepancy between centre and province, civilisation and 'barbarism', so that his works might be said to explore imaginatively the potential collapse of their own imperial designs. Johnson's poetic sensibility, in other words, often seems to be at odds with his political outlook: in *A Journey to the Western Islands of Scotland*, for instance, his theories of Augustan order come to be seen as merely hypothetical when set against the stark, mountainous landscape of rocks and thistles. In this sense, Johnson the empirical observer unravels the more abstract projections of Johnson the imperial speculator, so that his texts are shot through with pessimistic intuitions about the vanity of human wishes. Regarding emigration from the Scottish Islands to America, for example, he writes in a paradoxical, grimly comic vein about the self-defeating gestures of local chieftains: 'To hinder insurrection, by driving away the people, and to govern peaceably, by having no subjects, is an expedient that argues no great profundity of politics' (97). The remark is weighed down by Johnson's characteristic ballast of common-sense, but it also suggests ways in which

---

29   James Boswell, *The Journal of a Tour to the Hebrides*, ed. Peter Levi (London, 1984), p. 327.

30   Katie Trumpener, *Bardic Nationalism: The Romantic Novel and the British Empire* (Princeton, 1997), p. 69.

31   Robert Crawford, *Devolving English Literature* (Oxford, 1992), p. 185.

32   Ian Baucom, *Out of Place: Englishness, Empire, and the Locations of Identity* (Princeton, 1999), p. 27.

his account of the Scottish Islands is shadowed by the spectre of America as alterity, imagined here as a negative force lying in wait to undermine the British Empire, a lurking shadow which throws a dark reflection upon the spectrum of national unity. Johnson's writing is simultaneously attracted to and repelled by this vision of disorder, which is why Boswell's popular version of him as a conservative, clubbable dispenser of *bons mots* can never be entirely sufficient. And what America brings to the surface in Johnson's writing is the mixture of rational and irrational elements within his satirical polemics, the ways in which his fantasies of Augustan order are held in check by an implicit recognition of the impending collapse or inversion of that Anglocentric vision.

As Lewis Namier noted long ago, British responses towards America at the end of the eighteenth century overlapped significantly with attitudes towards the Dissenting Churches, with members of the Anglican establishment like Johnson seeking to consolidate the structural homology of church and state which nonconformist thinkers such as Richard Price did their best to dissolve.[33] Price, whose pamphlets on the American question sold in huge numbers, was another exemplification of links at this time between America and the Celtic fringes, being a Welsh preacher steeped in the religious traditions of personal liberty and the philosophical doctrines of enlightenment. In his tracts on America, Price envisages the new country as a beacon of hope, an emblem of that 'spirit of illumination' which will, so he hopes, induce Britain to follow America's example by acknowledging the value of moral self-improvement. Perceiving power as a corrupting influence *per se*, Price in 1778 urges his fellow Britons to abjure their lust for dominion and to pursue instead more rational policies of equality and contractual partnership:

> By exertions of authority which have alarmed [the Americans] they have been put upon examining into the grounds of all our claims and forced to give up their luxuries and to seek all their resources within themselves. And the issue is likely to prove the loss of all our authority over them and of all the advantages connected with it. So little do men in power sometimes know how to preserve power and so remarkably does the desire of extending dominion sometimes destroy it … The people of America are no more the subjects of the people of Britain than the people of Yorkshire are the subjects of the people of Middlesex. They are your fellow-subjects.[34]

Like Joseph Priestley and other supporters of America among the nonconformist clergy, Price became a frequent object of ridicule in Britain during the 1790s. In the midst of the British conflicts with America and France, Price's kind of middle-class radicalism became associated in the popular mind with eccentricity and neurosis, inclinations which reinvigorated the inherent anti-intellectualism of the British establishment.[35] Price's views on political liberty are characterised as absurdly abstract

---

33   Sir Lewis Namier, *England in the Age of the American Revolution*, 2nd ed. (London, 1961), pp. 38–9.

34   Richard Price, 'Two Tracts on Civil Liberty, the War with America, and the Debts and Finances of the Kingdom', in *Political Writings*, ed. D. O. Thomas (Cambridge, 1991), pp. 50, 70.

35   J. H. Plumb, 'British Attitudes to the American Revolution', in *The American Experience: The Collected Essays, Volume 2* (New York, 1989), p. 73.

and hypothetical in Burke's *Reflections on the Revolution in France* (1790), while a James Gillray caricature in the same year depicts a monarchical Burke looming over a cowering Price in the wake of the latter's last pamphlet, *A Discourse on the Love of our Country* (1789). Gillray's cartoon is entitled 'Smelling out a Rat; or, The Atheistical Revolutionist disturbed in his Midnight "Calculations"', and it lampoons as altogether too redolent of the inkhorn Price's final prophetic vision: 'Behold, the light you have struck out, after setting America free, reflected to France and there kindled into a blaze that lays despotism in ashes and warms and illuminates Europe!' Again, Price here conceives of the American Revolution as a model for subsequent reform movements closer to home, and in the final paragraph he specifically refers contemporary expressions of political dissent back to the spirit of the Protestant Reformation: 'Take warning all ye supporters of slavish governments and slavish hierarchies! Call no more (absurdly and wickedly) reformation, innovation.'[36]

In considering British reactions to American political independence, Price can be seen as a symptomatic figure in several significant ways. First, he places an extraordinarily high value on the importance of the American Revolution, declaring it in 1785 to be 'the most important step in the progressive course of improvement of mankind' since 'the introduction of Christianity'.[37] One of his prominent contemporaries who shared this view of America's significance was Adam Smith, the Scottish moral philosopher and economist, who championed freedom from all kinds of institutional restraint. Smith was of course a staunch advocate of free trade, and in *The Wealth of Nations* (1776) he anticipated Price by suggesting iconoclastically that 'the discovery of America and that of a passage to the East Indies by the Cape of Good Hope', both of which facilitated economic exchange, should be seen as 'the two greatest and most important events recorded in the history of mankind'.[38] Second, Price thinks of America as linked intellectually with the Glorious Revolution of 1688, which introduced a form of constitutional government in Britain, and so he is a keen proselytiser for 'Mr Locke and all the writers on civil liberty who have been hitherto most admired in this country'. Third, Price understands the new United States to be an incarnation of what Britain could and should have been if it had followed Locke's principles to their logical conclusion: 'The liberty of America might have preserved our liberty, and, under the direction of a patriot king or wise minister, proved the means of restoring to us our almost lost constitution.' In this sense, Price perceives America as a distant mirror of England, its alter ego, that model 'city upon a hill' which the exiled Englishman John Winthrop had imagined one hundred and fifty years earlier.[39] And fourth and finally, following on from this, Price conceives of the American Revolution as an opportunity to introduce the principles of the Reformation

---

36 Price, 'A Discourse on the Love of Our Country', in *Political Writings*, p. 96.

37 Price, 'Observations on the Importance of the American Revolution', in *Political Writings*, p. 119.

38 Adam Smith, *The Wealth of Nations, Books IV–V*, ed. Andrew Skinner (London, 1999), p. 209.

39 Price, 'Two Tracts on Civil Liberty', in *Political Writings*, pp. 20, 56; John Winthrop, 'A Model of Christian Charity' (1630), in Perry Miller, ed., *The American Puritans: Their Prose and Poetry* (New York, 1956), p. 83.

into a benighted England. Like Winthrop, Price sought to reform English institutions and to purify what he saw as the corruption at the heart of the British social, political and religious establishment. His 1759 essay, 'Britain's Happiness, and the Proper Improvement of it', assumes a direct teleological link between the Reformation and the Enlightenment by seeing them as both leading cumulatively towards an ethic of personal responsibility: 'The invention of printing followed by the reformation and the revival of literature; the free communication which has been opened between the different parts of the world, and the late amazing improvements in knowledge of every kind, have remarkably prepared the way for this joyful period.'[40]

This joyful period, those are Price's words, and they demonstrate how for him the Enlightenment was a religious rather than a purely secular phenomenon. For Price, Enlightenment should be seen as an extension of debates about the Reformation, not, as Roy Porter argued in 2000, as an example of the secular, pragmatic politics of eighteenth-century Britain. Porter maintained that while the English Enlightenment may not have had the self-consciously avant-garde panache of Diderot and the *philosophes*, it prided itself upon a more robust tradition of freedom and toleration, creating conditions of possibility whereby improved 'social prospects and agendas of personal fulfilment' could be achieved within a familiar social frame.[41] Porter's work on the British Enlightenment lays emphasis on its more empirical virtues: on the achievements of science, on the cherished freedom of the press and on the increasing importance of middle-class London, which took over control of cultural life at this time from the aristocratic court. The point is that Price's vision of Enlightenment and Porter's historical reconstruction of Enlightenment are two very different things, although, curiously enough, they are both performing intellectual acts of retrospective appropriation: Price looks back to the seventeenth century to justify his situation at the end of the eighteenth, just as Porter looked back to the eighteenth from a secularised position in the twenty-first. But the Enlightenment itself is revealed clearly as a slippery concept, dependent more on the projections of the observer than on the empirical data employed supposedly to justify these perspectives.

Not only, then, is cultural history riven with conflicts and contradictions, but interpretations of that cultural history are dependent implicitly upon extrapolations from an often anachronistic mode of nationalistic politics. The formalisation of American independence created a schism within the British state, so that subsequently the characteristics of freedom, mobility and republican iconoclasm, still common at least within Britain's conception of itself during the eighteenth century, were split off and came retrospectively to be identified more specifically with the American party. The English who gave their allegiance to the new American state, whether through actual emigration or not, identified themselves with a spirit of reformation and transformation; by contrast, the English who stayed literally and metaphorically at home began to retreat into more conservative postures and increasingly to

---

40   Price, 'Britain's Happiness, and the Proper Improvement of it', in *Political Writings*, p. 12.

41   Roy Porter, *Enlightenment: Britain and the Creation of the Modern World* (London, 2000), p. 14.

cherish the virtues of a settled, hierarchical society. Paul Langford dates the word 'Englishness' from about 1805, suggesting that it came at this time to be linked more with notions of practicality, prudence and stability rather than with that natural sense of adventurousness which typified the Englishman's self-image in the previous century.[42] After 1780, the notion of human behaviour moulding itself according to the contours of nature became increasingly equated intellectually with the experimental conditions of the New World—Crèvecoeur's *Letters from an American Farmer* (1782) is the most obvious example of this—with the result that Britain needed to define itself differently, to reposition itself not as nature's nation but as a country where more traditional social virtues still held sway.

Obviously the American Revolution was not the only reason for this new authoritarian mood in Britain at the end of the eighteenth century: the conflicts with France and various other social factors contributed to the general climate of reaction. Nevertheless, as Porter says, the war years up until 1815 were generally bleak times for the citizens of the British Enlightenment, who not only found themselves at odds with the nation and its government but who also, much to their dismay, found England now exulting in its role as the defender of Old World values.[43] When the American Declaration of Independence in 1776 accused the British Crown of exerting an 'absolute tyranny' over its subjects, this was the first time during the modern era that England had been forced into the position of an *ancien régime* oppressor; but it was a role to which the country was to become increasingly accustomed, indeed increasingly partial, during the nineteenth century. After 1800, English poets like Wordsworth and Coleridge refurbished the idea of knowledge as a form of revelation, a gift from God, not something to be achieved through the powers of human reason. As Ludmilla Jordanova argues, this served indirectly to reunite religion and politics, since the Wordsworthian poetic belief in immanent value could readily be transferred to the conception that the English landscape itself embodied certain kinds of divine values: not so much a divine right of kings, perhaps, but certainly a divine right of country.[44]

I argue, then, not only that the eighteenth-century Atlantic world witnessed a clash of many different forces and powers, but that the cultural history of this period has subsequently been written in the light of nationalist or other kinds of agendas which were ancillary and posterior to these sites of struggle themselves. Johnson and Price represent antithetical positions within eighteenth-century Britain, one Anglican and conservative, the other dissenting and radical, and it is the spectre of America that opens up these shades of alterity so far as English culture is concerned. In answer to the question 'Was there an Atlantic Enlightenment?', then, my answer would be, only half facetiously, that there was not one in the eighteenth century, but there is now. In the eighteenth century there were cultural civil wars of various kinds, and clashes between abstract ideas and conservative cultural formations were

---

42   Paul Langford, *Englishness Identified: Manners and Character, 1650–1850* (Oxford, 2000), p. 274.

43   Porter, *Enlightenment*, p. 474.

44   Ludmilla Jordanova, 'The Authoritarian Response', in Peter Hulme and Ludmilla Jordanova, *The Enlightenment and Its Shadows* (London, 1990), p. 213.

certainly part of these conflicts, which went to and fro across the Atlantic as well as dividing communities on either side of it. But to imagine, like Hegel, these cycles of conflict as involving a dialectical struggle between enlightenment and superstition is to underestimate what Raymond Williams used to call the 'residual' components affecting particular cultures: the way that progressive ideas become symbiotically intertwined with reactionary instincts.[45] The Atlantic world of the eighteenth century was a radically mixed-up environment, where the rational and the irrational joined hands for a *danse macabre* whose provenance involved darkness and light in equal measures.

---

45   Raymond Williams, 'Base and Superstructure in Marxist Cultural Theory', *New Left Review* 82 (Nov–Dec, 1973), 10.

Chapter 2

Where was the Atlantic Enlightenment?— Questions of Geography

Charles W. J. Withers

Introduction: Atlantic History, Atlantic Geography—Atlantic Enlightenment?

> Bougainville, Cook, Lapérouse, La Condamine, Pallas, Humboldt: this handful of names is all it takes to evoke the adventure of the century of the Enlightenment. These men completed the explorations of the oceans, launched the exploration of the continents, and provided Europe with the materials—maps, drawings, herbaria, and collections—for an encyclopedic knowledge of the world.[1]

In thus discussing 'The Explorer' as an Enlightenment figure, Bourguet captures a sense of the Enlightenment not as static, something fixed in space by national boundaries, but as something dynamic, a matter of enlarging knowledge about the world in ways that involved the production, reception and mobility of ideas and artefacts over land and sea. It is a view of the Enlightenment upon which this essay will elaborate. It is, moreover, a conception of the Enlightenment in which the Pacific figures prominently. For the British, the French and, to a lesser extent, the Spanish and the Russians, the Pacific Ocean was from the 1760s Enlightenment Europe's principal testing ground. Islands in the 'Southern Seas' were the source of new flora and fauna that intrigued and intoxicated European naturalists, the home of peoples whose existence and social structures raised profound questions to do with humanity's origins and differences and whose classification and depiction helped to usher in new 'modern' methods of understanding in art and in science. In short, the Enlightenment was in large measure 'made in the Pacific'—the result of sea-borne navigation, of new forms of 'ethnographic navigation' across the 'Great Map of Mankind' and the return of new world data to the metropolitan calculating centres of Enlightenment Europe.[2]

---

1   Marie-Noëlle Bourguet, 'The Explorer', in ed. Michel Vovelle, *Enlightenment Portraits* (Chicago: 1997), pp. 257–315, quote on p. 257.

2   In a voluminous literature, see John Dunmore, *French Explorers in the Pacific* (2 vols, Oxford, 1965–1969); Alan Frost, 'The Pacific Ocean: the Eighteenth Century's "New World"', *Studies on Voltaire and the Eighteenth Century*, 152 (1976): 779–822; David Mackay, *In the Wake of Cook: Exploration, Science and Empire, 1780–1801* (London, 1985); Roy MacLeod and Philip Rehbock, eds, *Nature in its Greatest Extent: Western Science in the Pacific* (Honolulu,1998); Peter Marshall and Glyndwr Williams, *The Great Map of Mankind: British Perceptions of the World in the Age of Enlightenment* (London, 1982); David Miller and Peter Hanns Reill, eds, *Visions of Empire: Voyages, Botany, and Representations of Nature* (Cambridge, 1996); Bernard Smith, *European Vision and the South Pacific, 1768–1850:*

If it is generally understood that the Pacific world helped challenge and enlarge the contemporary geographical consciousness in the Enlightenment, it is far from clear what role the Atlantic played and what might be signalled to in the term 'Atlantic Enlightenment'. For one thing, the Atlantic has few islands and island groups. None offered to Enlightenment *philosophes* and navigators the same sites and sights of natural significance and ethnographic diversity as the Pacific. The Azores and Cape Verde groups had been known since their discovery by Portuguese navigators in the mid-fifteenth century. In the south Atlantic, Ascension, St Helena and Tristan da Cunha were either uninhabited until the nineteenth century, lightly garrisoned (as St Helena was by the British during the 1700s), or they were stopping-off points only for whalers. Leaving aside the British Isles and excluding the Falkland Islands (occupied by the British from 1690, by the French in 1764, owned by the Spanish from 1766 until garrisoned by the British after 1833), the Atlantic had noteworthy islands only in its mid-western reaches—in the Caribbean. These, known to Europeans since Columbus's voyages, were the object of attention for several Enlightenment commentators regarding the Caribbean's economy, natural and civil history and geography.[3] Perhaps the best known such work, Abbé Raynal's *Histoire des Deux Indes*, argued for a liberalisation of trade and political culture in general and drew upon a diverse range of sources in doing so. But in being first published, anonymously, in Amsterdam in 1770 and in being a radical text about the geography of Asia and the Americas, Raynal's book was, as it were, a work from the Enlightenment's Atlantic margins.[4] Neither it nor others' enquiries considered the Atlantic itself a subject for discourse. Outside the Caribbean, there was no Enlightenment human 'Other' in the Atlantic. Coastal West Africa figured in circuits of international trade as the source of gold, ivory and, above all, slaves—the so-called 'Atlantic System'—but hardly at

---

A Study in the History of Art and Ideas, second edition (Sydney, 1985); Bernard Smith, *Imagining the Pacific: In the Wake of the Cook Voyages* (New Haven, 1992); Glyndwr Williams, 'The Pacific: Exploration and Exploitation', in ed. P. J. Marshall, *The Oxford History of the British Empire: Volume 2. The Eighteenth Century* (Oxford, 1998), pp. 552–75. On the Pacific as the 'test bed' of Enlightenment anthropology, see Bronwen Douglas, 'Seaborne Ethnography and the Natural History of Man', *Journal of Pacific History*, 38 (2003): 3–27 and Tom Ryan, '"Le Président des Terres Australes": Charles de Brosses and the French Enlightenment Beginnings of Oceanic Anthropology', *Journal of Pacific History*, 37 (2002), 157–86. On the idea of 'ethnographic navigation', see Michael Bravo, 'Ethnographic Navigation and the Geographical Gift', in David N. Livingstone and Charles W. J. Withers, eds, *Geography and Enlightenment* (Chicago, 1999), pp. 199–235.

3   For example, Bryan Edwards, *The History, Civil and Commercial, of the British Colonies in the West Indies* (London, 1793); Edward Long, *The History of Jamaica* (London, 1773) and Guillaume-Thomas-François [Abbé] Raynal, *Histoire Philosophique et Politique des Etablissements et du Commerce des Européens dans les Deux Indes* (Amsterdam, 1770). For one modern discussion of the Caribbean in the Atlantic Enlightenment, see Philip D. Morgan, 'The Caribbean Islands in Atlantic Context, circa 1500–1800', in Felicity A. Nussbaum (ed.), *The Global Eighteenth Century* (Baltimore, 2003), pp. 52–64.

4   One overview of Raynal and his *Histoire des Deux Indes* (which notes that he and the work have been unjustly marginalised), is Anthony Strugnell, 'Raynal, Guillaume-Thomas', in ed. Alan Kors, *Encyclopedia of the Enlightenment* (4 vols, New York and Oxford, 2003), vol. 3, pp. 398–9.

all in the contemporary intellectual imagination as part of an object of geographical and philosophical enquiry, namely something called the 'Atlantic Enlightenment'.[5]

Nor is it clear in modern scholarship what is understood by the term 'the Atlantic Enlightenment'. Acknowledging the pre-eminent place of the Pacific, even the Baltic has figured more evidently than the Atlantic as a space for Enlightenment knowledge.[6] There is, of course, a large volume of work on the Enlightenment in the Americas as there is on the Enlightenment's expression in different geographical contexts in Europe; elements of this work are touched on here. There is also a compendious literature in which the sea is central to eighteenth-century narratives of adventure and geographical encounter.[7] Yet it is generally true to say that questions to do with the Atlantic Enlightenment—and with what might be embraced by that term—have not featured widely in modern discussions of the nature and geography of the Enlightenment.

That this is so is perhaps surprising given the recent interest and strength of work in 'Atlantic history' and, to a lesser extent, in 'Atlantic geography'. With respect to the first—what has been called 'one of the most important historiographical developments of recent years'[8]—attention has been paid to British history in Atlantic perspective, and, more particularly, to notions of Atlantic history as something shared by the nations and territories bordering and connected by the

---

5   Pieter Emmer, 'The Myth of Early Globalization: the Atlantic Economy, 1500–1800', *European Review,* 11 (2003): 37–47; Patrick O'Brien, 'Inseparable Connections: Trade, Economy, Fiscal State, and the Expansion of Empire, 1688–1815', in Marshall, *Oxford History of the British Empire: Volume 2.,* pp. 53–77; David Hancock, *Citizens of the World: London Merchants and the Integration of the British Atlantic Community, 1735–1785* (Cambridge, 1985); Richard L. Kagan and Geoffrey Parker eds, *Spain, Europe and the Atlantic World* (Cambridge, 1995). On Africa's marginalisation in French Enlightenment thinking, see T. Carlos Jacques, 'From Savages and Barbarians to Primitives: Africa, Social Typologies, and History in Eighteenth-Century French Philosophy', *History and Theory,* 36 (1997): 190–215. Two studies that consider the relationships between trade, science and oceanic travel in the Enlightenment are: Simon Schaffer, 'Golden Means: Assay Instruments and the Geography of Precision in the Guinea Trade', in eds Marie-Noëlle Bourguet, Christian Licoppe and H. Otto Sibum, *Instruments, Travel and Science: Itineraries of Precision from the Seventeenth to the Twentieth Century* (London, 2002), pp. 20–50; and Larry Stewart, 'Global Pillage: Science, Commerce and Empire', in ed. Roy Porter, *The Cambridge History of Science. Volume 4: Eighteenth-Century Science* (Cambridge, 2003), pp. 825–44.

6   Lisbet Koerner, 'Daedalus Hyperboreus: Baltic Natural History and Mineralogy in the Enlightenment', in eds William Clark, Jan Golinski, and Simon Schaffer, *The Sciences in Enlightened Europe* (Chicago, 1999), pp. 389–422.

7   On this point, see Laura Brown, 'Oceans and Floods: Fables of Global Perspective', in Nussbaum, *The Global Eighteenth Century,* pp. 107–20; Phillip Edwards, *The Story of the Voyage: Sea-Narratives in Eighteenth-Century England* (Cambridge, 1994); Miles Ogborn and Charles W. J. Withers, 'Travel, Trade and Empire: Knowing Other Places, 1660–1800', in ed. Cynthia Wall, *New Perspectives on Literature: The Restoration and the Eighteenth Century* (Oxford, 2005), pp. 13–35.

8   J. H.Elliott, *Do the Americas have a Common History? An Address* (Providence, 1998), p. 19.

Atlantic Ocean.[9] Reviewing the field, David Armitage has proposed a 'threefold typology of Atlantic history': '*Circum*-Atlantic history—the transnational history of the Atlantic world; *Trans*-Atlantic history—the international history of the Atlantic world; [and] *Cis*-Atlantic history—national or regional history within an Atlantic context'.[10] Circum-Atlantic history is the history of the Atlantic 'as a particular zone of exchange and interchange, circulation and transmission. It is therefore the history of the ocean as an arena distinct from any of the particular, narrower, oceanic zones that comprise it' and, although encompassing the shores of the Atlantic, 'does so only insofar as these shores form part of a larger oceanic history rather than a set of specific or regional histories abutting onto the Atlantic'. By contrast, 'Trans-Atlantic history is the history of the Atlantic world told through comparisons'—an international history that is also an inter-*imperial* history—and 'Cis-Atlantic' history studies particular places as unique locations within an Atlantic world, seeking to define that uniqueness 'as the result of the interaction between local particularity and a wider web of connections (and comparisons)'.[11]

Geographers have likewise offered a three-fold typology in studying 'Atlantic geographies', Ogborn suggesting 'three different geographical epistemologies for Atlantic studies, three ways in which the Atlantic's spaces can be known: the survey, the network and the trace'. The survey takes 'a broad synoptic overview, often over a long time period, and it draws the whole Atlantic world together as if on a map or chart'. In the network, 'the accent is on the changing web of social relations and material connections between people, places and objects that bounded together the margins of the Atlantic and bounded the ocean itself'. In looking at 'the trace', the emphasis is upon 'movements and negotiation'—in, for example, individuals' journeys and journals, in learning new ways to live in and through displacement and so on.[12] Other geographers have examined the history of global hydrography in which notions of 'the Atlantic' as a single oceanic space emerge in mapmaking and, thus, in the European intellectual world, from the later-seventeenth century,[13] have reviewed sea and ocean basins as regional frameworks for historical study,[14] and have considered the Pacific as a 'new Mediterranean' in explaining America's rise to global hegemony.[15]

---

9   See for example Bernard Bailyn, 'The Idea of Atlantic History', *Itinerario*, 20 (1996): 19–44, and the forum 'The New British History in Atlantic Perspective', in *American Historical Review*, 104/2 (1999): 426–500.

10   David Armitage, 'Three Concepts of Atlantic History', in eds David Armitage and Michael J Braddick, *The British Atlantic World, 1500–1800* (Basingstoke, 2002), pp. 11–27.

11   Armitage, 'Three Concepts of Atlantic History', pp. 16–17, 18, 21.

12   Miles Ogborn, 'Editorial: Atlantic Geographies', *Social and Cultural Geography*, 6 (2005): 381–7.

13   Martin W. Lewis, 'Dividing the Ocean Sea', *Geographical Review*, 89 (1999): 188–214.

14   Jerry H. Bentley, 'Sea and Ocean Basins as Frameworks of Historical Analysis', *Geographical Review*, 89 (1999): 215–24. See also the work of the historian Elizabeth Mancke, 'Early Modern Expansion and the Politicization of Oceanic Space', *Geographical Review*, 89 (1999): 225–36.

15   Paul W. Blank, 'The Pacific: A Mediterranean in the Making?', *Geographical Review*, 89 (1999): 276–7. On this point, see also Neil Smith, *American Empire. Roosevelt's*

Thinking of 'Atlantic history' or 'Atlantic geography' as separate concerns—certainly, in any strictly disciplinary terms—is unhelpful, even misleading. Where historians such as Armitage recognise that 'The attraction of Atlantic history lies, in part, in nature ... The Atlantic might seem to be one of the few historical categories that has an inbuilt geography',[16] geographers such as Ogborn note that 'Atlantic geographies require perspectives that can encompass spatialities that include but exceed those of the local or of the nation-state, and historical periodizations that are attentive to the long term and to dynamic, circumnavigatory flows that disrupt notions of progress and development'.[17] As the leading Atlantic historian Bernard Bailyn notes in charting the contours of Atlantic history as part of his recent survey, 'The shift in historical perspective was essentially spatial'.[18] As historical geographer Donald Meinig put it, 'the Atlantic world was the scene of a vast interaction rather than merely the transfer of Europeans onto American shores'. For Meinig:

> Our focus is upon the creation of new human geographies resulting from this interaction, and that means those developing not only westward upon the body of America but eastward upon the body of Europe, and inward upon and laterally along the body of Africa. For it is certain that the geography of each was changed: radically on the American side ... more subtly on the European side, with new movements of people, goods, capital, and information flowing through an established spatial system and slowly altering its proportions and directions; slowly and unevenly on the African side, making connections with existing commercial systems but eventually grotesquely altering the scale and meaning of old institutions.[19]

Albeit that it has been but briefly outlined, such work in Atlantic history and geography—with its emphasis upon dynamic exchange, upon different scales and contested meanings, upon flows and their uneven consequences over time and space—has considerable utility in thinking about the 'Atlantic Enlightenment', not least given what we have noted of others' views of the Enlightenment as a matter of movement, travel and information exchange.

So what then might we understand by the 'Atlantic Enlightenment'? At the very least we should do more than simply regard the Atlantic Enlightenment as a sort of 'absent presence', a taken-for-granted space, an un-inscribed 'empty space', an empty 'time-space' even, which was occupied only temporarily as people and goods safely reached destinations on one side or the other. So, too, I would not want to propose that the term is used only to describe Enlightenment communities in Europe on the one side and in the Americas on the other on the unexamined assumption that they shared features held to be 'the Enlightenment'. Quite apart from variations within Europe and in America, we cannot ignore Africa's place in the Enlightenment or, indeed, leave unexamined just what the Enlightenment was more generally.

Geographer and the Prelude to Globalization (Berkeley, 2003).

16 Armitage, 'Three Concepts of Atlantic History', p. 11.

17 Ogborn, 'Editorial: Atlantic Geographies', p. 381.

18 Bernard Bailyn, *Atlantic History: Concept and Contours* (Cambridge, 2005), p. 55.

19 Donald Meinig, *The Shaping of America: A Geographical Perspective on 500 years of History* (4 vols, New Haven, 1996–1998), vol 1 *Atlantic America, 1492–1800*, pp. 64–5.

Given the work in Atlantic history and geography, questions to do with movement—of people, of ideas, of books to name but a few—should figure highly. So ought consideration of different scales, the differential impact of European ideas on the communities on the Atlantic's margins and the varying impact of the Atlantic 'new' upon the European mind. Rather than nations or, even, regions, particular places—particular institutions even—may be important as sites for the production and reception of ideas that crossed and re-crossed the Atlantic. In turn, we should allow that ideas of Enlightenment may have changed as they were made, worked with and relocated.

In posing here the question 'Where was the Atlantic Enlightenment?', I make a distinction between the Atlantic Enlightenment as a geographical phenomenon in general terms and the Atlantic *in* the Enlightenment as an object of specific study. In effect, this is to pose and to explore two related questions: 'Where was the Atlantic Enlightenment?', and 'Where was the Atlantic in the Enlightenment?'. In respect of the first and more conceptual question, I argue that the Atlantic Enlightenment should be seen neither as an empty space over which ships, people and ideas moved unhindered by the facts of geography nor as a simple shared entity transcending space. Rather, and as a preliminary typology, we might think of the Atlântic Enlightenment as sets of connected edges, a conceptual and geographical space defined both by sites on its margins and by the flows that moved between them. I elaborate upon these ideas in the first part of the essay.

In terms of the second question, whilst it is true that the Atlantic did not provide island laboratories for ethnographic speculation on the Pacific scale, it was as I shall show below far from neglected as an arena for Enlightenment science. To illustrate the view of the Atlantic as itself a flow between margins, the second part of this essay examines how the Gulf Stream was understood in the Enlightenment in the work of two Britons, Sir Charles Blagden and Thomas Pownall, in that of two Americans, Benjamin Franklin and Jonathan Williams and in a German-turned-American William De Brahm. I examine the mapping of the Gulf Stream by these men and show how, through its cartographic representation and ship-board analysis, the Gulf Stream was, so to speak, brought to the surface as a legitimate subject for philosophical enquiry. The focus of their work was not the 'ethnographic navigation' of their contemporaries in the Pacific, but 'thermometric navigation'. Studying the Gulf Stream as a dynamic flow involved these men in ocean-going science—in instrumental measurement whilst on the move—as well as in assessing at sea and on land the credibility of ships' captains and common deck hands. Such matters are important in looking at the Atlantic in the Enlightenment as a question of geography, a space for making science. Longitude for example—in its solution one of the great achievements of Enlightenment science either at sea or on land—was a matter of fixing the 'going rate' and knowing time distances between points in space. But it was not solved effectively as a practical problem until the 1770s and even then, reliable chronometers were not commonplace. Questions of Enlightenment knowledge moving securely over the sea—and, thus, of the Atlantic Enlightenment being a shared feature or not—again highlight the issue of movement, of translation as a geographical, epistemological and linguistic matter as well as the 'closure' of geographical space through the practical skills of navigation. This being so, thinking about the Atlantic Enlightenment as a space for knowledge's making and mobility involves issues of trust and of instrumentation to do with ships, sextants and log books, and of social type and intellectual authority to do with mariners' knowledge as well as the sharing of knowledge between intellectual communities on the ocean's margins. As Sorrenson has shown, ships were at once floating instruments and ordered social spaces, mobile laboratories which facilitated new knowledge for *voyageurs-naturalistes* but which necessitated cramped living amongst one's social inferiors.[20] For the handful of men engaged in measuring the Gulf Stream, the Atlantic Enlightenment was simultaneously a geographical space over which ships, men and knowledge moved between communities on its margins *and* a subject of Enlightenment geographical science. Let me turn first to the place of the Atlantic Enlightenment within Enlightenment studies more generally.

The Atlantic Enlightenment: a Space of Margins and of Flows

Until quite recently, considerations of the Enlightenment as a question of geography have largely focused upon the Enlightenment in national context. At one time or another in the eighteenth century, almost every country in Europe had its Enlightenment: Austria, Bohemia, England, France, Germany, Italy, Russia, Scotland, Sweden, Switzerland and the Netherlands.[21] Even as these national Enlightenments were being disclosed, other studies have laid bare the Enlightenment in the Americas and in countries and regions on the 'periphery' of the Enlightenment's Dutch, English, French and German 'heartlands'—in Greece, Hungary, Spain and Portugal, for example.[22] In such terms, the Enlightenment was both an essential 'thing' and considered at one geographical scale, the national.

Several different ways of interpreting the Enlightenment geographically are now more common. Some scholars have called for attention to the Enlightenment as a matter of international connections—the Enlightenment 'above national context'.[23] Others have discerned not one Enlightenment but many, 'a multiplicity of specific contexts, each one constituted by numerous (local and temporary) factors'.[24] At the same time, 'national' Enlightenments have come under closer scrutiny, revealing differences within national spaces as well as connections across national borders.

---

20   Richard Sorrenson, 'The Ship as a Scientific Instrument in the Eighteenth Century', *Osiris*, 11 (1996): 221–36.

21   These, with America, are the countries studied in Roy Porter and Mikuláš Teich, eds, *The Enlightenment in National Context* (Cambridge, 1981).

22   In a large literature, see Robert Ferguson, *The American Enlightenment, 1750–1820* (Cambridge, 1997), and the essays in ed. Kostas Gavroglu, *The Sciences in the European Periphery during the Enlightenment* (Dordrecht, 1999).

23   For example, John Robertson, 'The Enlightenment Above National Context: Political Economy in Eighteenth-Century Scotland and Naples', *Historical Journal*, 40 (1997): 667–97, and, at fuller length, his *The Case for Enlightenment: Scotland and Naples 1680–1760* (Cambridge, 2005).

24   Jan Golinski, 'Science *in* the Enlightenment', *History of Science*, 24 (1986): 411–24, quote from page 419.

The example of one nation on the Atlantic's margins—Scotland—will suffice to make this more general point.

Interpretations of the Scottish Enlightenment as an essentially urban, even Edinburgh-centric and philosophical affair have been replaced by studies which reveal the Enlightenment in Scotland to have been about questions of practical utility as well as aesthetics, gender as well as geometry, chemistry and crop yields as well as philosophical speculation. What was once taken as *the Scottish* Enlightenment has been shown to differ within and between the towns of Aberdeen, Edinburgh and Glasgow. Debates over the role of 'political economy' in civilised society took place not just in Glasgow's more commercially-oriented environment, but between particular people in certain institutions in Glasgow and between that city's intellectuals and like-minded counterparts in Europe and in the Americas. In short, the Enlightenment in Scotland was 'earthed' quite differently in different places. What took place *in* Scotland as 'Enlightenment', however and whereever locally understood, was also the result of connections *beyond* Scotland.[25]

The effect of such revisionism, even when differently articulated, has been that the Enlightenment's geography is now understood at a variety of scales and seen to be about the making, displacement and reception of different sorts of knowledge over geographical space.[26] Notions of *the* Enlightenment have been displaced. As Pocock notes, the point is not that there *cannot have been* a single Enlightenment shared by the cultures of Europe and America, it is that we should not take it for granted that there *was*. The use of the definite article encourages the presumption that there was such a thing as *the* Enlightenment, and that how we should think about it historically is to trace its origins and dissemination and modifications in different cultures. The merit of omitting the definite article is that it is liberating not constraining, and allows us to remember 'that the term "Enlightenment" is a tool, which we use to isolate a variety of phenomena which we suspect were similar, were interrelated, were the product of a shared history'.[27]

As historians and geographers have thus decisively challenged the notions of an essential Enlightenment reducible only to the scale of the nation, so historians of science have further contributed to an understanding of the Enlightenment as geographically dynamic. Such work, part of a more general 'spatial turn' in science studies, is distinguished by its attention to three features: the making of knowledge in particular sites and ways (contexts of discovery), the movement of knowledge between those sites, and the reception of knowledge in yet different places (contexts of justification). Study of the geography of science has called attention to the uneven distribution of scientific information, to the connections between 'locution and

---

25   This paragraph is distilled from the essays in Wood, *The Scottish Enlightenment*, and from Roger L. Emerson and Paul Wood, 'Science and Enlightenment in Glasgow, 1690–1802', in Withers and Wood, *Science and Medicine in the Scottish Enlightenment*, pp. 79–142.

26   Clark, Golinski, and Schaffer, *The Sciences in Enlightened Europe*; Livingstone and Withers, *Geography and Enlightenment*.

27   John G. A. Pocock, 'Enlightenment and Revolution: The Case of English-Speaking North America', *Studies on Voltaire and the Eighteenth Century*, 263 (1989): 249–61, quote from page 252.

location', to the venues in which different forms of knowledge have been made and to the varying social contours of its reception.[28] These concerns are apparent in what Harris has called the 'geography of knowledge'. For Harris, there are three related approaches to the geography of knowledge.

> In the first instance, it means a static geography of place: where did people 'do science'? Where were they when they aimed telescopes and recorded observations, logged positions and sketched in charts, performed dissections or prepared medicaments, executed experiments and calculations, or wrote and published the accounts of their activities? In the second, it means a kinematic geography of movement: whence came the constituents of scientific practice and knowledge, the measuring or cutting instruments, the authoritative texts or latest correspondence, the exotic natural curiosity or well-wrought experimental apparatus, the returning botanist or navigator? In the third sense, geography of knowledge also means the dynamics of travel: why and by what means did all these movements take place? What was the *anima motrix* responsible for the multiple peregrinations of the elements of knowledge?[29]

Together with those issues discussed above, these ideas have value in thinking about the Atlantic Enlightenment as a space of margins and of flows. Not least, they help dismiss once and for all notions of *the* Enlightenment moving east-west across the Atlantic as a single unproblematic phenomenon, a view encapsulated in Commager's claim that 'The Old World imagined, invented, and formulated the Enlightenment, the New World—certainly the Anglo-American part of it—realized and fulfilled it'.[30] Others have anyway challenged this. Pole long ago identified a more complex Enlightenment in America, to some degree a foreign and 'imported' object, to some degree not, an Enlightenment given local shape by varying emphases on Protestant Christianity, debates on rights and liberty and the virtue of others' enlightened ideas on the making of nationhood.[31] May's study of 'the Enlightenment in America' identified four Enlightenments. The 'Moderate Enlightenment' (which might also be called the 'Rational Enlightenment'), which preached order and religious compromise, was peculiarly English. The 'Skeptical Enlightenment', British in part, was distinctively French, its method wit, its 'grand master' Voltaire. The 'Revolutionary Enlightenment' had its origins in Rousseau, its culmination in Thomas Paine and William Godwin. And the 'Didactic Enlightenment'—opposed to the above—had Scotland as its

---

28 For reviews of these concerns, see Jan Golinski, *Making Natural Knowledge: Constructivism and the History of Science* (Cambridge, 1998); David Livingstone, *Putting Science in its Place: Geographies of Scientific Knowledge* (Chicago, 2003); Crosbie Smith and Jon Agar, eds, *Making Space for Science: Territorial Themes in the Making of Knowledge* (London, 1998); Charles W. J. Withers, *Geography, Science and National Identity: Scotland since 1520* (Cambridge, 2001), pp. 1–29.

29 Steven Harris, 'Long Distance Corporations, Big Sciences, and the Geography of Knowledge', *Configurations*, 6 (1998): 269–305, quote from pages 272–3.

30 Henry S. Commager, *The Empire of Reason: How Europe Imagined and America Realized the Enlightenment* (Garden City, 1978), p. xi.

31 J. R. Pole, 'Enlightenment and the Politics of American Nature', in Porter and Teich, *The Enlightenment in National Context*, pp. 192–214.

chief originating centre.[32] Regional differences were important. The 'Skeptical Enlightenment' was stronger in the slave owning 'Stoical South' than ever it was elsewhere. In New England, the new nation was forged out of the tension between the Moderate and Revolutionary versions of Enlightenment.[33]

In revealing the importance of geographical difference, these ideas help revise how we may think of North America as one western margin of the Atlantic Enlightenment in the same way as recent work has done for Scotland as one eastern margin. And as Brewer has shown of another eastern Atlantic margin, France, the Enlightenment varied not just across geographical space—between Paris and the provinces—but also in relation to social space, in what he terms 'epistemic space' (in the classification of knowledge used in the *Encyclopédie* for example), and in aesthetic space.[34] Rather, then, than think of the Atlantic Enlightenment's margins simply as geographical territory or assume it to be a phenomenon shared across space, we should consider that the Atlantic Enlightenment had numerous and different social and epistemic spaces and locally privileged sites. These may be as varied as pulpits in Boston, laboratories in Glasgow, publishers' offices in Edinburgh and in Philadelphia, *salons* in Paris or New Orleans. This is to call not just for attentiveness to different geographical *scales* within the Atlantic Enlightenment—away from the national and towards transnational connections with local expression. It is to recognise that there are different discursive *themes* making up the Atlantic Enlightenment, each (again to cite Harris) with different sets of 'measuring instruments' and 'authoritative texts'. I am not suggesting such work has not been done, merely pointing to the possibilities inherent in such a dynamic geographical conception. Richard Brown's exploration of the circuits of information movement in early America—between and among Virginia's 'Tidewater gentry', in port towns, and across rural New England, for example—offers one illustration of the intersection of local and regional spaces on the Enlightenment's margins.[35]

This to note that the Atlantic Enlightenment—understood as negotiated information flows across the space between continental margins and as knowledge made and received in places on those margins—meant different things to different people in different places. For some people, the Atlantic Enlightenment meant commercial transactions and financial security, for others religious salvation, for yet others the opportunity to heal or survey the stars through the arrival of new instruments, buy a book or learn to read. The Atlantic Enlightenment in natural history may not have been the same as that in rhetoric, political economy or moral philosophy, and may not have been accommodated in the same ways in Glasgow or by Boston merchants or amongst Virginia's 'Tidewater gentry' as it was on the Mississippi frontier. The strength and direction of the flows between the sites and social spaces on Atlantic margins should

---

32   Henry F. May, *The Enlightenment in America* (New York and Oxford, 1976).

33   May, *Enlightenment in America,* pp. 133–49, 181–96. See also David Jaffee, 'The Village Enlightenment in New England, 1760–1820', *William and Mary Quarterly,* 47 (1990): 327–46; John McDermott, 'The Enlightenment on the Mississippi Frontier, 1763–1804', *Studies on Voltaire and the Eighteenth Century,* 26 (1963): 1129–42.

34   Daniel Brewer, 'Lights in Space', *Eighteenth-Century Studies,* 37 (2004): 171–86.

35   Richard D. Brown, *Knowledge is Power: The Diffusion of Information in Early America, 1700–1865* (New York and Oxford, 1989).

not be presumed equal between places or unchanging over time. For Charles Elliot, for example, the leading Edinburgh bookseller of the 1780s, the medical book trade with the Americas 'was always one-way'. His customers in Charleston, New York and Philadelphia for Europe's medical texts were Americans returning home from medical education and booksellers who would sell on to these and other local customers.[36] For Jedidiah Morse in contrast, geographer and Congregational minister, his *Geography Made Easy* (1784) and *American Geography* (1799) offered an American's view of America's geography in opposition to the views expressed in 'imported geographies'. Morse used a locally produced geography in the late Enlightenment to forge a sense of American national identity from what he saw as persistent regional affiliations.[37] In Spanish-speaking Latin America too, what was taken to be Enlightenment was not simply transferred from Europe. The themes that were significant locally to the public in Spanish America had less to do with building new religious and political languages than with 'explicitly attempting to develop a critique of European epistemologies'. These centred not upon theories of reason or in the mobility of texts and artefacts but upon the interpretations that could be placed upon Aztec monuments and their inscriptions, interpretations which, in establishing a longevity to Amerindian culture that disproved Buffon, made the 'new' world older than the 'old' of Europe.[38] And for the Caribbean too, an altogether different sort of Enlightenment begins to emerge if we focus less on the works of contemporary intellectual commentators and more on the lives of those, notably slaves, whose experience figures in texts as part of Enlightenment theorisation about social development but whose voice does not.[39]

Thinking of the Atlantic Enlightenment as a space of margins and flows is thus consistent with new directions in the study of the Enlightenment's geographies, with work on the situated and mobile nature of science and with dominant trends in the historiography of Atlantic studies. Considered in this sense, the Atlantic Enlightenment may be seen not as a single entity but as a dynamic space, at once social, geographical and epistemological. Its characteristics were different depending on where on its margins Enlightenment knowledge was made and received, by whom, in what form and in how such knowledge and its makers and audiences moved, if at all, between one place and another.[40] With these ideas in mind, I return to my second question.

---

36   Warren McDougall, 'Charles Elliot's Medical Publication and the International Book Trade', in Withers and Wood, *Science and Medicine in the Scottish Enlightenment*, pp. 215–54, especially 228–32.

37   Martin Brückner, 'Lessons in Geography: Maps, Spellers, and Other Grammars of Nationalism in the Early Republic', *American Quarterly*, 51 (1999): 311–43, and, at greater length, his *The Geographic Revolution in Early America: Maps, Literacy, & National Identity* (Chapel Hill, 2006).

38   Jorge Cañizares-Esguerra, *How to Write the History of the New World: History, Epistemologies, and Identities in the Eighteenth-Century Atlantic World* (Stanford, 2001), 266–345, quotes from pp. 266–7.

39   Laurent Dubois, 'An Enslaved Enlightenment: Rethinking the Intellectual History of the French Atlantic', *Social History*, 31 (2006): 1–14.

40   For a fuller discussion of the Enlightenment considered geographically, see Charles W. J. Withers, *Placing the Enlightenment: Thinking Geographically about The Age of Reason* (Chicago, 2007).

The Atlantic in the Enlightenment: The Gulf Stream as a Question of Geography

The Pacific may have been the Enlightenment's premier socio-natural laboratory, but the Atlantic was not an empty scientific space in the Enlightenment. The experiments of Robert Boyle and the voyages between 1698 and 1700 of the English astronomer Edmund Halley to measure variations in terrestrial magnetism were amongst the first expressions of Enlightenment marine science.[41] The French established their Dépôt des Cartes et Plans de la Marine in 1720 as part of their Navy Ministry. As for their Spanish and British counterparts, French mapping of the Atlantic was important for commercial and military reasons as well as of scientific importance.[42] St Helena provided an island site for the observation by European astronomers of the Transit of Venus in 1761 and in 1768, and its environmental degradation was a concern for naturalists and Navy officials alike.[43] Caribbean islands provided measuring points for the testing of longitude.[44] Hebridean waters provided important sites for the emergence of definitive standards in British maritime survey.[45] The Atlantic occupied enlightened minds on land. In Edinburgh University, the Rev. Dr John Walker, Professor of Natural History from 1772 until 1803, included hydrography, 'the history of the waters of the globe' in his teaching.[46]

The presence in the mid Atlantic of a large current of warm water with its source in the Strait of Florida—what we know as the Gulf Stream—has been known since the sixteenth century, but what was not recognised until much later was that the Gulf Stream flowed north-eastwards up the American Coast and far out into the Atlantic. The attention given to its study through at-sea experimentation and observation in the last quarter of the eighteenth century reflects a growing interest in marine science of which the reports and maps of Franklin, Blagden, Pownall and others are part. Enlightened knowledge about the sea was not, however, the preserve of the land-bound philosopher. What for these men was a matter of real substance demanding empirical examination was for mariners and ship owners a matter of time, safety and money.

---

41 Margaret Deacon, *Scientists and the Sea 1650–1900: A Study of Marine Science* (London, 1971).

42 French hydrographic science in the Enlightenment is best evident in the work of Bellin: Jacques Nicolas Bellin, *Recueil des Memoires qui ont été publiés avec les cartes hydrographiques* (Paris, 1751); Jacques Nicolas Bellin, *Hydrographie Française* (2 volumes, Paris, 1792). More generally, see Daniel R. Headrick, *When Information Came of Age: Technologies of Knowledge in the Age of Reason and Revolution, 1700–1850* (Oxford, 2000), pp. 108–15.

43 On the environmental degradation of St Helena in the Enlightenment, see Richard Grove, *Green Imperialism: Colonial Expansion, Tropical Island Edens and the Origins of Environmentalism, 1600–1860* (Cambridge, 1995), pp. 108–25. On St Helena as an astronomical observatory, see Rob Iliffe, 'Science and Voyages of Discovery', in Porter, *The Cambridge History of Science. Volume 4: Eighteenth-Century Science*, pp. 618–48.

44 Jim Bennett, 'The Travels and Trails of Mr Harrison's Timekeeper', in Bourguet, Licoppe and Sibum, *Instruments, Travel and Science,* pp. 75–95.

45 Diana C. F. Smith, 'The Progress of the *Orcades* Survey, with Biographical Notes on Murdoch Mackenzie Senior (1712–1790)', *Annals of Science*, 44 (1987): 277–88.

46 Walker's surviving 'Hydrography' lectures form volume 4 of his natural history syllabus: they are in the care of the Royal College of Physicians, Edinburgh.

Understanding the Gulf Stream as a problem of Enlightenment geography highlights questions not just about social warrant and intellectual credibility and the places where reliable knowledge was made, but also about the different values and uses attaching to such knowledge.

The Gulf Stream was commented upon (but not named as such) in 1705 by William Dampier and, in 1726, by Benjamin Franklin, who reported upon it following his voyage that year from London to Philadelphia. Yet despite Franklin's claims to the contrary in his later writings (see below), he was not the first to study the Gulf Stream. That claim belongs to the German-born John Gerar William De Brahm, who, between 1765 and 1771, was His Majesty's Surveyor General of the Southern District of North America. Dr Brahm's responsibilities as a surveyor demanded that he make 'authentic discoveries' as he put it—that is, worked from direct observation and on mathematical precepts—of what would become the southern states of the United States. This required shipboard triangulation of headlands and, thus, firsthand encounter with coastal waters and with the Gulf Stream. His account of his survey work, much of it a natural history of Florida and surrounding islands, was brought together in his *The Atlantic Pilot* (1772). De Brahm there included a map of the Gulf Stream. This is reproduced here as Figure 2.1.

De Brahm's map is the first to bring the Gulf Stream into view as a dynamic trans-Atlantic flow, albeit in stylised form. It posits a North Atlantic merger with currents from the Gulf of St Lawrence (themselves being studied by French and British hydrographers) and represents the Gulf Stream as a directional line of uniform thickness with associated instrumental bearings. His interest in the phenomenon lay not in investigating the measurable quantities of the Stream but in its position as an aid to coastal navigation.

Franklin's interest in the Gulf Stream was based on attempts to measure this dynamic flow. His interest began as he put it 'about the year 1769 or 70', and is detailed in a letter of 1785 concerning 'Maritime Observations' arising from his last Atlantic crossing that same year and addressed to Alphonsus Le Roy, the French chemist.[47] Franklin's interest in the sea extended over many years, however, and included practical experiments—on Clapham Common, Derwent Water and, in association with Charles Blagden and others, in Portsmouth harbour—to test Pliny's account of how oil could be cast on waves to calm them and thus ease a ship's passage.[48] In 1769 and 1770, Franklin was engaged in the management of the American post office. His interest in the Gulf Stream was piqued when officials in Boston complained to Treasury officials in London about the time taken in different Atlantic routes. '[T]he packets between Falmouth and New-York' ["packets" were ships used for mail rather more than passengers and goods], 'were generally a fortnight longer in their passages, than merchant ships from London to Rhode-Island.'

---

47   [Benjamin Franklin], 'A Letter from Dr. Benjamin Franklin, to Mr. Alphonsus le Roy, Member of several Academies, at Paris. Containing sundry Maritime Observations', *Transactions of the American Philosophical Society*, 2 (1786): 294–324 [hereafter cited as 'Maritime Observations'].

48   Deacon, *Scientists and the Sea*, pp. 198–201.

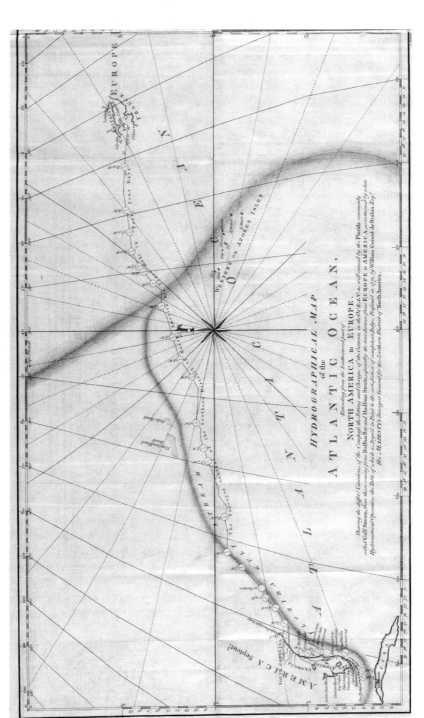

Figure 2.1   William De Brahm's 'Hydrographical Map of the Atlantic Ocean', from his *The Atlantic Pilot* (1772)

Part of Franklin's 1785 letter discussing why this was, and how it was to be explained, merits quotation at length:

> [I]t appearing strange to me that there should be such a difference between two places, scarce a day's run asunder, especially when the merchant ships are generally deeper laden, and more weakly managed than the packets, and had from London the whole length of the river and channel to run before they left the land of England, while the packets had only to go from Falmouth, I could not but think the fact misunderstood or misrepresented. There happened then to be in London, a Nantucket sea-captain of my acquaintance, to whom I communicated the affair. He told me he believed the fact might be true; but the difference was owing to this, that the Rhode-Island captains were acquainted with the gulf stream, which those of the English packets were not. We are well acquainted with that stream, says he, because in our pursuit of whales, which keep near the tides of it, but are not to be met with in it, we run down along the sides, and frequently cross it to change our side: and in crossing have sometimes met and spoke with those packets, who were in the middle of it, and stemming it. We have informed them that they were stemming a current, that was against them to the value of three miles an hour; and advised them to cross it and get out of it; but they were too wise to be counselled by simple American fishermen. When the winds are but light, he added, they are carried back by the current more than they are forwarded by the wind: and if the wind be good, the subtraction of 70 miles a day from their course is of some importance. I then observed that it was a pity no notice was taken of this current upon the charts, and requested him to mark it out for me, which he readily complied with, adding directions for avoiding it in sailing from Europe to North-America. I procured it to be engraved by order from the general post-office, on the old chart of the Atlantic, at Mount and Page's, Tower-hill; and copies were sent down to Falmouth for the captains of the packets, who slighted it however; but it is since printed in France, of which edition I hereto annex a copy.[49]

The map to which Franklin makes reference was incorporated in the published version of his 1785 letter together with 'Remarks upon the Navigation from Newfoundland to New-York, in order to avoid the Gulph Stream'. Both the map and the 'Remarks' are here reproduced as Figure 2.2.

In documenting how Rhode Island ships' captains knew about the Gulf Stream (but others did not), and where and how Franklin came to encapsulate his understanding in map form, this map and text extract highlight themes that cut across the two key questions framing this essay. Our question might now become 'How and where was knowledge about the Atlantic made in the Atlantic Enlightenment?' Different answers are possible, each embracing issues of geographical, social and epistemic space. One answer is 'at sea', as ships crossed the ocean and one another's path, even if English captains refused to acknowledge the experiential knowledge of their American counterparts, 'simple American fishermen', whose navigational practices in the Gulf Stream were based on whale watching. Another might be 'on a map', initially produced in London by an American statesman-scientist, who derived his information from the verbal testimony of a Nantucket sailor (one Captain Folger), even allowing that the map in question was 'slighted' by its intended first audience, Falmouth-based captains, and was finally printed and distributed in France. Yet a

---

49   [Franklin], 'Maritime Observations', pp. 314–15.

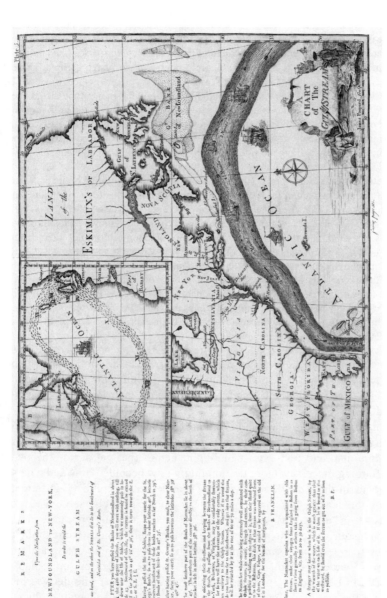

Figure 2.2   Benjamin Franklin's 'A Chart of the Gulf Stream' and accompanying 'Remarks Upon the Navigation from Newfoundland to New-York, in order to avoid the Gulph Stream' (1786). (NB: The inset map of the Atlantic Ocean to the left of Franklin's is not associated with Franklin's 'Maritime Observations' but illustrates an essay by Mr John Gilpin, 'Observations on the Annual Passage of Herrings', which appeared in *Transactions of the American Philosophical Society* 2 (1786): 236–9)

third answer would be 'in different publications'—first but differently by De Brahm, later by Franklin in a Philadelphia-based periodical publication. Discussing the different circuits of information in eighteenth-century American port towns, including Franklin's Philadelphia, Brown has noted that 'for merchants the foremost need was to be up-to-date'. 'Among lawyers it was breadth and depth of knowledge of people and the law that was more often critical than a command of current events.'[50] For Enlightenment natural philosophers at sea and in port it was different still. Their knowledge of this natural phenomenon was derived not from credible witnesses from amongst their own social rank, but from translating others' lived experiences and spoken words on board moving ships into fixed lines on a map (Franklin) and from mathematical triangulation of the flow in relation to the American south-east coastal margin (De Brahm).

Franklin continued his discussions of the Gulf Stream in his 'Maritime Observations' by speculating upon its causes—which he saw (rightly) to be related to the airflow of tropical trade winds—and by turning to yet a different form of measurement. These were his observations on the heat of the Atlantic and the Gulf Stream: 'I annex hereto the observations made with the thermometer in two voyages, and may possibly add a third'[51] (he never did). These allowed him not just to corroborate other evidence, but to offer practical advice:

> The conclusion from these remarks is, that a vessel from Europe to North-America may shorten her passage by avoiding to stem the stream, in which the thermometer will be very useful; and a vessel from America to Europe may do the same by the same means of keeping in it. It may often have happened accidentally, that voyages have been shortened by these circumstances. It is well to have command of them.[52]

Franklin was not the only one arguing thus. The English physician Charles Blagden, author of several papers on temperature, had published an essay on the heat of the Gulf Stream in 1781.[53] The subject of thermometry was high on the agenda of the Royal Society at this time. Given that Blagden and Franklin had conducted marine experiments together in 1783, it is scarcely conceivable that Franklin was unaware of the former's essay, yet he does not mention it in his 'Maritime Observations'. Blagden understood that the Gulf Stream mattered to different audiences: 'Since all ships going from Europe to any of the southern provinces of North America must cross this current, and are materially affected by it in their course, every circumstance of its motion becomes an object highly interesting to the seaman, as well as of great curiosity to the philosopher.'[54] His method of assessing the extent of the Gulf Stream combined the thermometry of the Atlantic's waters, in and out of the Stream, with measurements of air temperature given that, as he put it, 'An opinion prevails among

---

50   Brown, *Knowledge is Power*, p. 117.
51   [Franklin], 'Maritime Observations', p. 316.
52   [Franklin], 'Maritime Observations', pp. 316–17.
53   Charles Blagden, 'On the Heat of the Water in the Gulf-Stream', *Philosophical Transactions of the Royal Society of London*, 71 (1781): 334–44.
54   Blagden, 'On the Heat of the Water in the Gulf-Stream', p. 336.

seamen, that there is something peculiar in the weather about the Gulf-stream'.[55] These combined temperature readings, taken at different seasons of the year, could then be linked to latitudinal measurements. Navigation by temperature would then become the basis to increased safety on the American side of the Atlantic both because it was an instrumentally derived form of natural knowledge capable of easy repetition and because it was capable of being understood and used by sailors themselves:

> As the course of the Gulf stream becomes more to be accurately known, from repeated observations of the heat and latitude, this method of determining the ship's place will be proportionably more applicable to use. And it derives additional importance from the peculiar circumstances of the American coast, which, from the mouth of the Delaware to the southernmost point of Florida, is every where low, and beset with frequent shoals, running out so far into the sea that a vessel may be aground in many places where the shore is not to be so distinguished even from the mast-head. The gulf-stream, therefore, which has hitherto served only to increase the perplexities of seamen, will now, if these observations are found to be put into practice, become one of the chief means of their preservation upon that dangerous coast.[56]

Although it is unclear whether Franklin was acknowledging Blagden in remarking upon the value of Atlantic thermometry, Franklin certainly directed others' endeavours, and may even have benefited from them. A 1790 'Memoir' by one Jonathan Williams on this topic notes 'In the months of August and September, 1785. I was a fellow passenger with the late Doctor Franklin from Europe to America, and made, under his direction, the experiments mentioned in his description of the course of the gulph stream, an account of which was annexed to his maritime observations'.[57] Williams and Franklin were more than fellow passengers and ocean-going experimenters. Franklin was Williams' great-uncle and Williams had acted as Franklin's private secretary for five years from 1775. Williams was prompted by his relative's interest in the Atlantic and may have refrained from publishing his own observations until after Franklin's death in 1790. As Williams later put it, 'Doct. Franklin's observations had the knowledge of currents for their object, and this extension of his discovery did not occur; but as I am indebted to his instructive discovery and example, for my inducement to pursue philosophical researches when in my power to do so, he may be considered as the original author of what is now presented for examination'.[58] Williams's significance here rests both in the fact that he repeated his experiments in four further voyages to and from north America and Europe and along the American coast—experiments whose sites he turned into a map—and on a later voyage to

55 Blagden, 'On the Heat of the Water in the Gulf-Stream', p. 342.

56 Blagden, 'On the Heat of the Water in the Gulf-Stream', pp. 343–4.

57 [Jonathan Williams], 'Memoir of Jonathan Williams, on the Use of the Thermometer in Discovering Banks, Soundings, &c', *Transactions of the American Philosophical Society*, 3 (1793): 82–99, quote from pages 82–3.

58 [Jonathan Williams], 'Memoir of Jonathan Williams', pp. 83–4.

Oporto. The results of his Portuguese trip he read before the Society in 1792 and later published.[59]

In illustrating his north Atlantic voyages in 1789 and 1790 (and that with Franklin in 1785), Williams's lines and sites constituting his thermometric gradients provide for us now a series of transatlantic information flows and routes of experimentation (see Figure 2.3).

Williams's instrumental measurement was also a means to corroborate his relative's earlier work. Referring to Franklin's thermometry on board the *Reprisal* in November 1776, Williams reports how 'it agrees with my journal, in nearly the same place made nine years afterwards'. Further, Williams's work, when used in combination with other forms of measurement, had different geographical application, a point that extends Blagden's observations on the utility of Atlantic thermometry for American sailors. 'It is well known, by sounding' [noted Williams]:

> that the English coast extends with a very gradual descent to a great distance. It is also known that the American coast does not extend very far, and the water is suddenly deep. Let these facts be compared with the changes in the thermometer, on the two coasts, and they will agree with what has been said about the usefulness of that instrument.... If my apprehension of the accuracy of thermometrical observation is well founded, it would be an easy thing to make a general survey of the coast under water, more particularly than has hitherto been, or could be done by sounding.[60]

Williams brought together his lines and sites of experimentation as a practically useful guide—something neither Franklin nor Blagden did—in his *Thermometrical Navigation*, published in Philadelphia in 1799.[61]

The case for the Atlantic Enlightenment as a dynamic space of information flow between margins—a space in which geographical knowledge was differently made and represented—is perhaps most clearly illustrated in the map that accompanied Thomas Pownall's 1787 pamphlet *Hydraulic and Nautical Observations on the Currents in the Atlantic Ocean* (see Figure 2.4).

Pownall shows the Gulf Stream as a 'plume-like' arc across the Atlantic. Lines of travel are indicated: 'from Britain to St. John in Newfoundland', 'the Upper Course from Britain to Carolina and Virginia', and the 'Usual Course from Britain to the West Indies Carolina, and Virginia for sake of the Trade Winds'. The route of French ships bound for West Africa is shown, with the remark that it is one 'Prescribed by an order of their Governments'. The Cape Verd [sic] Island group is shown stylised, in sectional form as shipboard observers might have seen it above the Atlantic's swell.

Pownall's *Hydraulic and Nautical Observations* were based not on thermometry but on conversation and observation. They arose, as he put it, from 'his comparing notes (if he may so express himself) with several of his Majesty's Commissioned

---

59   [Jonathan Williams], 'A Thermometrical Journal of the Temperature of the Atmosphere and Sea, on a Voyage to and from Oporto, with Explanatory Observations thereon', *Transactions of the American Philosophical Society*, 3 (1793): 194–202.

60   [Jonathan Williams], 'Memoir of Jonathan Williams', pp. 86–7.

61   The work—of ninety-eight pages—was a compilation of Franklin's 'Maritime Observations', Williams's papers of 1792 and 1793 and a few 'additions and improvements'.

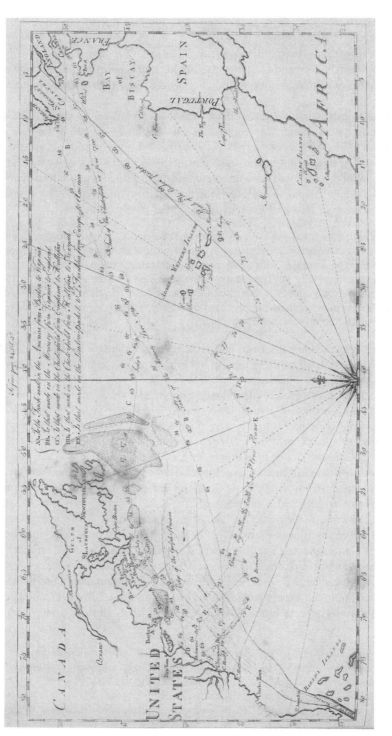

Figure 2.3   Jonathan Williams's untitled map of the Gulf Stream accompanying his 'Memoir … on the Use of the Thermometer in Discovering Banks, Soundings, &c', *Transactions of the American Philosophical Society* 3 (1793): 82–99, facing p. 84

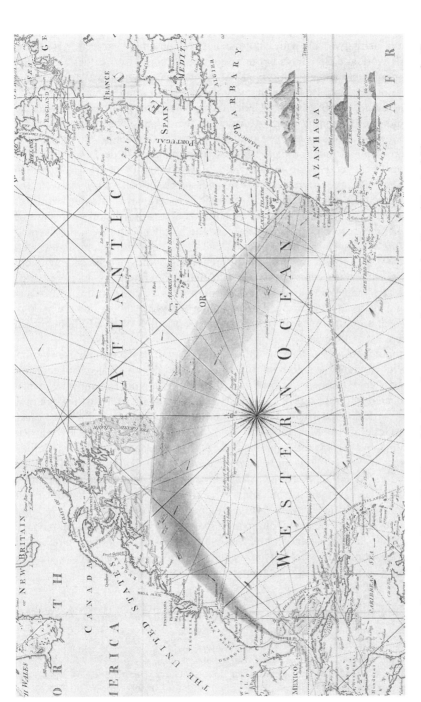

Figure 2.4   Extract from Thomas Pownall's 'Chart of the Ocean' accompanying his *Hydraulic and Nautical Observations on the Currents in the Atlantic Ocean* (London: Printed for Robert Sayer, 1787), facing p. 1

and Warrant Officers, in the frequent passages he hath had occasion to make across the Atlantic in his Majesty's ships' as well as from 'the reports of American masters of trading and fishing vessels with whom he hath talked on the subject'.[62] He knew of Franklin's work and Blagden's but does not cite at length from either. Pownall's emphasis upon 'facts actually observed'—his own and others—was to the same end as those others discussed here, namely natural philosophy about the sea with a view to practical benefits at sea. 'Under this predicament he begs to submit the following mode of reasoning on the Currents in the Atlantic Ocean; as leading *to practical rules for the navigation* of that sea; and as a foundation for queries the investigation of which may be of the highest importance to a decisive facility of the intercourse between Europe and America.'[63] His discussion of what was known led him to speculation concerning what remains to be known and, in turn, to the possibility of reducing the time for an Atlantic crossing. 'By an examination of the Currents in the higher latitudes of the Northern parts of the Atlantic, and of their course along the coasts of Greenland, and the Eskimaux shores, if they should prove such as the reasoning in this paper leads to, a much quicker passage yett may be found'.[64] Thorough study of the different geographies of the Enlightenment Atlantic—'still more accurate examination of the Northern and Southern edge of the Gulf Stream' and 'knowledge of the Western edge of the Current which sets South along the Coasts of Africa' as Pownall put it—could make natural philosophy more reliable and sailing times shorter. From such work, the Atlantic Enlightenment would become a smaller space.

A geographical chart of Pownall's life—a more evidently biographical circum-Atlantic Enlightenment—would support the argument too, for his was one of constant movement between Atlantic margins. Pownall was born into the Lincolnshire gentry in 1722, educated at Cambridge in England, became private secretary to the Governor of New York in 1753, was Lieutenant Governor of New Jersey, and, for three years from 1757, Governor of Massachusetts. In 1760, he was appointed Governor of South Carolina, but he never took up the post, electing instead to work for Britain's military forces in Europe. Pownall's *Administration of the Colonies* (1764), which was enlarged in five editions between 1765 and 1777, is a commentary on colonial rule, but his advocacy there of an 'imperial Parliament' was at odds with most political thinking in Britain. Pownall was a Member of Parliament between 1767 and 1780 and, until the American Revolution, he maintained a private correspondence with many leading New Englanders and was in almost constant communication with Franklin in London.[65] Thus did personal and scientific worlds intersect across the far-from-empty space that was the Atlantic (in the) Enlightenment.[66]

---

62   Thomas Pownall, *Hydraulic and Nautical Observations on the Currents in the Atlantic Ocean* (London, 1787), pp. 3–4.

63   Pownall, *Hydraulic and Nautical Observations*, p. 8.

64   Pownall, *Hydraulic and Nautical Observations*, p. 15.

65   John A. Schutz, 'Pownall, Thomas', in John A. Garraty and Mark C. Carnes, eds, *American National Biography* (24 vols, New York and Oxford, 1999), vol. 17, pp. 798–9.

66   This section is based on my 'Science At Sea: Charting the Gulf Stream in the Late Enlightenment', *Interdisciplinary Science Reviews*, 31 (2006): 58–76.

Conclusion

Answers to the question 'Where was the Atlantic Enlightenment?' will of course reflect particular disciplinary interests and discursive practices. In two distinct but related senses, this essay has offered answers that cohere around notions of geography, the role of mapping in particular and matters of on-board instrumental measurement, first-hand observation, conversation, correspondence and journal publication. Maps of the Gulf Stream and their accompanying texts have been used to reveal the Atlantic itself as an object of Enlightenment enquiry. Of course, maps do not so much 'represent' the world as they act to 'constitute' it. These maps served to translate numbers derived from thermometrical navigation on the move and words derived from the testimony of others into a yet different form of geographical knowledge. Maps allowed sights at sea differently arrived at to be understood in different sites on land. This empirical evidence supports the view of the Atlantic Enlightenment as a space of dynamic enquiry. But it does not define that space nor seek to prescribe how others may see and approach study of the Atlantic Enlightenment.

Mapping the Gulf Stream was one expression of how nature's dynamic forces were brought into philosophical view in the Enlightenment and in the Atlantic world. The activities of men like Franklin and Pownall are consistent with the wider epistemic making of geographical space in the Enlightenment. Pownall for example had connections with Lewis Evans, the Welsh-born Philadelphia map maker (whose 1755 'A General Map of the Middle British Colonies in America' was used by the British General Braddock in the French and Indian War).[67]

If the evidence and typologies outlined here have any wider purchase, several implications follow. It ought to be possible to think of the Atlantic Enlightenment as much more than a shared entity and of the Atlantic in the Enlightenment as much more than an empty space over which knowledge moved from one 'marginal' community to another and in which knowledge making did not occur. Indeed. thinking of the Enlightenment in terms of dynamic spaces and flows means we need to be careful with terms like 'core' and 'margin'. In some university sites within the British Atlantic Enlightenment's 'margins', the Atlantic was, as we have seen, a part of philosophical enquiry: where in Edinburgh John Walker taught his students with reference to Daniel Solander's work off the Brazilian coast and to Forster's work to name but two, in Aberdeen the philosopher Thomas Reid paid explicit attention to 'Trade Winds' as part of his geography teaching.[68] Such evidence is testimony to a more than marginal interest in the Enlightenment in the natural and commercial geography of the world's oceans. In Philadelphia, in London and on the sea itself, men like Franklin and Jonathan Williams experienced more directly the

---

67   On Enlightenment mapping in general, see Matthew Edney, 'Cartography: Disciplinary History', in ed. Gregory A. Good, *Sciences of the Earth: An Encyclopedia of Events, People and Phenomena* (2 vols, New York: Garland, 1998), vol 1, pp. 81–5; Charles W. J. Withers, 'Mapping', in Kors, *Encyclopedia of the Enlightenment*, vol 3, pp. 18–20. On Pownall and Evans, see [Anon.], (Review of) 'A Topographical Description of the Dominions of the United States of America', *Pennsylvania Magazine of History and Biography*, 74 (1950): 410–12.

68   Charles W. J. Withers, 'Toward a Historical Geography of Enlightenment in Scotland', in Wood, *The Scottish Enlightenment,* pp. 63–98.

constitution of Enlightenment science, helping promote 'thermometrical navigation' as a particular objective in safely and more quickly crossing the Atlantic.

More broadly, the Atlantic Enlightenment may, like Atlantic history and Atlantic geography, take different shape depending upon what exactly is being studied and how knowledge in the Enlightenment was then made and represented to the communities concerned. Thinking geographically about the Atlantic Enlightenment is, then, less a question of 'Where was the Atlantic Enlightenment?' as a single question permitting simple answers. It is, perhaps, more a question of 'Where was the Enlightenment in the Atlantic?' Answers would include (but not be limited to): at sea, in the practices of 'thermometric navigation' rather than 'ethnographic navigation', in the words of sailors, on maps, and as published and circulated reports amongst men of science and letters resident in different sites around the Atlantic's edges but connected by what they did across that Ocean's spaces.[69]

69   I am grateful to Susan Manning and Frank Cogliano for their invitation to contribute to this volume. For permission to quote from materials in their care, I thank Ian Milne of the Royal College of Physicians, Edinburgh, Roy Goodman, Librarian of the American Philosophical Society, Philadelphia and the Librarian of the University of Edinburgh. Thanks are due to staff of the Special Collections Division of the University of Edinburgh Library for their assistance in the reproduction of the figures and to the Librarian for permission to reproduce the figures. Parts of the paper draw upon material first published in *Interdisciplinary Science Reviews* 31 (2006): 58–76 and I am grateful for the editor's permission to incorporate them here. The research on which this essay is based was undertaken whilst in receipt of a British Academy Research Readership and I acknowledge this support with thanks.

Chapter 3

John Witherspoon and the Transatlantic Enlightenment

Daniel W. Howe

I

Eighteenth-century America encountered the Enlightenment in different versions. A secular, anticlerical Enlightenment found expression in the writings of Thomas Paine; embraced by Thomas Jefferson, it became an aspect of the political tradition Jefferson founded. This kind of Enlightenment sympathised initially with the French Revolution and breathed a skepticism of prescription and authority, whether temporal or spiritual. But America also nurtured a Christian Enlightenment, less well remembered today but in fact durable and pervasive in its influence. This version of the Enlightenment actually drew strength from the cultural tradition of the Protestant Reformation and synthesised rational empiricism with Christian piety. In America, this Protestant Enlightenment effected a reconciliation between religion and republicanism that Europeans found astonishing. The Protestant Enlightenment was chiefly responsible for the American antislavery movement, for the American system of popular education, and ultimately for the large role that organised religion has continued to play in American society and politics.[1] It is even arguable—and will here be argued—that the Protestant Enlightenment influenced the framers of the Constitution. A central figure in this version of the Trans-Atlantic Enlightenment was the Scottish-American John Witherspoon.

John Witherspoon was born 5 February 1722 (which would become 15 February 1723 after the reform of the calendar) in Guilford, East Lothian, Scotland, the son of a Church of Scotland minister named James. John's mother had been a minister's daughter, and one of her grandfathers had signed the Solemn League and Covenant in 1643. The youth attended the University of Edinburgh, took his M.A. in 1739, completed postgraduate theological studies in 1743, and was licensed to preach.[2] His time at the University exposed Witherspoon to cosmopolitan influences, Whig politics, and the ideas of the larger European world of the Enlightenment. Edinburgh University's extraordinarily broad curriculum at the time included not only the theology of the Reformation, strengthened by its Dutch contacts, but also such

---

1   On the Christian Enlightenment, see Peter Gay, *The Enlightenment: The Rise of Modern Paganism* (New York, 1967), 322–35; on the American Protestant Enlightenment, see Henry May, *The Enlightenment in America* (New York, 1976); Nina Reid-Maroney, *Philadelphia's Enlightenment: Kingdom of Christ, Empire of Reason* (Westport, Ct., 2001); and Mark Noll, *America's God: From Jonathan Edwards to Abraham Lincoln* (New York, 2002).

2   College students were typically younger in those days. The M.A. was (and still is) the first degree in Scottish universities.

diverse aspects of the Enlightenment as Newtonian science, polite literature, and the renewed interest in classical republican political thought.[3] Witherspoon, who learned French as well as the classical languages, absorbed what went on in his surroundings and participated in the excitement of Scotland's Enlightenment. He approved of the Union of 1707 with England and defined himself as a North Briton rather than a provincial Scot. When civil war broke out in 1745 he joined up on the Hanoverian side. Captured by the Stuart forces after the Battle of Falkirk, he was held prisoner in Castle Doune, near Stirling. Witherspoon's formative years demonstrated to him the possibility of reconciling Enlightenment learning and politics with Christian, and specifically Calvinist, devotion. The rest of his career would be devoted to forging, sustaining, and perpetuating that synthesis.

With the return of peace to Scotland Witherspoon served as pastor of the parish of Beith until 1757, when he moved to a more distinguished pulpit for the next eleven years: Paisley, an expanding community near Glasgow whose textile industry produced shawls with a pattern named after the town. During the time of his parish ministry, Witherspoon won a name for himself as a formidable controversialist. Surprisingly to us, his sympathy with Enlightenment principles did not extend to any modification of the Calvinist doctrines of humanity's total depravity and God's unconditional election of some to salvation. In Scottish ecclesiastical politics of the period, John Witherspoon sided firmly with the Evangelical Popular party who defended Calvinist orthodoxy against the Moderates, who tried to introduce greater respect for human autonomy and the possibility of natural human virtue. Witherspoon made his choice both on theological and political grounds: the Evangelicals represented the views of the majority of Presbyterian parishioners, the Moderates depending on the patronage of liberal aristocrats. Then, in 1768, Witherspoon accepted an invitation, partly negotiated through Benjamin Rush, to come to the American colonies and assume the presidency of the College of New Jersey, a Presbyterian institution.[4] Other invitations had come to positions in Dundee, Dublin, and Rotterdam, for by this time Witherspoon possessed an international reputation. In 1764 the University of St. Andrews had awarded him an honorary doctorate of divinity.

Witherspoon's college presidency proved to be enormously influential, not only within what became Princeton University, but for American higher education as a whole. The lectures he gave on moral philosophy and rhetoric helped shape the minds of a particularly influential generation of Americans and set patterns in American philosophy and social thought that would hold for a hundred years. When the Revolution broke out, Witherspoon supported it, presided over his local committee of correspondence, and attended the Continental Congress in Philadelphia. There, in 1776, he became the only clergyman to sign the Declaration of Independence. He published essays justifying the revolutionary cause under the pen name 'Druid'. He remained in Congress throughout the war and served on several key committees,

---

3   On the Scottish universities in these years, see Douglas Sloan, *The Scottish Enlightenment and the American College Ideal* (New York, 1971), 14–35.

4   For the protracted negotiations, see L. H. Butterfield, *John Witherspoon Comes to America: A Documentary Account* (Princeton, 1953).

notably the one on Foreign Relations, a conspicuous figure in his black clerical gown and white bands, surrounded by gentry and merchants in colourful knee breeches and tailed coats. While in Congress he nurtured a friendship with his colleague and former student, the Virginian James Madison. Throughout this public service Witherspoon remained president of Princeton, though when he was across the river in Philadelphia he delegated much to the vice president, his son-in-law Samuel Stanhope Smith.

After the Revolution, Witherspoon played a leading role in drawing up the form of government for the newly independent American Presbyterian church and acted as temporary Moderator of its first General Assembly.[5] In his mature years, Witherspoon proved as staunch an advocate of a stronger union among the states as he had been of union between Scotland and England in youth—and for much the same reasons, commercial and cultural. He participated in the New Jersey convention that ratified the United States Constitution in 1788. In 1790, as a member of the New Jersey state legislature, he chaired a committee charged to address the problem of slavery; his report recommended against a plan for gradual emancipation on the grounds that slavery was disappearing of its own accord. (Witherspoon's own estate included two slaves).[6] In 1794 he died at the age of seventy-one.

II

Across his eventful lifetime, John Witherspoon had an important part in many different contexts—in a number of different stories, we may call them. In the first place, there is the story of Scottish-American social and cultural relations, of migrations to the New World from highlands and lowlands, from both Scotland and Ulster, of Scottish influences on American education and literature, and in particular, the history of the American Presbyterian church.[7] One of several influential Scottish immigrants of the revolutionary generation (they included James Wilson and Francis Alison as well as, on the Tory side, William Smith) Witherspoon prominently urged his fellow Scots to move to America and invested in land for resale to them.[8] He also persuaded Thomas Jefferson to remove an ethnic slur against the Scots from the text of Declaration of Independence. Contemporaries noticed that he never lost his thick Scots accent.[9]

Secondly, there is the story of Presbyterian ecclesiastical politics, of Witherspoon's role in the rivalries between Evangelicals and Moderates in Scotland and between the Old Side and New Side in America. The Scottish Moderates having made effective use of satire against the Evangelicals, Witherspoon turned the tables on them.

5   Thomas J. Wertenbaker, 'John Witherspoon, Father of American Presbyterianism', in *Lives of Eighteen from Princeton*, ed. Willard Thorp (Princeton, 1946), 68–85.

6   Varnum Lansing Collins, *President Witherspoon* (Princeton, 1925), vol. 2, pp. 167–8, 181.

7   See Ned C. Landsman, ed., *Nation and Province in the First British Empire: Scotland and the Americas, 1600–1800* (Lewisburg, Pa., 2001).

8   See Bernard Bailyn, *Voyagers to the West* (New York, 1986), 390–93; 610–16.

9   Manassah Cutler, upon hearing Witherspoon preach a sermon in 1787, quoted in Collins, *President Witherspoon*, vol. 2, p. 161.

His pamphlet *Ecclesiastical Characteristics* (1753), 'an humble attempt to open the mystery of moderation', mocked the Moderates by pretending to be a statement of their principles. ('The Confession of Faith, [to] which we are now all laid under a disagreeable necessity to subscribe, was framed in times of hot religious zeal; and therefore it can hardly be supposed to contain anything agreeable to our sentiments in these cool and refreshing days of moderation.'[10] Reprinted in Edinburgh, Glasgow, London, Philadelphia, and Utrecht, the pamphlet made its author a Calvinist celebrity. In England it was welcomed by critics of Latitudinarianism. Encouraged by its success, Witherspoon published more polemical pamphlets and engaged in one controversy after another, both ecclesiastical and legal. As these confrontations grew ever sharper and more personal, eventually the pastor overstepped permissible lines and left himself vulnerable to a lawsuit for libel. Loyal friends had to help him pay the resulting judgement against him.[11] Yet despite his deserved reputation as a controversialist, Witherspoon never seceded altogether from the Church of Scotland, as many embittered Evangelical Calvinists did.

In America, this Scotsman who had made himself famous for acerbic partisan rhetoric successfully reconciled the pro-revival New Side and anti-revival Old Side Presbyterians in common support of his work at Princeton. During the generation between its founding during the religious Great Awakening of the 1740s and Witherspoon's arrival in 1768, Princeton had been dominated by the New Sides. During Witherspoon's presidency, however, the Old Sides gradually became more numerous, and their domination of Princeton then continued for generations.[12]

Of more general interest today than Presbyterian factionalism is the story of American independence and the place of religion within that struggle. Witherspoon found his new countrymen no less proud and disputatious than the Scots, and their Revolution provided ample scope for his combative zeal. Contemporaries called the American Dissenting clergy 'the black regiment' within the Patriot cause. Witherspoon and his fellow Calvinist ministers, who denounced the Church of England and British colonial policies before the war and preached firm resolve to the rebels during it, would have been astonished by the argument of the present-day historian Jonathan Clark that the American Revolution was based on liberal theological heresy.[13] American Protestant Dissenters tended to rally together against the Anglican clergy in support of the Revolution, so differences among them over theology and ecclesiology that would have loomed large in other situations did not surface in wartime. Witherspoon's inclination for heavy-handed satire, which he had indulged at the expense of the Scottish Moderates, he turned to even more savage caricatures of American Loyalists.[14]

---

10   *The Selected Writings of John Witherspoon*, ed. Thomas Miller (Carbondale, 1990), 57, 69.

11   Collins, *President Witherspoon,* I, 59–62.

12   James McLachlan, *Princetonians, 1748–1768* (Princeton, 1976), xxiv.

13   J. C. D. Clark, *The Language of Liberty, 1660–1832: Political Discourse and Social Dynamics in the Anglo-American World* (New York, 1994).

14   See Timothy M. Barnes and Robert M. Calhoun, 'Moral Allegiance: John Witherspoon and Loyalist Recantation', *American Presbyterians* 63 (1985): 273–83.

Another important, but very different, story is the history of moral philosophy. The lectures Witherspoon delivered at Princeton played a crucial part in spreading what is called the Scottish philosophy of common sense in the United States.[15] They demonstrate the extent to which he participated in the eighteenth-century project of creating a science of human nature. Witherspoon not only introduced Americans to the philosophy of the Scottish Enlightenment but critically mediated among the different schools of thought within that diverse Enlightenment. He turned Princeton philosophy away from the metaphysical idealism of his predecessor Jonathan Edwards and toward the common-sense realism that became characteristic of Scottish and American academic philosophy for generations to come. In fact, a short essay that Witherspoon published in 1753 is one of the earliest statements on record of the position that became known as Scottish common sense.[16]

In the history of American education, Witherspoon is also significant for curricular innovation. He applied the example of the Scottish universities in their openness to new branches of learning like science and modern languages along with classics and theology. In 1771, he established a professorship of mathematics and natural philosophy and proudly acquired for his college the orrery of David Rittenhouse: a mechanical model of the solar system, showing the motions of all the (known) planets and their satellites. He also introduced the Scottish practice of lecturing to college students, significantly reshaping a pedagogy previously based on tutorials and recitation classes. A well spent year travelling about the country fund-raising doubled the university's endowment (to a modest five thousand pounds).[17]

Witherspoon's presidency set Princeton on the road to becoming one of the most influential of American universities, with an academic empire of feeder academies and imitative colleges. At a time when all other American colleges recruited their students mainly within their own colony/state, Princeton drew upon a wide geographical base, and the new president particularly nurtured its ties with the South.[18] (He even tried to recruit students from the West Indian planter class, but with less success.) Witherspoon's visibility was such that he modelled the role of the college president to the nation at large, combining academic administration with teaching, and in particular with teaching a required course in moral philosophy to the senior class, a practice that became standard in American colleges until after the Civil War.[19]

One of the interesting stories involving Witherspoon has to do with the influence he exercised through his students. John Witherspoon's Princeton nurtured American statecraft. The 469 Princeton graduates during his presidency (1768–94) included a

---

15   *An Annotated Edition of Lectures on Moral Philosophy by John Witherspoon* has been edited by Jack Scott (Newark, 1982).

16   J. W. [John Witherspoon,] 'Remarks on an Essay on Human Liberty', *Scots Magazine* 15 (April 1753), 165–70. The subject is more fully explored in Matthew Phelps, 'John Witherspoon and the Transmission of Common Sense Philosophy from Scotland to America', D.Phil. Thesis, Oxford University, 2002.

17   For a fine overview of Witherspoon's impact at Princeton, see Sloan, *Scottish Enlightenment and American College Ideal*, 103–45.

18   See Richard A. Harrison, *Princetonians: 1769–1775* (Princeton, 1980), xxii–iii.

19   See George Schmidt, *The Old Time College President* (New York, 1930); and Wilson Smith, *Professors and Public Ethics: Studies of the Northern Moral Philosophers* (Ithaca, NY, 1956).

United States president, a vice-president, ten cabinet secretaries, six members of the Continental Congress, six members of the Constitutional Convention, twenty-one United States senators, thirty-nine members of the House of Representatives, twelve state governors, fifty-six state legislators, and thirty judges, three of whom became justices of the US Supreme Court.[20] The present essay will look only at James Madison, called 'Father of the Constitution'. Witherspoon and Madison had a close relationship at Princeton, where the college president acted as moral preceptor to undergraduate 'Jemmy', and they remained lifelong friends and political associates.[21]

Finally, there is the story of the rise of polite culture in the eighteenth century.[22] Often Calvinists in both Britain and America embraced austerity and regarded genteel politeness with suspicion. ('We can often determine to which sect a man belongs by his looks, tone, and gait,' remarked an American religious magazine as late as 1829. Theological liberals 'incline to the amiable and pacific virtues', Calvinists 'to the stern and self-denying virtues').[23] At Princeton, however, the two value systems effected a reconciliation. Just as Witherspoon mediated between New Sides and Old, so did he also mediate between Calvinist severity and the new cult of politeness.[24] Princeton college life included not only classical learning, early-modern Protestant piety, and the natural science of the Scottish Enlightenment, but also most forms of *belles lettres*. Witherspoon himself gave lectures on 'eloquence' (including composition, rhetoric, and aesthetics) that invoked both classical and neoclassical models.[25] They make an interesting comparison with the more famous lectures on rhetoric of his University of Edinburgh contemporary Hugh Blair; Witherspoon showed more interest in the application of rhetorical principles to the practical needs of lawyers, clergymen, and prospective republican statesmen.[26] Gentlemen's literary societies formed at Princeton for 'mutual improvement': the American Whig and the Cliosophic societies. These societies enjoyed official recognition, and most students belonged to one or the other. They encouraged American nationalism, classical tradition, standards of decorum, and polite letters.[27] Princeton University provided a hospitable environment to many young men from the southern planter aristocracy, anxious to acquire the trappings of refinement while remaining staunchly Calvinist in theology.

---

20   Collins, *President Witherspoon*, vol 2, p. 229.

21   Harrison, *Princetonians, 1769–1775*, 161. A 'moral preceptor' assumed a pastoral and advisory role with an individual student.

22   See Paul Langford, *A Polite and Commercial People: England 1727–1783* (New York, 1989); and Richard Bushman, *The Refinement of America: Persons, Houses, Cities* (New York, 1992).

23   Boston *Christian Examiner*, 7 (1829), 234.

24   See the sophisticated analysis of Ned Landsman, 'Witherspoon and the Problem of Provincial Identity in Scottish Evangelical Culture', eds. Richard B. Sher and Jeffrey R. Smitten in *Scotland and America in the Age of the Enlightenment,* (Edinburgh, 1990), 29–45.

25   Reprinted in *Selected Writings of John Witherspoon*, ed. Miller, 231–318.

26   See Thomas P. Miller, 'Witherspoon, Blair, and the rhetoric of Civic Humanism', eds. Sher and Smitten, *Scotland and America*, 100–114.

27   See James McLachlan, 'The *Choice of Hercules*: American Student Societies in the Early 19th Century', in *The University in Society*, ed. Lawrence Stone (Princeton, 1974), vol. 2, pp. 449–94.

III

Notwithstanding the central role he played in so many different aspects of the Atlantic Civilization of his time, no scholarly biography of John Witherspoon has appeared since 1925. In that year Varnum Lansing Collins published *President Witherspoon*, an accurate and laudatory work based on extensive research, but inevitably dated in its point of view. Collins concerned himself much with the College of New Jersey as an institution, but showed less interest in intellectual and cultural history, and particularly little in the history of philosophy. In 1973 a Princeton University archivist published a manuscript memoir of Witherspoon written in 1835 by Ashbel Green, who himself had served as president of Princeton from 1812 to 1822.[28] Two popular, inspirational biographies aimed at Christian audiences have appeared, good books of their kind.[29] However, serious modern scholarship on Witherspoon has appeared chiefly in the form of articles, often excellent but necessarily fragmentary; most of the important ones are cited in the notes to this essay.

Mark Noll's book *Princeton and the Republic* (1989) provides one of the most significant modern treatments of Witherspoon, yet even it focuses not on the Scottish emigrant himself but on the career of his son-in-law and successor at Princeton, Samuel Stanhope Smith. Within this framework, Noll treats Witherspoon's presidency as background for the personalities and issues that primarily concern him.[30] Smith pushed even harder than Witherspoon for curricular modernisation. This, and the tendency for graduates of the College to heed a call to public service rather than to the ministry, provoked the Presbyterian General Assembly to establish a separate institution, the Princeton Theological Seminary, in 1811–12. Noll interprets this foundation as marking the failure of the goal, shared by Witherspoon and Smith, of integrating Christian with Enlightenment principles in education. Noll concludes that 'Witherspoon's achievement was personal and temporary rather than intellectual and lasting'.[31]

This judgement seems to me too narrow in focus. In fact, both the College of New Jersey and the new Princeton Theological Seminary proudly maintained their ties of direct lineage from John Witherspoon. Princeton Seminary stood as a bastion of Old School Calvinist theology and Scottish common sense philosophy well into the twentieth century. Its most famous scholars, Archibald Alexander and Charles Hodge, remained as confident as Witherspoon himself had been that natural science

---

28   Ashbel Green, *The Life of the Revd John Witherspoon, with a Brief Review of his Writings and a Summary Estimate of his Character and Talents*, ed. Henry Lyttleton Savage (Princeton, 1973).

29   Martha Lou Lemmon Stohlman, *John Witherspoon, Parson, Politician, Patriot* (Philadelphia, 1974); L. Gordon Tait, *The Piety of John Witherspoon: Pew, Pulpit, and Public Forum* (Louisville, Ky, 2001).

30   Mark Noll, *Princeton and the Republic, 1768–1822: The Search for a Christian Enlightenment in the Era of Samuel Stanhope Smith* (Princeton, 1989).

31   Ibid., 258–71; quotation from p. 292. For a more favourable assessment of Smith's career at Princeton, see Sloan, *Scottish Enlightenment and American College Ideal* (cited above, n. 3), 146–84.

would prove compatible with true religion.[32] More significantly, throughout American academia beyond Princeton, the common sense philosophy that Witherspoon had brought from Scotland to synthesise Christianity with the Enlightenment would reign supreme for most of the nineteenth century—and harmonised, to general satisfaction, with the American republicanism that Witherspoon also championed.[33]

The most extended recent work on Witherspoon comes from a scholar of the American political tradition, Jeffrey Morrison. *John Witherspoon and the Founding of the American Republic* (2005) aspires to restore its subject to his proper rank among the founders. In keeping with this intention, it calls attention to his role as Revolutionary patriot and American nationalist. It ignores his Scottish career, and its treatments of Witherspoon's philosophical and religious ideas are derivative and somewhat dated. Morrison demonstrates the central place Witherspoon occupied within the community of the founders and the high regard in which they held him. But for all its commendable purpose, the book illustrates the very problem it seeks to remedy: the difficulty of achieving a full appreciation for its subject's influence. To recreate and properly assess John Witherspoon's life and impact requires locating him in more than simply a political context, and in more than an American one.[34]

If John Witherspoon was so important, why have historians not done better by him? To that question, several answers present themselves. In the first place, there seems to be a paucity of sources, particularly relating to his personal life, though historians have found ways around such difficulties in other cases. More importantly, history has generally been studied in the context of the nation-state, and Witherspoon's career cannot be understood save in conjunction with both its Scottish and American situations.[35] With historians expected to be either British or American in focus (a distinction compounded by the degree of separation between Scottish and English history), there might have been no professional pay-off commensurate with the effort for studying Witherspoon's life as a totality. This inhibiting factor should finally be overcome with the rising interest in the history of the Atlantic World, for Witherspoon was a quintessentially Atlantic figure.

The most serious reason for Witherspoon's neglect, however, is that the philosophical school associated with him, Scottish common sense, has suffered from a derogatory historiographical tradition that goes all the way back to H. T. Buckle in the nineteenth century.[36] This interpretive tradition, essentially repeated by I. Woodbridge Riley, Herbert Schneider, and Donald Harvey Meyer, has characterised

---

32   Brooks Holifield, *Theology in America* (New Haven, 2003), pp. 380–81. On the Witherspoon-Smith tradition at Princeton, see also Fred J. Hood, *Reformed America: The Middle and Southern States, 1783–1837* (Tuscaloosa, Al., 1980), pp. 7–26.

33   The classic treatment is Sydney Ahlstrom, 'Scottish Philosophy and American Theology', *Church History* 24 (1955): 257–72.

34   Jeffrey H. Morrison, *John Witherspoon and the Founding of the American Republic* (Notre Dame, Ind., 2005).

35   When a graduate student at Oxford undertook a doctoral thesis treating Witherspoon, he needed two supervisors: Dr. John Robertson for the Scottish side and myself for the American. See Matthew Phelps, 'John Witherspoon', cited in n. 16.

36   H. T. Buckle, *On Scotland and the Scotch Intellect* (Chicago, 1970; originally published 1861).

common sense philosophy as dogmatic and shallow, a prostitution of philosophy to the service of conservative religious and social objectives. Instead of seeing the philosophers of common sense as *participants* in the Scottish Enlightenment, historians have cast them as the rear-guard religious resistance *against* the Enlightenment, a kind of Protestant Counter-Reformation.[37] As a result of such misinterpretation, Witherspoon has not seemed to historical scholars an exciting person to study. He has been the ultimate example of the 'dead white male': the boring spokesman for a lost and unlamented world view. He has remained, as Mark Noll correctly observed in 1985, 'an enigma'.[38] Significantly, the recovery of respect for the Scottish and American common sense philosophy has been led by philosophers rather than by intellectual historians.[39]

In reality, Witherspoon involved himself in the Scottish Enlightenment as much as he did with ecclesiastical controversies. His support for the Scottish Union with England, like his support for Union among the American states, derived from a thoroughly Enlightened approval of commercial expansion and economic development. He possessed a wide familiarity with seventeenth- and eighteenth-century thought, secular as well as religious, and drew upon it in his lectures at Princeton. There he intended, as he put it, 'to meet [infidels] on their own ground, and to show from reason itself, the fallacy of their principles'.[40]

In his use of reason to justify religion, Witherspoon could draw inspiration from a Genevan Calvinist theologian named Benedict Pictet (1655–1724). Witherspoon had studied Pictet in his theology classes; in later years at Princeton, he still treasured his copy of the French translation of Pictet's *Theologia Christiana*. Pictet emphasised, much as Witherspoon did later, the harmony between reason and revelation; he pioneered the reconciliation of Calvinist theology with natural science and moral philosophy that Witherspoon would continue.[41] Pictet showed Witherspoon that it was not necessary to adopt the laxity of the Moderates in order to take account of

---

37　I. Woodbridge Riley, *American Philosophy, the Early Schools* (New York, 1907); Herbert Schneider, *A History of American Philosophy* (New York, 1957; originally published 1946); Donald Harvey Meyer, *Democratic Enlightenment* (New York, 1976). Matthew Phelps, in the thesis cited above at n. 16, commendably counteracts this tradition.

38　Mark Noll, 'The Irony of the Enlightenment for Presbyterians in the Early Republic', *Journal of the Early Republic* 5 (Summer 1985): 149–75; quotation from p. 153.

39　The reevaluation for common sense philosophy in America, including that of John Witherspoon, was led by Elizabeth Flower and Murray G. Murphey, *A History of Philosophy in America* (New York, 1977), vol. 1, pp. 203–73. The Common Sense philosophers of Scotland had already been accorded respect in, e.g., D. Daiches Raphael, *The Moral Sense* (London, 1947) and S. A. Grave, *The Scottish Philosophy of Common Sense* (Oxford, 1960). For more recent appreciative analyses, see Knud Haakonssen, intro. to Thomas Reid, *Practical Ethics: Being Lectures and Papers on Natural Religion, Self-Government, Natural Jurisprudence, and the Law of Nations* (Princeton, 1990); and William Rowe, *Thomas Reid on Freedom and Morality* (Ithaca, NY, 1991).

40　*Lectures on Moral Philosophy*, 64.

41　See Martin I. Klauber, 'Reformed Orthodoxy in Transition: Benedict Pictet (1655–1724) and Enlightened Orthodoxy in Post-Reformation Geneva', *Later Calvinism: International Perspectives* ed. W. Fred Graham, (Kirkville, Mo., 1994), 93–113.

secular moral philosophy. Witherspoon's outlook constituted an eighteenth-century updating of Pictet's.

Significantly, what Witherspoon most disliked about the Moderates was not their use of reason but their sentimentality and indulgent attitude toward human emotions and failings. In 1756 the Moderate Presbyterian clergyman John Home wrote a dramatic play called *Douglas: A Tragedy*, which enjoyed popular runs in both Edinburgh and London. Whether it was appropriate for a Christian even to attend the theatre, much less for a minister of the gospel to write for it, sharply divided Scottish opinion at the time. Witherspoon weighed in against it. Theatres then were sites of prostitution and their actors notorious for loose morals. Witherspoon doubted that what went on in theatres, either on stage or off it, could be cleaned up enough to transform them into an innocent recreation for Christians. He considered it scandalous for a minister to so indulge public passions as to write a script for performance.[42] Many in the colonies shared his opinion; in 1774 the First Continental Congress banned theatrical performances along with horse-racing and cock-fighting.[43]

In politics, Witherspoon retained the belief, handed down from the ancients via Renaissance and early-modern authorities, in the need to ground free government on patriotic virtue. Self-interest would not suffice as the basis of self-government, he was convinced. Nor did he accept the brazen theory of Bernard Mandeville that private vices, such as luxury, constituted public virtues because they promoted consumption and thus encouraged trade. Witherspoon retained a classical belief in self-discipline, tempered but not distorted by his acceptance of polite standards of good taste. He praised the ancient Greek ideal of 'moderation in every thing how good soever'.[44] To this venerable foundation he added modern elements drawn from a range of authors including Pufendorf, Locke, Montesquieu, and even his Scottish Moderate antagonist Francis Hutcheson. He defended natural rights, government by consent, and a series of compacts establishing first society, then civil government, and finally the particular relationship between ruler and ruled.[45]

However old-fashioned some of his views, on the subject of economics Witherspoon seems thoroughly modern. He shared the outlook of his famous countryman and contemporary, Adam Smith, and endorsed free enterprise as a means to facilitate commerce.[46] Actually, such a combination of liberalism with

---

42 John Witherspoon, *A Serious Inquiry into the Nature and Effects of the Stage* (Glasgow, 1757; reprinted in New York, 1812). For the controversy as a whole see Alice Gipson, *John Home: A Study of His Life and Works* (New Haven, 1916).

43 Ann Fairfax Withington, *Toward a More Perfect Union: Virtue and the Formation of American Republics* (New York, 1991), pp. 11, 20–37.

44 *Lectures on Moral Philosophy*, 114.

45 For analyses of Witherspoon's political philosophy, see James McAllister, 'John Witherspoon: Academic Advocate for American Freedom', in *A Miscellany of American Christianity*, ed. Stuart C. Henry (Durhanm, NC, 1963), 183–224; and Roger Fechner, 'The Godly and Virtuous Republic of John Witherspoon', in *Ideas in America's Cultures*, ed. Hamilton Cravens (Ames, IA, 1982), pp. 7–26.

46 On Witherspoon's endorsement of commerce during both his Scottish and his American periods, see Landsman, 'The Two Worlds of John Witherspoon', in *Scotland and America*, cited above, n. 21.

Calvinism and classical republican political values appeared frequently among American Revolutionaries. The logical distinction between Enlightenment liberalism and classical republicanism, which has been has been pointed out by historians, did not much bother people in the late eighteenth century. The thinkers and doers of Witherspoon's generation drew freely upon both traditions.[47]

IV

Witherspoon composed his *Lectures on Moral Philosophy* at Princeton between 1770 and 1772, and then (like many another university lecturer), continued to deliver them to student audiences for years thereafter. They were not published until 1801, several years after his death, but in the meantime they had circulated widely in the form of notes by his students, many of whom went off to found colleges, academies, and churches of their own. Witherspoon treated not only the philosophy of ethics but also political theory and jurisprudence in these lectures.

Like Jonathan Edwards, John Witherspoon knew Francis Hutcheson's philosophy thoroughly. Since Hutcheson was the leader of the Moderate clergy, Witherspoon despised his theology. As a philosopher, however, Witherspoon accorded him a measure of respect. Indeed, Witherspoon followed Hutcheson's sequence of topics for presentation so closely that some modern readers have carelessly jumped to the conclusion that he was accepting the substance of Hutcheson's opinions.[48] In fact, Witherspoon accepted much of Hutcheson's psychology of the human faculties but ultimately rejected his ethical sentimentalism in favour of a rational basis for moral knowledge. (He had earlier savaged Hutcheson's ethical theory in his satiric *Ecclesiastical Characteristics*).

Witherspoon's Princeton lectures proved instrumental in shifting learned Calvinist opinion away from the emotive or sentimentalist theory over to ethical rationalism; thereafter, Edwards's version of Calvinist ethical sentimentalism began to lose adherents. Witherspoon rejected the theory that ethical distinctions rested only on human feelings (or 'affections', to use the contemporary term); he particularly objected to Hutcheson's treatment of moral values as akin to aesthetic ones. Witherspoon insisted that morality was objective, immutable, and 'in the nature of things'. While recognising that moral judgements had an emotional component, he maintained that they also had a rational basis. 'Probably both [reason and affection] are necessary' components of the moral life, he declared at one point; presumably the rational insight came first, followed by a motivating feeling. If Witherspoon seemed then to mediate between ethical sentimentalism and ethical rationalism, in

---

47   See (among many articles on the subject) Daniel Walker Howe, 'European Sources of Political Ideas in Jeffersonian America', *Reviews in American History* 10 (December 1982): 629–64; and James Kloppenberg, 'The Virtues of Liberalism: Christianity, Republicanism, and Ethics in Early American Political Discourse', *Journal of American History* 74 (June 1987): 9–33.

48   As Garry Wills implies in *Inventing America: Jefferson's Declaration of Independence* (New York, 1978), 176.

later lectures he came down unequivocally on the side of rational intuition as the source of moral judgements.[49]

By calling attention to the role of reason in the moral life, Witherspoon prepared the way for the favourable reception Americans accorded to the rationalist theory of Thomas Reid's *Essays on the Active Powers of Man*, which appeared in 1788. Reid was an Arminian (that is, a believer in human free will), not a Calvinist, and he belonged to the Moderate wing of the Church of Scotland. The widespread acceptance of Reid's philosophy throughout American Calvinist seminaries and colleges constituted one of the surprising features of antebellum American religious culture. John Witherspoon helped overthrow the philosophical influence of the Scottish Moderate Francis Hutcheson only to have it replaced with that of another Scottish Moderate, Thomas Reid.[50]

Some people, both in Witherspoon's day and ours, have claimed that basing ethical judgements on feeling is more 'democratic' than basing them on rational judgement. Their assumption is that everybody has feelings but only an educated elite can apply reason to moral problems. But Witherspoon, Reid, and their supporters looked at it differently. To them, our sense of obligation is intuitive, known by 'simple perceptions', without elaborate argument. We know that a promise should be kept in the same way that we know that the whole is equal to the sum of its parts. Confusingly, both Hutcheson and Reid used the term 'moral sense' to mean the faculty of making moral judgements, but whereas Hutcheson thought the moral sense was a feeling, a sentiment, Reid characterised it as a rational power. Reid declared that moral sense is not an emotion but a form of 'common sense', that is, the sense common to all. It is not a refined sentiment but the kind of down-to-earth quality we have in mind when we say, 'You show good sense'.[51] Witherspoon's younger contemporary Jane Austen used the term in this way when she distinguished in her novel between *Sense* and *Sensibility*.

Witherspoon's lectures on moral philosophy as well as his polemical writings display an attitude toward human nature typical of the mainstream of Enlightened writers. He thought in terms of a hierarchy of faculties constituting motives that governed human actions. This psychology of the human faculties would be most explicitly and fully laid out by Thomas Reid, but it is already implicit in Witherspoon. Human nature may be diagrammed as a pyramid. At the apex is conscience or the moral sense; at the base, the passions. Intermediate between them lies prudential self-interest. Tragically, the strength of these faculties varied *inversely* with their legitimacy and reliability. It was one thing to *know* the Good, another thing entirely to *act* upon it. Conscience, the highest motive and the one people ought to follow,

---

49 *Lectures on Moral Philosophy*, 71, 86–7.

50 See also Daniel W. Howe, *The Unitarian Conscience: Harvard Moral Philosophy, 1805–1861* (Cambridge, 1970), pp. 31–2, 45–9; and E. Brooks Holifield, *The Gentlemen Theologians: American Theology in Southern Culture, 1795–1860* (Durham, NC, 1978), pp. 129–37.

51 Witherspoon, *Lectures on Moral Philosophy*, 87; Thomas Reid, *Works*, ed. Sir William Hamilton (Edinburgh, 1863), vol. 1, pp. 478–81. See also S. A. Grave, *The Scottish Philosophy of Common Sense* (Oxford, 1960), chap. 7.

constituted the weakest motive. The passions, base and undependable as guides, were nevertheless massively powerful. As Alexander Pope put it, 'The ruling passion conquers reason still'.[52] The faculty of self-interest, less authoritative than conscience but stronger, could be either rational (when taking a broad and long-term view) or passionate (when governed by narrow and short-term interests).

Witherspoon looked upon the strength of the passions as manifesting original sin; 'human passions, since the fall, are all of them but too strong'.[53] Powerful and dangerous as the passions were, however, God had made human beings to be guided by their conscience and reason. Witherspoon believed that we had a duty to practise self-discipline, or the cultivation of a properly balanced, moderate character, trying to strengthen conscience and rational prudence rather than indulging the easy gratification of the passions.[54] He applied these principles in his defence of American rights, carefully arguing from natural law and the British constitution, speaking respectfully of the King even while criticising his ministers, and cautioning other colonists to make sure that 'it is not passion but reason that inspires you'.[55]

An excellent practical application of Witherspoon's model of human nature appears in his sermon, 'The Dominion of Providence over the Passions of Men'. Witherspoon preached this on 17 May 1776, a day of fasting and evangelical humiliation proclaimed by the Continental Congress, and he dedicated the sermon to John Hancock, president of the Congress. He took his text from Psalm 76, verse 10: 'Surely the wrath of man shall praise thee.' Even corrupt human nature, even the disorderly passions of men, serve God's providential purposes, Witherspoon assured his audience. The Scottish moral philosophers famously emphasised the unintended consequences of human actions. Witherspoon gave this a Christian twist: God could turn even the most violent human passions, such as those of warfare, to His own ends, such as the triumph of liberty. His view of human nature confirmed his Whig politics. He did not accuse Members of Parliament of any unusual degree of passionate evil. Americans must resist 'their unjust claims' to rule those whom they do not represent, for the simple reason that 'they are men, and therefore liable to all the selfish bias inseparable from human nature'. Witherspoon called upon his fellow Patriots to keep their own passions in order, not to manifest a 'turbulent' spirit but to wage a war on behalf of self-discipline, 'industry', and 'frugality', demonstrating all the while 'a dignity in virtue'.[56]

---

52 Alexander Pope, *Moral Essays*, epistle 3, line 153.

53 *Nature and Effects of the Stage*, 54.

54 *Lectures on Moral Philosophy*, 66–7, 114–16.

55 'On Conducting the American Controversy', *The Works of John Witherspoon* (Edinburgh, 1805), vol. 9, p. 85.

56 'The Dominion of Providence over the Passions of Men', in *Selected Writings of John Witherspoon*, ed. Miller (cited above, n. 11), 126–47. I have discussed this sermon in *Making the American Self: Jonathan Edwards to Abraham Lincoln* (Cambridge, Mass., 1997), 65. See also Richard B. Sher, 'Witherspoon's *Dominion of Providence* and the Scottish Jeremiad Tradition', in *Scotland and America* (cited above, n. 21), 46–64.

V

Fifteen years before the framers of the national Constitution met in Philadelphia, before Madison and Hamilton penned *The Federalist Papers*, even before the drafting of any of the revolutionary state constitutions, John Witherspoon's *Lectures on Moral Philosophy* laid out the principles of a government based on checks and balances to an audience of future American leaders. After describing the systems of monarchy, aristocracy, and democracy, pointing out the deficiencies of each, the Princeton president concluded:

> Hence it appears that every good form of government must be complex, so that the one principle may check the other. It is of consequence to have as much virtue among the particular members of a community as possible; but it is folly to expect that a state should be upheld by integrity in all who have a share in managing it. They must be so balanced, that when every one draws to his own interest or inclination, there may be an over poise upon the whole.[57]

The lecturer's line of argument echoed that of the Roman Polybius, who had influenced Calvin; but to young James Madison, Jr., who heard it in 1771, it must have seemed fresh and relevant, for he would later turn it to imaginative account.

Witherspoon did not attend the Constitutional Convention where Madison played such a central role, but most of the delegates shared an outlook broadly similar to his. Many of them had studied moral philosophy either in the colonies or Scotland; indeed fully one-fifth of them, representing about half the states, had done so at Princeton itself.[58] The basic law they drafted respected the principles of mixed and balanced government that Witherspoon had defended. As members of the Continental Congress, Princeton's president and his former student James Madison had not always seen eye to eye. A delegate from New Jersey, Witherspoon looked out for the interests of the small states, while Madison, coming from Virginia ('the Prussia of the American confederation') of course advocated those of the large states. In religion Madison was a deist. But when expounding fundamental political principles, he concurred in the view of human nature that his old mentor taught.[59]

Madison's contributions to *The Federalist Papers* demonstrate this congruence. It is generally impossible to say with assurance that Madison got this or that specific idea from Witherspoon, if for no other reason than that such attitudes about human nature were commonplaces of the gentry class in the eighteenth century, on both sides of the Atlantic. If Madison did not recall them from Witherspoon's lectures, he could have picked them up in any number of other ways. His collaborator Alexander Hamilton, graduate of King's College in New York City (now Columbia University),

---

57　*Lectures on Moral Philosophy*, 144.

58　David M. Kirkham, '"Inflamed with Study"': Eighteenth-century higher education and the formation of the American constitutional mind' (Ph.D. thesis, George Washington University, 1989), 93, 103, 105, 196.

59　Much of the argument in this section draws upon that of Matthew Phelps, 'John Witherspoon and the Transmission of Common Sense Philosophy', cited above in n. 16.

in his contributions to *The Federalist*, employed the same set of assumptions about human motivation as Madison.

In *The Federalist*, Madison and Hamilton see the science of government as analogous to the psychology of the faculties. 'Publius' (their collective pseudonym) treats lawmaking as a process analogous to the decisions reached by a wise person. He argues for a government whose components or branches will be balanced in much the same way as the faculties of a well balanced character conduce to right decisions. The executive constitutes the 'will', the legislature the 'understanding', and the judiciary the 'conscience' of the commonwealth.[60] Within the legislative branch, the House of Representatives, whose members serve short terms, will be more susceptible to passions, while the Senators will take the longer, more rational view.[61] The balanced mind of a wise individual will weigh many motives before acting; reason will overcome momentary passions. In a well structured government, too, there will be repeated deliberations before action is taken. A poorly constructed government, like a weak mind, will be prone to fall under the tyranny of some capricious passion. Within the commonwealth as Madison conceives it, the analog to 'passion' is 'faction'.[62]

So far, the application of faculty psychology to political philosophy appears to yield a classical republican model. The body politic needs to follow the precepts of virtue, and to achieve this end needs to impose self-discipline in the form of a written constitution mandating balanced government. However, the thinkers of the Scottish Enlightenment also integrated elements of liberalism into this framework. They did so by paying attention to the intermediate kind of motives, those of prudential self-interest. Scottish moral philosophers showed that prudence could ally with conscience, thereby strengthening greatly the incentive to virtue. This partial legitimating of self-interested motives was an essential precondition to the liberal world view. Witherspoon insisted that God commanded things because they were right, not the other way around (that is, they were not right simply because of God's arbitrary will). Furthermore, God in His Providence ordained that if we did that which was right, it would ('in ordinary cases') be advantageous for us.[63] This line of argument indicated that prudential calculation could lead to conclusions agreeable to conscience. Long-term self-interest, scrupulously identified, could be a guide to moral action, and could be enlisted in the cause of public virtue. 'Private and public interest', Witherspoon concluded, 'should be made to assist, and not destroy each other'.[64] Publius would invoke this principle.

Adam Smith showed how divine providence could use the selfishness of individuals to help the whole community. The baker supplies us with bread out of self-seeking motives, yet performs a valuable service for all. 'By pursuing his own

---

60 *The Federalist,* numbers 70 (executive/will), 56 (legislative/understanding), and 84 (judiciary/conscience).

61 Ibid., numbers 62 and 63.

62 I pursue this line of analysis in more detail in 'The Political Psychology of *The Federalist*', *William and Mary Quarterly*, 46 (1987): 485–509.

63 Witherspoon, *Lectures on Moral Philosophy,* 85, 93.

64 Ibid., 87.

interest', Smith noted with a fine sense of irony, a person often promotes the welfare of society 'more effectually than when he really intends to promote it'.[65] The selfish pyramid of human nature, though it posed grave problems, could also be turned to advantage by the invisible hand of God's providential design.

The Federalist acknowledged that a good commonwealth hoped to find wise and virtuous citizens to lead it, though it must take precautions against the chance of getting leaders of another sort. Witherspoon had warned, 'It is folly to expect that a state should be upheld by integrity in all who have a share in managing it'. Madison, speaking as Publius, was more pithy: 'Enlightened statesmen will not always be at the helm.'[66] What safeguards existed, then?

Balanced government provided the time-honoured answer, but Madison had another idea as well. The very large extent of the new republic offered cause for hope. A large constituency is more likely to yield wise and virtuous candidates than a small one, he pointed out. Furthermore, he argued in his famous Tenth *Federalist Paper* (elaborating on a point that had been made by David Hume), a diverse constituency is less likely to fall under the spell of some faction or demagogue simply because its many interest groups will act as checks on the ability of any one element (even a numerical majority) to oppress the rest.[67]

Out of the clash of rival interests, Madison hoped, there might emerge a result approximating justice. 'When every one draws to his own interest or inclination', old Witherspoon had taught, 'there may be an over poise upon the whole'.[68] With the aid of an argument Witherspoon had made for balanced government, Madison could see beyond the classical republican model of a city-state whose citizens had a direct involvement with their commonwealth, to envision a federal government for a large and diverse national republic.

VI

What, then, do we learn by studying the case of John Witherspoon? Much, certainly, that is helpful for the newly emerging field of Atlantic studies. In the first place we find out about the early-modern Atlantic world of learning, and in particular about the wide ranging, almost all-encompassing subject called 'moral philosophy'. So broad was the conception of moral philosophy in Witherspoon's day that many who treated it encompassed not only epistemology and ethics but also what we would consider psychology, sociology, and anthropology. In fact, all of the modern social sciences, including economics, are daughters of this old moral philosophy.[69] (When the great Adam Smith wrote on ethical theory as well as political economy,

---

65   Adam Smith, *An Inquiry into the Nature and Causes of the Wealth of Nations*, eds. R. H. Campbell and A. S. Skinner (Indianapolis, 1981), vol. 1, p. 456.

66   Witherspoon, *Lectures on Moral Philosophy*, 144; *The Federalist*, no. 10, par. 9.

67   *Federalist* no. 10, pars. 2–6. David Hume, 'Idea of a Perfect Commonwealth', *Essays: Moral, Political, and Literary*, ed. Eugene Miller (Indianapolis, 1987), 528.

68   Witherspoon, *Lectures on Moral Philosophy*, 144.

69   See Gladys Bryson, *Man and Society: The Scottish Inquiry of the Eighteenth Century* (Princeton, 1945).

he was only doing the job, as then defined, of a professor of moral philosophy at Glasgow University.)

Another aspect of the Atlantic world of learning that Witherspoon illustrates is the compatibility of Evangelical Christianity with rationality. We should not identify the Scottish Moderates exclusively with reason and the Popular Party exclusively with emotional revivalism.[70] Witherspoon saw himself as a defender of the rightful supremacy of reason over the passions. The Princeton president's insistence on the rational component in value judgements and scorn for the Moderates' cultivation of refined sensibility typified a certain kind of rigorous, austere Protestantism. His objections to John Home's authorship of the play *Douglas* illuminate the point: a pastor should teach his flock how to control their passions, not pander to them.[71] When Witherspoon moved from Scotland to a country where Presbyterians divided principally over their attitude toward revivalism, he came to favour (at least tacitly) the anti-revival Old Side.

In the third place, we can see in the case of Witherspoon how the American revolutionaries synthesised Lockean liberalism with older habits of mind derived from Christianity and classical republicanism. Scottish moral philosophers facilitated the process by discovering that prudential self-interest could be rational, that the social affections could benefit society, and that selfish actions could unintentionally serve the common good.[72] These new principles of moral philosophy helped legitimate individualism and self-interest, thus giving liberalism a toe-hold within a culture still governed to a large extent by traditional, religious, and communal modes of thought. Knowledge of these principles helped American statesmen like James Madison devise and justify a novel system of government for a new nation that still drew upon the experience and wisdom of the past.[73] Witherspoon's mind-set, so conveniently and comprehensively summarised in his lectures, provides a handy point of reference for those who would understand the outlook of America's constitutional founders.

The study of John Witherspoon is also essential for understanding the history of American education. Not only did he introduce into America the Scottish common sense philosophy, both in its epistemological and ethical aspects, he also set the pattern for American college presidents as fund-raisers, public intellectuals, and specifically as teachers of moral philosophy. The most influential textbook in the antebellum United States, *Moral Science* (1835) by Francis Wayland, the president of Brown University, still showed the influence of Witherspoon's old lectures. And a hundred years after John Witherspoon's election, another Scotsman, James McCosh, was also elected president of Princeton; he too was a moral philosopher of the

---

70 Of the kind described so sympathetically and well in Leigh Eric Schmidt, *Holy Fairs: Scottish Communions and American Revivals in the Early Modern Period* (Princeton, 1989).

71 *Nature and Effects of the Stage*, 54–9.

72 See Albert O. Hirschman, *The Passions and the Interests: Political Arguments for Capitalism Before Its Triumph* (Princeton, 1977); John Dwyer, *The Age of the Passions: An Interpretation of Adam Smith and Scottish Enlightenment Culture* (Edinburgh, 1998).

73 The broader issues are discussed in Daniel W. Howe, 'Why the Scottish Enlightenment was Useful to the Framers of the American Constitution', *Comparative Studies in Society and History*, 31 (July 1989): 72–87.

common sense school. In an even larger sense, Witherspoon's career reminds us how much American education in general owed to religious impulses and to overseas examples; if these two sources of inspiration were taken away from educational development in the young republic, precious little would be left. Thomas Jefferson's vision of secular public education sponsored by the state had surprisingly little to show by way of achievement until after the Civil War.[74]

Important as Witherspoon is to the history of American philosophy and higher education, we should not forget his personal contribution to the creation of American nationalism. He carried over from Scottish discussions of the Union of 1707 a strong sense of the advantages of both commercial and cultural unification into the American debates of the 1780s. He deplored the economic effects of the inflation of the Continental currency and demanded that the central government be empowered to tax. A Union stronger than the Articles of Confederation, he insisted, was necessary to preserve the achievement of the Revolution. (When it came to language, however, Witherspoon favoured the United States adhering to the standards of metropolitan English, not encouraging the development of 'Americanisms', a word he seems to have invented).[75]

The study of Atlantic history has largely, and necessarily, emphasised the study of parallels among the countries it treats. Scotland and America shared a common Calvinist heritage, a contrast between their cosmopolitan centres and their primitive, violent backcountry, and a provincial cultural relationship to the English metropolis.[76] The fact that a single person like John Witherspoon could play a prominent role in both countries underscores some of the things the two had in common. However, we should note that treating John Witherspoon as a case study in Atlantic history can also illuminate differences between Scotland and America. Much of what provoked Witherspoon to criticism of the Moderate wing of the Church of Scotland related to the ecclesiastical patronage system. No such system existed in America, which helps explain the absence of a Moderate movement in American Presbyterianism. An analogous movement existed in New England Congregationalism, called Liberalism, but Witherspoon did not engage with it. He did, however, form a friendship and alliance with the middle-of-the-road Old Calvinist president of Congregationalist Yale, Ezra Stiles.[77] In the absence of Moderate Presbyterian antagonists, Witherspoon may have felt free to make concessions to polite culture in America that he would have shunned in Scotland. Though maintaining his disapproval of the theatre to his

---

74   See Daniel W. Howe, 'Church, State, and Education in the Young American Republic', *Journal of the Early Republic*, 22 (2002): 1–24.

75   See Ned Landsman, 'The Legacy of British Union for the North American Colonies', in ed. John Robertson, *A Union for Empire: Political Thought and the British Union of 1707* (Cambridge, 1995), pp. 297–317.

76   As pointed out in the now classic article of John Clive and Bernard Bailyn, 'England's Cultural Provinces: Scotland and America', *William and Mary Quarterly* 11 (1954): 200–13.

77   Stiles is the subject of a masterful biography by Edmund S. Morgan, *The Gentle Puritan* (New Haven, 1962).

dying day, he tolerated dramatic performances by Princeton students, including even the production of a play by John Home.[78]

Witherspoon made himself a key figure in several transitions of momentous significance not just for Princeton but for American culture as a whole. Starting as a mediator between New Side and Old Side Presbyterians, he ended up favouring the Old Side and initiating their long-term dominance at Princeton and indeed within American Presbyterianism as a whole. Seeming at first glance to mediate between ethical sentimentalism and ethical rationalism, his lectures on moral philosophy had the effect of preparing the way for the dominance of the latter school of thought throughout American academia. Intending no doubt to mediate between Calvinist austerity and polite culture, his influence turned out to provide the entering wedge for the rising new politeness. At first seeking only the reform of the British overseas empire, not its dissolution, he came to embrace independence with fervour. Devoted to the classical republican ideas of self-discipline and citizen virtue, Witherspoon also encouraged rise of modern liberal politics. One of the major contributions of Scottish moral philosophers to modern social analysis was their recognition of the importance of the unintended consequences of human action. The career of John Witherspoon actually illustrates a quite number of such unintended consequences.

---

78 Collins, *President Witherspoon*, vol. 2, pp. 155–6. Witherspoon's last publication, in 1793, was an open letter denouncing professional 'play-actors'. It is printed as an addendum to the New York edition of the *Nature and Effects of the Stage*, cited in n. 39.

Chapter 4

David Hume and the Seagods of the Atlantic

*Emma Rothschild**

David Hume, who grew up a few miles inland from the small North Sea port of Berwick-upon-Tweed, and whose most westerly adventure was in the course of an expedition to the French port of Lorient, is at first sight a distinctively unAtlantic figure. He was large and plump and indolent; his greatest pleasures were having conversations with women, reflecting on his own sentiments, and 'reading and sauntering and lownging and dozing, which I call thinking'.[1] He was dressed, in the portrait by Allan Ramsay which hung in his house in Edinburgh, and which is now in the Scottish National Portrait Gallery, in a vast red and gold brocade coat; an elaborate, antiquated, unAtlantic sort of coat.

The idea of an Atlantic world, which has been at the heart of North American colonial history for almost a century, has been extended, in recent years, from Rio de la Plata to the Danube to Mozambique. It has also come to include the idea of a community of values, or states of mind, or ways of thinking. These are the values which were so unlike Hume's; values of newness and vehemence, of the transient and the anti-historical and the enthusiastic. But Hume, too, lived in an Atlantic world, and his writings were profoundly influenced by the Atlantic conflicts which began in 1739, and continued until his death in 1776. It is these Atlantic connections, and their relationship to the larger or global world of the eighteenth century, with which I will be concerned in what follows. Hume's own life, I will suggest, is an illustration of the extent to which even individuals in the interior of the eighteenth-century provinces of Europe were surrounded by information about distant opportunities. His *Political Discourses* of 1752 was an evocation, in turn, of the distinctively Atlantic world of commerce, credit, empire and conquest; and of an Atlantic politics of distance which was at the heart of his political and economic thought.

The estate of Ninewells in Berwickshire, to which David Hume was brought as a young child, and where he wrote most of his two *Enquiries*, the *Dialogues concerning Natural Religion*, and many of his essays and discourses, was at the periphery of the Atlantic world of the eighteenth century. It is hidden in a little valley, in the uplands between the Cheviot and the Lammermuir hills. But it is almost in sight of a vast and oceanic scene. Berwick-upon-Tweed, nine miles to the east, and across the frontier

* I am most grateful for helpful comments from the editors of this volume, and from Bernard Bailyn, William O'Reilly, Nicholas Phillipson, and Amartya Sen. A longer version of the chapter will be published in *Atlantic Soundings*, ed. Bernard Bailyn.

1   Letters to Hugh Blair of April 1 1767, in *The Letters of David Hume*, ed. J. Y. T. Greig (2 vols., Oxford, 1969), vol. 2, p. 134.

into England, was situated, in the description of a late eighteenth century historian, where the 'transparent Tweed, with stately majesty … disembogues its waters into the German ocean.' The traveller who descends from Ninewells on the Chirnside road comes suddenly, near a hamlet called 'Brow of the Hill', upon this vista of the German ocean.[2]

Hume's first extended journey, at the age of 23, was to the larger seascape of the English Atlantic. In February 1734 he was 'tempted, or rather forced, to make a very feeble Trial for entering into a more active Scene of Life'. He set out to London, and on to Bristol, where he launched himself on a mercantile career, in the house of some 'eminent merchants'; merchants trading to the West Indies, as will be seen, in this high season of the Bristol commerce in sugar and slaves. Hume's new life only lasted for some four months. But his hopes, at first, had been high, as he wrote at the time; 'having got Recommendation to a considerable Trader in Bristol, I am just now hastening thither, with a Resolution to forget myself, & every thing that is past, to engage myself, as far as is possible, in that Course of Life, & to toss about the World, from the one Pole to the other, till I leave this Distemper behind me'.[3]

From Bristol, Hume continued to France, where he settled in a little town on the river Loir, near where it flows into the Loire, and to Nantes, and where he wrote his *Treatise of Human Nature*. But even at home, in the east of Scotland, Hume lived in a milieu which was open to the world. One of his early friends, James Oswald of Dunnikier, introduced him to the seaside life of Fife, and to 'the whole Oeconomy of the Navy'; Oswald, who was Commissioner of the Navy for Scotland, parliamentary manager of the Board of Trade, and an expert on Canadian affairs, represented the parliamentary constituency of the Dysart Burghs, Kirkcaldy, Kinghorn, Dysart and Burntisland, the 'low, sea-salted, wind-vexed promontory', with its 'little towns, posted along the shore as close as hedges, each with its bit of harbour', of which Robert Louis Stevenson wrote that 'History broods over that part of the world like the easterly *haar*'.[4]

Through his 'oldest and best friend', William Mure of Caldwell in Renfrewshire, and Mure's sister Elizabeth, Hume also came to know the commercial and official scenes of the west of Scotland. 'I shall come down early in the Spring to the Borders of the Atlantic Ocean, & rejoice the Tritons & Seagods,' he wrote to Mure in 1742, of a proposed visit to John Boyle, the Earl of Glasgow and the heir to a fortune in shipping and the administration of Customs and Excise; in this newly prosperous world of the post-Union economy, he acquired a 'whole Circle of my West countrey Acquaintances'. 'About the 40 riches began to incress considerably. Many returned from the East and West Indias with good fortune who had gone abroad after the Union,'

---

2   John Fuller, M.D., *The History of Berwick Upon Tweed, including a Short Account of the Villages of Tweedmouth and Spittal, &c.* (Edinburgh, 1799), pp. 54–5.

3   Letter of March or April 1734 to Dr George Cheyne, in Hume, *Letters*, vol. 1, p. 18; 'The Life of David Hume, Esq. Written by Himself' ['My Own Life'], in David Hume, *Essays Moral, Political, and Literary*, ed. Eugene F. Miller (Indianapolis, 1987), p. xxxiii.

4   Letter of August 4 1744 to William Mure, in Hume, *Letters*, vol. 1, p. 58; 'The Coast of Fife', in Robert Louis Stevenson, *The Scottish Stories and Essays*, ed. Kenneth Gelder (Edinburgh, 1989), p. 261.

Elizabeth Mure wrote of the change of manners in her lifetime; 'It was then that the slavery of the mind began to be spocken off; freedom was in everybody's mouth … For their Girls the outmost care was taken that fear of no kind should enslave the mind; nurses was turned off who would tell the young of Witches and Ghosts.'[5]

Hume's own Atlantic expedition, and his long, frequently interrupted venture into public life, began in 1746. In the winter of 1745, he had spent a 'melancholy & unsociable' period in Hertfordshire, as companion to an unhappy young landowner, the Marquess of Annandale. On his way back to Scotland he encountered a distant relation, General James St Clair, a proprietor of coal mines in the same sea-side promontory of Fife as the Oswalds. General St Clair was at the time preparing an expedition to Canada, and he offered the position of secretary to his young kinsman. 'Such a Romantic Adventure, & such a Hurry, I have not heard of before,' Hume wrote to another cousin, in a letter sent from the naval base of Portsmouth, 'before my departure for America'; 'I knew not a word of this Matter till Sunday last at Night.'[6]

In Portsmouth, as the expeditionary force awaited 'the first fair wind [which] carries us away', Hume reflected on his future life in America. The force was bound for Boston, where they were to spend the winter, before proceeding to Canada. It might be possible, Hume concluded, to become an army officer in America, at a sufficiently distinguished rank (for 'at my years I could not decently accept of a lower commission than a company'); his prospect would be 'to procure at first a company in an American regiment, by the choice of the Colonies'. But destiny intervened once more, and General St Clair's expedition was 'detain'd in the Channel, till it was too late to go to America'. The ministry then dispatched them 'to seek Adventures on the Coast of France'. Their somewhat uninstructive directions were to 'make an attempt on L'Orient, or Rochefort, or Rochelle, or sail up the river of Bourdeaux; or … to sail to whatever other place on the western coast they should think proper'.[7]

The General found himself, in Hume's description, to be 'without intelligence, without pilots, without guides, without any map of the country to which he was bound, except a common map, on a small scale, of the kingdom of France, which his Aid-de-camp had been able to pick up in a shop at Plymouth …'. The officers responded to an enquiry about the coast of France, 'as if the question had been with regard to the coast of Japan or of California'; the expedition was even without money ('except a few chests of Mexican dollars, consigned to other uses'). But it was eventually determined, on the basis of an admiral's recollection of something he had 'once casually heard' from a member of parliament for Southwark, that their objective should be the Brittany

---

5   Letters to William Mure of November 14 1742 and September 10 1743, in Hume, *Letters*, vol. 1, pp. 44, 54; Elizabeth Mure, 'Some remarks on the change of manners in my own time 1700–1790,' in *Selections from the Family Papers preserved at Caldwell* (Glasgow, 1874), vol. 1, p. 270.

6   Letter of November 26 1745 to Captain Philip Vincent and of May 23 1746 to Alexander Home, in Hume, *Letters*, vol. 1, pp. 69, 90.

7   Letters of June 6 1746 to Sir James Johnstone, of May or June 1746 to Henry Home, and of October 4 1746 to John Home, in Hume, *Letters*, vol. 1, pp. 94–5; 'Fragments of a paper in Hume's handwriting, describing the descent on the coast of Brittany, in 1746, and the causes of its failure', in John Hill Burton, *Life and Correspondence of David Hume* (Edinburgh, 1846), vol. 2, p. 443.

town of Lorient.[8] Lorient, in this first world-wide war of commerce, was the principal port of the French Compagnie des Indes, and it was at Lorient that Hume's American expedition was abandoned, in September 1746.

'The General sent a Summons to the Town, who seemed to prepare for their Defense, by burning all their Suburbs,' Hume wrote on September 22, in a little notebook he kept on board ship. Three deputations, from the military, the town and the 'India Company', offered to surrender, if their houses were secured from pillage, and the military were permitted to remove. These conditions were refused, and the expedition's 'Engineers engag'd with a Mortar, & two 12 pounders to set the Town in a Flame, in one afternoon'. But the weather, once more, did not favour the British. 'Every Body much discourag'd, especially on account of the Rain, which fell all day as well as yesterday & the day before,' Hume wrote on September 25; the engineers 'in general shoud themselves confusd & ignorant in their Business. They forgot the Grate to heat their Ball.' On September 30 the General proposed 'some other attempt on the Coast of France', which the 'Sea Officers unanimously declined'.[9]

The expeditionary force was then ordered to Cork, which was the western extremity of its Atlantic adventure, and in January 1747 it was recalled to England. Hume listed the orders received in the course of the journey: '... 9. To disembark at Dover 10. To disembark at Gravesend 11. I omitted an Order to wait till further orders ...' He also listed the material detritus of the Atlantic expedition, with its ordering of rank and comfort: 'One Trunk D. Hume Esq One Box Mr Hume's Books Box Paper Mr Hume One Trunk the General Canvas Bed One Trunk of the Generals with a Mat & a Bed Stead.'[10] He stayed in London for a short time, 'to see, if anything new will present itself', as he wrote to yet another kinsman. But by August 1747, he had returned to Ninewells, and to the life of a 'poor Philosopher', in the familiar conditions of the Newcastle coastal shipping: 'Our Ship was dirty: Our Accomodation bad: Our Company sick: There were four Spies, two Informers, & three Evidences who saild in the same Ship with us.'[11]

In 1748, Hume was offered a new official position. He travelled, also with the unfortunate General St Clair, down the Maese, the Rhine and the Danube to Vienna, and thence to Turin, where they arrived, once more, in time to receive news of the negotiation of the treaty of Aix-la-Chapelle, and instructions to return to England. On his return from Ireland in the summer of 1747, Hume had reported to a friend that he was 'well provided of good Cloaths'. On his return from Italy, too, he was equipped with a 'great store of linnens and fine Cloaths'. (It is possible that this included his Italian coat, with its military deportment and its red almost velvety sleeves, that he wore for Allan Ramsay's portrait.) But his clothes, and the experience, as he

---

8   'Fragments of a paper', pp. 444, 446.

9   David Hume, 'Notebook', British Library, Add. Mss. 36638, pp. 8r, 8v, 9r, 13v, 14r, 18v.

10   David Hume, 'Notebook', pp. 12v, 22r.

11   Letters of January 1747 and June 1747 to Henry Home, in *New Letters of David Hume*, ed. Raymond Klibansky and Ernest C. Mossner (Oxford, 1969), pp. 24, 26; letter of August 7 1747 to Colonel Abercromby, in Hume, *Letters*, vol. 1, p. 105.

described it to James Oswald, of having seen 'Courts & Camps', were all he had to show, once again, for his diplomatic existence.[12]

Hume's circumstances changed very much for the better in 1752, with the publication of his *Political Discourses*, and later of his *History of England*. His next return to official life, too, was to the much improved position, in 1763, of a member of the household of the new British Ambassador to France, with a pension of £200 a year for life. In Paris, in the postwar world of 1763, Hume found himself celebrated as an 'English philosophe', or as 'one of the greatest geniuses in the world' (as he reported to Adam Ferguson). When he attended the Ambassador to Versailles in November 1763, he was welcomed by the 9-year-old Duc de Berri (later Louis XVI), who said how much he had enjoyed reading 'many passages in my works', by the 8-year-old Comte de Provence (later Louis XVIII), who said how much he looked forward to reading 'my fine History', and by the 6-year-old Comte d'Artois (later Charles X), of whom Hume wrote that 'I heard him mumble the word *Histoire*, and some other terms of panegyric'.[13]

The world of French politics into which Hume settled was itself a universe of oceanic connections. Hume's duties, in the frenzy of inter-imperial exchange in which Canada was ceded by the French to the British, Louisiana was ceded by the French to the Spanish, Martinique was ceded by the British to the French, Grenada was ceded by the French to the British, and Florida was ceded by the Spanish to the British, were concerned to a great extent with maritime relationships. He wrote a memorandum to the French Ministry about illicit cutting of timber in Newfoundland, and illicit fishing in 'intermediate seas' by the inhabitants of the French islands of St Pierre and Miquelon; he investigated the jetties at Dunkirk and the legal proceedings, which extended to 'Dunkirk, Calais & Boulogne', of a former merchant from New Hampshire; he wrote another memorandum about the devaluation of French paper money in Canada, and the 'hardship and injustice' imposed on English merchants.[14]

Hume's life as a 'philosophe', too, was surrounded by the minutiae of colonial and oceanic existence. He first encountered D'Alembert, who became his closest friend in Paris, and to whom he left £200 in his will, when D'Alembert wrote to him on behalf of 'a poor Canadian family' who were living as refugees on an island off the Atlantic Coast of France, and who wished to return to 'English domination'. Diderot wrote to recommend a 'jeune Pensylvain', who was a student of medicine, and a married couple, of whom the wife was placed by Hume as 'gouvernante' in the home of Sir George Colebrooke, war contractor, husband of an Antigua heiress, proprietor in Grenada and Lanarkshire, and chairman, later, of the East India Company. La Condamine, the mathematician and Amazon explorer, wrote to ask

---

12 Letter of June 1747 to Henry Home in Hume, *New Letters*, p. 26, and of January 29 1748 to James Oswald and June 22 1751 to Michael Ramsay in Hume, *Letters*, vol. 1, pp. 109, 161.

13 Letters of September 13 1763 to Adam Smith, of November 9 1763 to Adam Ferguson, of November 23 1763 to Alexander Wedderburn, and of December 1 1763 to William Robertson, in Hume, *Letters*, vol. 1, pp. 395, 410, 415, 416.

14 'Mémoire' of August 22 1765 and letters of August 28 1765, September 5 1765, and October 3 1765, in Hume, *New Letters*, pp. 105–8, 110–13, 122–4, 223–4; 'mémoire' of September 25 1765, in Hume, *Letters*, vol. 2, pp. 405–6.

for his help in respect of a young man who had fallen foul of 'an Oydor of Quito (this is a very respected idol in Spanish America)', because he had refused to marry his daughter.[15]

When Hume left Paris for England in January 1766, his intention was to return to Edinburgh, and to live in retirement on the proceeds of his investments. But a year later, he was again in London, and again 'from a Philosopher, degenerated into a petty Statesman'.[16] This was his last public office, as Under-Secretary of State for the Northern Department (responsible for Russia and France), under the patronage of General H. S. Conway, the brother of his patron in Paris, and the theorist, at the time of the Stamp Act crisis, of the sentiments of the American colonists.

The new way of life, as Hume wrote to Hugh Blair, was 'by no means disagreeable. I pass all the Forenoon in the Secretary's House from ten till three, where there arrives from time to time Messengers, that bring me all the Secrets of this Kingdom, and indeed of Europe, Asia, Africa and America'. He was in touch with his new friends from Paris, and his old friends from Scotland; he was part of what Edmund Burke described at the time as 'Conways chain', in which 'His family get every thing'. But eventually, in January 1768, he left office for the last time, having requested 'the Liberty, after my Dismission, of inspecting all the public Records and all the Papers in the Paper-Office'. He considered the possibility of going to live in Paris, but decided against it, in part because he feared that he would be expelled when the next war broke out between France and England. In August 1769 he returned to Edinburgh, and to the life he so cherished, of reading and dozing.[17]

Hume was an observer, in all these vicissitudes, these journeys by ferry and barge and Newcastle shipping, of the Atlantic crises of the middle of the eighteenth century, and the new crises of the times were of profound importance to his historical and political ideas. 'I am an American in my Principles, and wish we would let them alone to govern or misgovern themselves as they think proper,' he wrote in 1775 to his old friend William Mure. J. G. A. Pocock has described these and other observations on empire as the 'dying thoughts of a North Briton', and Hume indeed returned to the 'late war', and its 'extremely frivolous object', in the revisions he made to his *History of England* in the last months of his life. 'Our late delusions have much exceeded anything known in history, not even excepting those of the crusades,' he wrote of the national debt 'in the present year, 1776,' in a footnote

---

15   Letter from D'Alembert, National Library of Scotland, MS 23153, no. 2, f. 365; letters from Diderot, undated and of February 22 1768, in *Letters of Eminent Persons addressed to David Hume*, ed. John Hill Burton (Edinburgh, 1849), pp. 283, 287; letters to the Rev. John Gardner of March 4 1768 and August 3 1769, in Hume, *New Letters*, pp. 181, 187. On Colebrooke, see Sir Lewis Namier and John Brooke, *The History of Parliament: The House of Commons, 1754–1790* (London, 1964), vol. 2, pp. 235–7.

16   Letter of March 13 1767 to the Marquise de Barbentane, in Hume, *Letters*, vol. 2, p. 128.

17   Letters to Hugh Blair of April 1 1767, to Andrew Millar of July 17 1767, and to the Comtesse de Boufflers on November 27 1767, in Hume, *Letters*, vol. 2, pp. 133–4, 151, pp. 171–2; letters of December 23 1766 and October 27 1767 to Charles O'Hara, in *The Correspondence of Edmund Burke*, ed. Thomas W. Copeland (Cambridge, 1958), vol. 1, pp. 287, 331. On Conway, see Namier and Brooke, *House of Commons*, vol. 2, pp. 244–7.

about Queen Elizabeth's revenues; 'we have even lost all title to compassion, in the numberless calamities that are waiting us.'[18]

But Hume's dismal view of imperial power was already well established. 'O! how I long to see America and the East Indies revolted totally & finally,' he had written to another old friend, Sir Gilbert Elliot, in 1768; to the publisher William Strahan, in 1769, he anticipated 'the total Revolt of America, the Expulsion of the English from the East Indies'. The *Political Discourses* of 1752—of which Hume wrote at the end of his life that it 'was the only work of mine that was successful on the first publication'—was itself an extended diatribe against the colonial and mercantile system, and against the corruptions of distant dominion. Hume's essays and discourses, and his *History of England*, are at the heart of his science of human nature, as Pocock and Nicholas Phillipson have shown.[19] The *Political Discourses* was in turn at the heart of his contemporary history, and the relationships it depicted were ones, above all, of long-distance commerce, and distant power.

The *Political Discourses* existed under that title for little more than a year. It was subsumed, by 1753, in Hume's *Essays and Treatises on Several Subjects*, and in the intricate publishing history of his various shorter works. But the title itself was an indication of Hume's philosophical purpose; of his intention, as in Machiavelli's *Discorsi* and James Harrington's *Political Discourses*, to which he refers in the concluding discourse of the book, to revive speculation about principles of government. These principles, in turn, were to a substantial extent principles of the government of economic connections, or of political economy. Commerce, luxury, money, interest, the balance of trade, the balance of power, taxes, public credit: these were the preoccupations of Hume's political masterpiece, and it was an investigation, in particular, of the new circumstances of global commerce; a eulogy to 'free communication and exchange'.[20]

The idyll at the heart of the *Political Discourses* is of a peaceful exchange of commodities and ideas, in which 'commerce is extended all over the globe', 'innocent luxury' flourishes, 'men naturally flock to capital cities, sea-ports, and navigable rivers', and the 'middling rank of men' are respected. It is in this civilised world that the 'tempers of men are softened', and that even government, once 'human reason has refined itself by exercise', can become mild and moderate. Human nature is itself improved. 'It is impossible but they must feel an encrease of humanity, from the very habit of conversing together, and contributing to each other's pleasure and entertainment.' This was Hume's most extended evocation of the disposition of

---

18   Letter to William Mure of October 27 1775, in Hume, *Letters*, vol. 2, pp. 302–3; David Hume, *The History of England* (1778) (Indianapolis, 1983), vol. 4, p. 373, note c.; J. G. A. Pocock, 'Hume and the American Revolution: The dying thoughts of a North Briton',' in J. G. A. Pocock, *Virtue, Commerce, and History* (Cambridge, 1985): 125–41.

19   Letters of July 22 1768 to Sir Gilbert Elliot and of October 25 1769 to William Strahan, in Hume, *Letters*, vol. 2, pp. 184, 210; Hume, 'My Own Life', pp. xxxiv, xxxvi–vii; and see J. G. A. Pocock, *Barbarism and Religion: Narratives of Civil Government* (Cambridge, 1999), pp. 177–221, and Nicholas Phillipson, *Hume* (London, 1989), pp. 137–41.

20   'Of the Balance of Trade', in Hume, *Essays*, p. 324.

enlightenment; 'thus *industry, knowledge,* and *humanity,* are linked together by an indissoluble chain'.[21]

But the tranquil world of commerce—and this is the most important polemical point of the *Discourses*—was at the same time in deadly peril from the spirit of conquest and empire. The *Discourses* was a work of the moment, or of the interwar world of 1752, between the universally misundertood treaty of Aix-la-Chapelle, which ended the War of the Austrian Succession (and Hume's Italian diplomacy) in 1748, and the new misunderstandings which led to the outbreak of the Seven Years' War in 1756. It was imbued with the recollection of the 'last war', or the 'late wars', and with the expectation of wars to come. Its direst prospect was that these wars, with their conflicts in Cape Breton and Madras and Lorient, would be pernicious, in multiple respects, for the spirit of humanity.

'War is attended with every destructive circumstance; loss of men, encrease of taxes, decay of commerce, dissipation of money, devastation by sea and land,' Hume wrote; it led inevitably to taxes; it was the outcome of 'our own imprudent vehemence'; it tended, if funded by public borrowing, to 'dissolution and destruction'. The freedom of government was itself in peril in a world of imperial conquest. In the Roman republic, the public had been 'almost in continual alarm'; the Roman empire had declined not because of luxury but because of the 'unlimited extent of conquests'. In the American colonies, the British ruled over a system of domestic slavery as barbarous as that of ancient times. In the system of '*pressing of seamen*' into naval service, 'a continued violence is permitted in the crown ... the wild state of nature is renewed'. The last paragraph of the *Political Discourses*, like the last paragraph of the *Wealth of Nations*, was an excoriation of empire: 'extensive conquests, when pursued, must be the ruin of every free government'.[22]

Hume's description of commercial exchange, and of its opposite, the world of colonial conquest, is an evocation, in part, of the Atlantic life he had observed or imagined in Berwick and Bristol and London. The *Political Discourses* includes a mass of details of commercial existence: the mines in America, the bullion of Cadiz, the rate of interest in Batavia and Jamaica, the expansion of paper money in the colonies, the taxation of brandy in the interest of the southern colonies, the provincial splendour of Bordeaux and Toulouse, the prices of bank stocks and India bonds. Its most extended metaphor is of the communication of commerce as an immense and global body of water. In the Atlantic ocean, money drains from the Indies to Spain and France; in the Asiatic commerce, 'the immense distance of CHINA, together with the monopolies of our INDIA companies' cannot obstruct the flow of commerce; there is even a confluence of all oceans, and 'were it not for the

---

21 'Of Refinement in the Arts' ('Of Luxury'), 'Of Interest', 'Of the Balance of Trade', in Hume, *Essays*, pp. 269, 271, 273–4, 277–8, 304, 314.

22 'Of Commerce', 'Of Refinement in the Arts', 'Of Public Credit', 'Of the Balance of Power', 'Of Some Remarkable Customs', 'Idea of a perfect Commonwealth', in Hume, *Essays*, pp. 259, 276, 339, 351, 363, 374–6, 529; David Hume, *Political Discourses* (Edinburgh, 1752), p. 304; and see Adam Smith, *An Inquiry into the Nature and Causes of the Wealth of Nations*, ed. R. H. Campbell and A. S. Skinner (Oxford, 1976), p. 947.

continual recruits, which we receive from AMERICA, money would soon sink in EUROPE, and rise in CHINA, till it came nearly to a level in both places'.[23]

The 40 years' war of the eighteenth century was in these vistas the dominating circumstance of Hume's public life, as it was of so much of the political life of the late enlightenment. If the period from the outbreak of the War of the Austrian Succession in 1739 to the end of the War of American Independence in 1783 is conceived of as a single conflict, with its interwar periods and its postwar periods and its periods of false or imagined or expected war, then it was this conflict which formed Hume's political ideas, and the world of information in which he lived. It was a global conflict: the 'most frivolous Causes', Hume wrote to his intimate friend and translator in France, Trudaine de Montigny, in 1767, had during the last war 'spread the Flame from one End of the Globe to the other'; the disputes between the Spanish and the English in the South Atlantic, he wrote to Strahan in 1771, threatened to throw 'almost the whole Globe into a Ferment'. It was also a war of intelligence, or of the failure of intelligence. 'That horrible, destructive, ruinous War; more pernicious to the Victors than to the Vanquished', was 'fomented by some obscure designing Men', he wrote to Trudaine, and it might have been prevented by 'the Explication of a few Points'.[24]

The eighteenth-century wars have been described, as they were described at the time by Dupont de Nemours and Adam Smith, as virtual or offshore conflicts, subjects of amusing conversation, in Paris or London, or of 'the amusement of reading in the newspapers' about the exploits of distant fleets and armies. They were conflicts of information and misinformation. But they were at the same time conflicts which transformed the financial organisation of the Atlantic world, in the empire of public credit which was Hume's great subject in his *Political Discourses*, as it was Dupont's and Smith's great subject as well. They also transformed the individual existences of the hundreds of thousands of young men who were subject, or who feared they might be subject to the lotteries for the royal militia which Hume's friend A. R. J. Turgot tried to reform in the Limousin, or to the pressing of seamen by which, in Hume's own description, 'a continued violence is permitted in the crown'. They were distant conflicts, which imposed themselves, in multiple ways, on the interior lives of societies.[25]

Hume was fascinated, from his earliest youth in Berwickshire, with information and intelligence, and with the sentiments of individuals in respect of different kinds of news. The discursive, inquisitive men and women who are at the heart of his description of human nature are continuously recounting and receiving information; they are also continuously looking for new sources of intelligence, and trying to decide whether pieces of information are true. They 'love to receive and communicate

---

23 'Of the Balance of Trade', in Hume, *Essays*, pp. 312–13.

24 Letters of May 23 1767 to Trudaine de Montigny in Hume, *New Letters*, p. 235, and of March 11 1771 to William Strahan in Hume, *Letters*, vol. 2, p. 237.

25 'Of some Remarkable Customs', in Hume, *Essays*, pp. 374–6; Smith, *The Wealth of Nations*, p. 920; and see Emma Rothschild, 'Global Commerce and the Question of Sovereignty in the Eighteenth-Century Provinces', *Modern Intellectual History*, 1 (2004): 1–25.

knowledge'; they live in a 'conversible World', in which everyone 'mutually gives and receives Information'.[26]

This was the world in which Hume himself lived, from his childhood to the end of his official life, amidst the secrets of Asia, Africa and America. His correspondence, throughout his life, was full of observations about correspondence; about clubs to get down newspapers from London, letters which were sent by the common carrier, and (in 1745) about the 'universal practice of opening all letters ... a clerk in the post-office opens a letter, runs it over, and, finding it concerns only private business, forwards it presently'. In Paris, Hume was anxious for political news from England; you 'promisd, to correspond', he wrote to William Strahan, and 'I have long expected to hear from you and to learn your Sentiments of English Politics'. In London, with all his secrets, he was anxious for news of his old friends in Paris; he felt as isolated 'as I should be in Westphalia or Lithuania', he wrote to the Comtesse de Boufflers.[27]

The Atlantic world of information was of dominating importance, more generally, to the politics of distance which was at the heart of Hume's philosophical and moral thought. The idea of distance (and the word 'distance') is everywhere, in the *Treatise* and in the *Political Discourses*. The individual is surrounded by what Hume describes as 'distance or outness (so to speak)'; he exists in a universe of near or distant objects, of which he has more or less reliable information, and to which he is connected in more or less accidental ways. The nearby is more important, in general, than the distant. But the relationships of contiguity and distance are very far from orderly, and distance in time has a more powerful effect on the imagination than distance in space. 'Our situation, with regard both to persons and things, is in continual fluctuation; and a man, that lies at a distance from us, may, in a little time, become a familiar acquaintance'; in the immense universe of people and things and relationships, the very distant—or the objects which are at the very edge of our vision—can suddenly, dizzyingly, be transformed into the very near.[28]

These ideas of distance and connectedness were illustrated, even in the *Treatise*, by the relationships of the Atlantic world of commerce. The distance between Hume, in the Loire valley, and a friend in Scotland, was filled in imagination by the 'continu'd existence of posts and ferries'; the uniformity of human life was the outcome of 'industry, traffic, manufactures, law-suits, war, leagues, alliances, voyages, travels, cities, fleets, ports'. Individuals spent much of their lives in making judgements about other people, as 'a merchant looks for fidelity and skill in his factor or super-cargo'. Even 'the greatest distance of place this globe can admit' was sometimes insufficient to distract the mind, and 'a *West-India* merchant will tell you, that he is not without concern about what passes in *Jamaica*'.[29]

---

26   'Of Refinement in the Arts', 'Of Essay Writing', in Hume, *Essays*, pp. 271, 533–4.

27   Letters of 1745–1746 to Sir James Johnstone, of October 14 1763 and March 20 1764 to William Strahan, and of March 1 1767 to the Comtesse de Boufflers, in Hume, *Letters*, vol. 1, pp. 82, 406, 426, vol. 2, p. 124.

28   David Hume, *A Treatise of Human Nature* (1739) (Oxford, 1978), pp. 191, 581.

29   Hume, *Treatise*, pp. 196, 402, 429.

In the *Political Discourses*, Hume described a good sort of distance; the 'great extent' of the Roman empire under the Antonine Emperors, which was for Hume (as it was later for Edward Gibbon and Adam Smith) the very image of a profound peace; or the mildness of a republican government in an 'extensive country', which later so inspired James Madison, and in which 'the parts are so distant and remote, that it is very difficult, either by intrigue, prejudice, or passion, to hurry them into any measures against the public interest'.[30]

But there was also a bad sort of distance. The imagination of distance, or the failure of imagination, was in foreign relationships far more insidious. It was subject, even more than in domestic politics, to the empire of chance. Of all the revolutions of the state, Hume wrote in 1742, 'the foreign and the violent' were particularly unsusceptible of reasonable observation, because they were 'more influenced by whim, folly, or caprice'. 'Foreign politics' were far more dependent on 'accidents and chances, and the caprices of a few persons'. They were dependent, too, on distant connections, or on long chains of consequences and coincidences, endlessly imagined and endlessly disconcerted. The failure of imagination of distance was a cause—the most fatal of all causes—of errors in human conduct.[31]

The tenuous freedom of modern commercial societies was continuously at risk, in Hume's dismal prospect, from the evil opposing forces of enthusiasm or superstition, faction or corruption. But it was in the direst of peril in the conditions of empire and conquest. 'Enormous monarchies are, probably, destructive to human nature,' he wrote in his discourse on the balance of power; their wars 'carried on at a great distance', and their idiosyncratic combination of faction (in some colonies) and corruption (in others, or in the Asiatic luxury described by Sallust) was destructive of all political virtue. 'Arbitrary Power can extend its oppressive Arm to the Antipodes; but a limited Government can never long be upheld at a distance,' Hume wrote to Willian Strahan in 1775. Even the good distance of republican government in an 'extensive country' would be destroyed by the bad distance of empire, as in the peroration of the *Discourses*: 'extensive conquests, when pursued, must be the ruin of every free government'.[32]

The new politics of distance was evident, even, in Hume's own failures of imagination. In the *Political Discourses*, Hume described the slavery of antiquity in horrific detail; he questioned the simile of arbitrary power as being like slavery; he added a homily to the equity of modern times ('a bad servant finds not easily a good master, nor a bad master a good servant; and the checks are mutual, suitably to the inviolable and eternal laws of reason and equity'). But in a later passage—a footnote which he added in 1754 to his essay 'Of national Characters'—he expressed a view

30   'Of the Populousness of Ancient Nations', 'Idea of a perfect Commonwealth', in Hume, *Essays*, pp. 458, 527.

31   'Of the Rise and Progress of the Arts and Sciences', 'Of Commerce', in Hume, *Essays*, pp. 112, 254–5; *Treatise*, p. 538.

32   'On Refinement in the Arts', 'Of the Balance of Power', 'Idea of a Perfect Commonwealth', in Hume, *Essays*, pp. 275–6, 340–41, 529; letter of October 26 1775 to William Strahan, in Hume, *Letters*, vol. 2, p. 300.

of the natural inferiority of Africans which became one of the founding texts, even within his own lifetime, of the defence of slavery.[33]

Hume's footnote was very far from being insouciant, or unintended. 'I am apt to suspect the negroes, and in general all the other species of men (for there are four or five different kinds) to be naturally inferior to the whites,' he wrote in 1754; in a version of the essay prepared not long before his death, and published in 1777, the capacious assertion of white superiority was reduced to the assertion of black inferiority. 'I am apt to suspect the negroes to be naturally inferior to the whites,' Hume wrote in 1776; he likened the 'one negroe' in Jamaica (Francis Williams, the Latin poet) who was supposed to be 'a man of parts and learning', to 'a parrot, who speaks a few words plainly'.[34]

Hume's sentiments in respect of African slavery have been considered, rightly, as one of the most disturbing evils of enlightenment thought, and they are difficult to understand. Even in his own lifetime, the footnote was the subject of intense interest, of which he must to at least some extent have been aware. He was undoubtedly aware of the devastating criticism of his views by James Beattie in his *Essay on Truth* of 1770. Another of his eloquent critics, the physician Benjamin Rush, was the 'jeune Pensylvain' about whom Diderot had written to him some years earlier.

Hume may even have followed the uses of his essay in the conflict of pamphlets over the famous Somerset case of 1772, which established, in a judgement by Lord Mansfield, that there was no right of slave-owners in England to transport their slaves by force to the other slave societies of the British empire. 'In looking into Mr Hume's Essays,' one of the opponents of the 'Negroe Cause', Samuel Estwick, 'Assistant Agent for the Island of Barbados', wrote in 1773, 'I was made happy to observe the ideas of so ingenious a writer corresponding with my own.' The great abolitionist Granville Sharp actually described Hume in 1776, in a response to Estwick, as the 'first broacher of that uncharitable doctrine', that 'Negroes are "*an inferior species of men*"' 'The learned Dr. Beattie, in his *Essay on Truth*, has fully refuted the insinuations of Mr. Hume,' Sharp wrote, 'so that Mr. Estwick's subsequent attempt, which was prompted only by the authority of Mr. Hume, needs no further confutation.'[35]

Hume's footnote poses difficult questions, in these circumstances, about his idyll of commercial and civilised society. He seems easily, or effortlessly, to forget the 'natural equality' to which he referred from time to time, or the 'laws of reason and equity'. His generalisations are founded on the slightest of empirical investigation. As Beattie wrote, they would not, even if true, prove the point in question, 'except it were also proved, that the Africans and Americans, even though arts and sciences were introduced among them, would still remain unsusceptible of cultivation'. As to their truth, 'no man could have sufficient evidence, except from a personal acquaintance with all the negroes that now are, or ever were, on the face of the earth.

---

33 'Of the Populousness of Ancient Nations', in Hume, *Essays*, p. 384.

34 'Of National Characters', in Hume, *Essays*, p. 208; David Hume, *Essays and Treatises on Several Subjects* (London: T. Cadell, 1777), vol. 1, note [M], pp. 550–51.

35 Samuel Estwick, *Considerations on the Negroe Cause*, 2nd edition (London, 1773), pp. 77–9, note [p]; Granville Sharp, *The Just Limitation of Slavery* (London, 1776), p. 27, note 27.

Those people write no histories; and all the reports of all the travellers that ever visted them, will not amount to any thing like a proof of what is here affirmed.' In respect of the 'empires of Peru and Mexico', meanwhile, 'we know that these assertions are not true'.[36]

Even Hume's own personality comes to seem less charming, in the footnote and in his revisions to it. Hume is one of the individuals of the eighteenth century who is easiest to know, or to imagine that one knows. He was interested in his own and his friends' 'characters'; one of the merriments of Christmas, at Balcarres on the coast of Fife—'as a gambol of the season they agreed to write each his own character, to give them to Hume'—was to describe one's own personality. He described at great length the events of his inner life and his inner thoughts; he wrote a large number of letters, which survive, to his intimate friends; he had a large number of friends, and an exceptional gift, which was much commented upon, for what he described as the virtue of friendship, 'that seems principally to ly among *Equals*, and is, for that Reason, chiefly calculated for the middle Station of Life. This Virtue is FRIENDSHIP'. But he was quite uninterested, or so it seemed, in the exercise by which Smith and Turgot were so intrigued, of imagining oneself to be someone else; a slave, or a day-labourer, or a woman in childbirth. He was also very little interested in evidence about these other people. He was, as Turgot described him, 'very insensitive' [*très peu sensible*].[37]

Hume's footnote is of interest, too, in relation to the circumstances of his life, and of his successive and oceanic milieux. For Hume's own Atlantic world was a world full of slaves, and of information about slaves. His earliest Atlantic adventure, in 1734, brought him to Bristol at the height of its dominance in the European-African-American slave trade, following the acquisition of the 'Asiento', or the right to supply slaves to the Spanish colonies. 'His Master dealt in sugar,' Josiah Tucker told the antiquarian and lawyer David Dalrymple, of Hume's period in Bristol.[38] The mercantile house of Michael Miller, in which he is reported to have been employed, was involved in the Jamaica trade; the Bristol parliamentary election of May 1734, while he was there, turned on Walpole's excise bill in respect of tobacco, and on processions of horsemen with 'knots of gilded tobacco in their hats'.[39]

---

36   James Beattie, *An Essay on the Nature and Immutability of Truth; in Opposition to Sophistry and Scepticism* (Edinburgh, 1770), pp. 480–81; and see Colin Kidd, 'Ethnicity in the British Atlantic world, 1688–1830', in *A New Imperial History: Culture, Identity and Modernity in Britain and the Empire 1660–1840*, ed. Kathleen Wilson (Cambridge, 2004), pp. 260–77 and Aaron Garrett, 'Hume's Revised Racism Revised', *Hume Studies*, vol. 26, no. 1 (April 2000).

37   David Hume, *Dialogues concerning Natural Religion* (1779) (London, 1990), p. 28; 'Of the Middle Station of Life', in Hume, *Essays*, p. 547; letter of December 1773 from Turgot to Condorcet, in *Correspondance inédite de Condorcet et de Turgot 1770–1779*, ed. Charles Henry (Paris, 1883), p. 144; on Lady Anne Lindsay's reminiscences of Christmas in Fife, see Ernest Campbell Mossner, *The Life of David Hume* (Edinburgh, 1954), pp. 568–70.

38   'A volume of anecdotes, facetiae, &c., collected by Lord Hailes', Charles Dalrymple mss., in *Fourth Report of the Royal Commission on Historical Manuscripts* (London, 1874), p. 532.

39   Kenneth Morgan, *Bristol and the Atlantic Trade in the Eighteenth Century* (Cambridge, 1993), pp. 132–3, 195; John Latimer, *The Annals of Bristol in the Eighteenth Century* (Bristol,

Even on his return to Scotland, Hume was surrounded by the consequences of the slave economy. A substantial proportion of Hume's oldest friends, in the enlightened and commercial society of mid-eighteenth century Scotland, were connected, indirectly or directly, to the Atlantic slave economy. William Mure was in 1763 granted 'the Reversion of the office of Receiver General of Jamaica'; James Oswald was the kinsman, and patron in office, of the West African and West Indian merchant dynasty of Richard Oswald; Oswald's son 'Jemmy' became secretary of the Leeward Islands. The family of Sir James Johnstone of Dumfriesshire, through whom Hume was connected to his erstwhile patron Lord Annandale, was a bonanza of colonial interests: one brother, George, established a new system of government for slave plantations in West Florida, with the help of James 'Ossian' Macpherson (of whom Hume wrote to Smith that 'he has the most anti-historical head in the Universe'); the oldest brother, James, inherited the negroes, slaves, and boiling houses of a third brother, Alexander, in the island of Grenada; three other brothers, in this post-Union world of large families and large expectations, were servants of the English East India Company in Bengal.[40]

These were not, even, distant ills. Hume's acquaintances lived off the wealth of slave property, and they lived in close proximity to slaves. Benjamin Franklin settled in Covent Garden with an English landlady and two slaves. James Grant, who was one of General St Clair's secretaries, together with Hume, in the 1740s, returned to Sutherland from East Florida with a retinue of attendants, a state coach, and a black cook. One of the legal scandals of Hume's last period in Edinburgh was the divorce proceeding of Houston Stewart Nicholson against his wife Margaret, in 1770. Nicholson was a cousin of William Mure; one of the witnesses was 'Latchimo, a negro', about whom the defendant objected 'in respect he was a slave, and not a Christian', to which the pursuer countered that 'there was no proper slavery known in this country', and 'it was no objection to a witness that he was not a Christian; it was enough that he believed in a God and a future state'.[41] The case which eventually established that there was no slavery in Scotland was brought, in Perth and Edinburgh in 1773–1778, by Joseph Knight, the slave of one of the Johnstone sisters' son-in-law, Sir John Wedderburn of Jamaica. Even the Somerset case of 1772 involved another respectable figure in the official milieu of the Scottish Atlantic; Charles Stuart, the owner of James Somerset, was Cashier of the Customs office in Boston, and the brother of an Edinburgh publisher. Scotland in the eighteenth century was

---

1893), pp. 100, 145–7, 184–90.

   40 Letter of March 17 1763, in *Selections from the Family Papers preserved at Caldwell* (Glasgow: The Maitland Club, 1874), vol. 2.i, p. 273; letter of October 17 1767 to Adam Smith, in Hume, *Letters*, vol. 2, p. 169; and see Emma Rothschild, 'The Inner Life of Empires', forthcoming 2008.

   41 Gordon S. Wood, *The Americanization of Benjamin Franklin* (New York, 2004), p. 85; letter of April 18 1750 to John Clephane, in Hume, *Letters*, vol. 1, p. 142; Namier and Brooke, *A History of Parliament*, vol. 2, p. 531; Case of December 6 1770, reported in *Decisions of the Court of Sessions, from November 1769 to January 1772, collected by Hamilton* (Edinburgh, 1803), pp. 158–61; and see P. J. Marshall, 'Presidential Address: Britain and the World in the Eighteenth Century: IV, The Turning Outwards of Britain', *Transactions of the Royal Historical Society*, 6th series, 11 (2001), 1–15, pp. 2–3, 15.

not a slave society, or a slave-owning society. But it was a society in which Atlantic slavery was at the edge of Hume's and Mure's and the Oswalds' experience, and of their imagination.

Hume's fluctuating view of the enslavement of Africans was an interesting example, in these circumstances, of the politics of distance. The lives of 'Africans and Americans' were far-off, for Hume, on most occasions; illustrations of large generalisations about the causes of sentiments, or the ancient population, or the nature of redemption. But these distant lives could also come, suddenly, into view. The Atlantic and its dangers were near as well as far, and the object of particular as well as general reasoning. Or, in the question posed in a poem of 1773 called *The Nabob*, about Hume, Beattie, the East India Company, and the Atlantic slave trade,

Concerns it you who plunders in the East?
In blood a tyrant, and in lust a beast?
When ills are distant, are they then your own?[42]

David Hume, as I have tried to suggest, lived in an Atlantic milieu, or in a succession—a 'fluctuating, uncertain, fleeting' succession, in his own expression—of Atlantic milieux. The world of the mid-eighteenth century, even for this indolent and uncommercial 'philosophe', was an Atlantic world. He was familiar, from his earliest youth, with the bustling life of English, Scottish and French ports; his friendships, also from his early period in Scotland, were with individuals whose interests and connections extended around the world; he was connected to the most extravagantly colonial of Scottish families; he set off to go to America himself, in the expedition of 1746 to Canada which ended in Lorient; the work of his which was most celebrated in his lifetime, the *Political Discourses* of 1752, was an extended investigation of oceanic commerce and conflict; he was concerned, in all his official positions in 'the English ministry', with Atlantic policies; he lived, like so many others, in an information society, which was also a society of news and intelligence about the forty years war of the mid-eighteenth century; he lived, too, in a society of Atlantic slavery.

Hume's life is an interesting illustration, for all these reasons, of the ways in which the Atlantic world of the eighteenth century extended far inland, into the interior of provinces and into the interior of individual existence. I have been concerned, in general, with Hume's 'life and times', rather than with his 'life and work', and I do not wish to suggest that the Atlantic scenes in which he found himself were of determining or decisive importance in respect of his philosophical or historical or political ideas. (The *Treatise*, which he wrote in his mid-20s in the Loire valley, is indeed one of the most extraordinary examples in the entire history of philosophy of the extent to which philosophical invention is the outcome of individual genius, and not of a cultural or intellectual 'context').

The political ideas with which I have been concerned—the ideas about economic relationships in the *Political Discourses*—were of great importance to Hume's literary success, and to his reputation in the century following his death, although they have

---

42   [Richard Clarke], *The Nabob, or Asiatic Plunderers* (London, 1773), p. 3.

been of much less subsequent interest. But it is his life, above all—a life which was well-documented, and for which the documentary evidence has survived reasonably well—which seems to provide a window, like his own window, in his room in the Loire valley, into the Atlantic world of the eighteenth century. The Atlantic was a source of possibility, as it was for Hume in the summer of 1746, and a source of information, and a source of official power; it was continuous with other oceans of worldwide commerce; it was inspiring and horrific. This was Hume's world, and it was the world of his imagination, of his inquisitive, discursive men and women of enlightenment, as well.

Chapter 5

The Atlantic Enlightenment and German Responses to the American Revolution, *c.*1775 to *c.*1800

Thomas Ahnert*

The German territories in the eighteenth century were part of the Atlantic Enlightenment.[1] True, no German state had founded a colony in America; there was no German mercantile organisation comparable to the trading companies of the British, French, Dutch, or Danish;[2] and the Holy Roman Empire was an almost entirely landlocked entity, whose direct access to trans-oceanic trade was limited to a few ports on the coast of the Baltic and the North Sea. Yet many Germans were deeply involved in the eighteenth-century's Atlantic networks of social, economic, and cultural exchange. Hamburg was Europe's primary location for sugar refining and reshipping in the eighteenth century, due to its political neutrality;[3] important German trading colonies had been established in foreign ports, such as Bordeaux and Cadiz, where they played a crucial role in connecting the proto-industrial production of the German hinterland to the world of maritime commerce.[4]

There was also large-scale emigration from the German territories to North America, from the early eighteenth century: it has been estimated that around 85,000 Germans crossed the Atlantic between 1700 and 1775, making them the second-largest group of voluntary migrants, behind the Scots-Irish.[5] Native Germans and

* I am especially grateful to the Max-Planck-Institute for History in Göttingen for electing me to a visiting fellowship in June 2005 and June 2006. Most of the research for this chapter was conducted during my stay at the Institute.

1   For recent work on the American Revolution in its transatlantic contexts, see M. A. Morrison and Melinda Zook, *Revolutionary Currents. Nation Building in the Transatlantic World* (Lanham, MD., 2004) and Eliga H. Gould and Peter S. Onuf (eds), *Empire and Nation: The American Revolution in the Atlantic World* (Baltimore, 2005). There is, however, no discussion of the German states in either of the two volumes.

2   For a recent examination of the failed attempt by Frederick the Great to set up a rival trading company, operating from the East Frisian port of Emden, see F. Schui, 'Prussia's "Trans-oceanic Moment": the Creation of the Prussian Asiatic Trade Company in 1750', *Historical Journal* 49 (2006): 143–160.

3   Klaus Weber, *Deutsche Kaufleute im Atlantikhandel 1680–1830. Unternehmen und Familien in Hamburg, Cadiz und Bordeaux* (Munich, 2004), p. 311.

4   Ibid., p. 313.

5   Francis D. Cogliano, *Revolutionary America, 1763–1815. A Political History* (New York, 2000), p. 12. The forced immigration of African slaves was greater than total European immigration.

their children probably composed around a tenth of the North American colonies' population on the eve of independence.[6] One common motive for leaving Europe was religious persecution. Evangelical organisations such as the *Herrnhuter Gemeinde* or the Halle Pietists developed sophisticated pan-European and transatlantic networks to manage the transfer of German Protestants to the New World, where many of them settled in Pennsylvania and Georgia, especially.[7] Other migrants, above all from the Rhineland and the Palatinate, left for economic reasons, and were often persuaded to do so by recruiting agents for Dutch shippers and American landowners.[8]

Since 1714 the Elector of Hanover had also been the King of England. During the War of American Independence George III used his German connection to recruit around 30,000 'Hessian' mercenaries from a variety of German principalities to fight on the British side.[9] Letters by German officers, serving in the colonies, were published in political-literary journals at home.[10] On the side of the rebel colonists a former Prussian officer, Friedrich Wilhelm von Steuben, was instrumental in raising and training a disciplined army capable of fighting the British.

The extent to which Germans were part of the Atlantic world of the eighteenth century is reflected in the attention which the political crisis in Britain's North American colonies from the mid-1760s and the subsequent formation of a new free state received from the German reading public. 'Everybody', wrote the *Frankfurter Gelehrte Anzeigen* in 1777, 'now wants to judge on the American war'.[11] North American events generated a variety of responses from educated Germans. The radical pro-American political theorist Johann Christian Schmohl (1756–1783), for example, embarked for the New World towards the end of the War of Independence,

---

6   Bernard Bailyn, *From Protestant Peasants to Jewish Intellectuals: the Germans in the Peopling of America*. German Historical Institute Annual Lecture Series 1 (Oxford, 1988), p. 3.

7   Bernard Bailyn, *Atlantic History. Concept and Contours* (Cambridge, MA, 2005), p. 99. See also W. R. Ward, *The Protestant Evangelical Awakening* (Cambridge, 1992), pp. 141–4, 255–8.

8   William O'Reilly, 'Migration, Recruitment and the Law: Europe Responds to the Atlantic World', in ed. Horst Pietschmann, *Atlantic History. History of the Atlantic System 1580–1830* (Göttingen, 2002), pp. 119–37. O'Reilly has pointed out that, for legal reasons, religious persecution was often used as a pretext for emigration.

9   For German interest in the exploits of the 'Hessians' mercenaries in America, see, for example, Anon., *Ein grosser Sieg welche die Braunschweig- u, Hessischen Truppen in Amerika bey Neu-York den 31. August gegen die Amerikanischen Truppen durch ihre Tapferkeit erhalten haben* (s.l., 1776).

10   In his *Briefwechsel, meist historischen und politischen Inhalts* (Göttingen, 1779), for example, the Göttingen professor August Schlözer published letters from German officers serving in America.

11   'Jedermann will jetzt über den amerikanischen Krieg urteilen' (quoted in Horst Dippel, *Germany and the American Revolution, 1770–1800: A Sociohistorical Investigation of Late Eighteenth-Century Political Thinking*, trans. Bernhard A. Uhlendorf, with a foreword by R. R. Palmer (Chapel Hill, 1977), p. 206). Dippel's study is still the most important work on the German response to the American Revolution, but is rather narrowly focused on the question of whether Germans understood the democratic character of that Revolution. Dippel concludes that, on the whole, they did not.

but died at sea when he fell overboard and drowned near the Bermudas.[12] Between 1795 and 1800 the Brunswick botanist and civil servant E. A. W. Zimmermann published a two-volume treatise, comparing the new free state of North America, its inhabitants, climate, and geography with the situation of France, while the German traveller Dietrich von Bülow (1757–1808) wrote a fierce polemical diatribe against the recently formed United States of America, which he had visited twice, returning from his second journey as a very strong critic of the new free state.[13]

Historians have often focused on the possible contribution of the American Revolution to a more general political crisis of Europe's *anciens régimes* towards the end of the eighteenth century, in the period leading up to and during the French Revolution.[14] In the territories of the Holy Roman Empire '[e]vents such as the American War of Independence … provoked an examination of fundamental constitutional issues',[15] a process for which Hans-Erich Bödeker has coined the concept of a 'politicization' of the German public sphere in the second half of the eighteenth century.[16] Much of the German debate over the American Revolution, however, did not address constitutional issues in the Holy Roman Empire at all. Even praise for the American Revolution did not necessarily imply a demand for political, let alone radical, anti-monarchical reform in the German states.[17] The American crisis and its outcome were important, not so much because they provided a model for political reform, but because the German states and North America were connected to each other as members of the same Atlantic world created by migration, travel, commerce, and war. German authors were not only keenly aware of the events in North America. They also interpreted them in an Atlantic context. They discussed, for example, the legal nature of the transatlantic relationship between Britain and the North American colonies. They compared North America and its development with that of the European states. They also considered the impact of the American Revolution on the Atlantic networks of communication and exchange, which connected the Old and the New World.

---

12   See the introduction by Rainer Wild to J. C. Schmohl, *Über Nordamerika und Demokratie. Ein Brief aus England*, ed. Rainer Wild. Kleines Archiv des achtzehnten Jahrhunderts 14 (St. Ingbert, 1992). The original work was published in 'Kopenhagen' (i.e. Königsberg) in 1782.

13   D. von Bülow, *Der Freistaat von Nord-Amerika in seinem neuesten Zustand* (Berlin, 1797).

14   F. Venturi, *The End of the Old Regime in Europe, 1768–1776. The First Crisis*, trans. R. Burr Litchfield (Princeton, 1989).

15   E. Hellmuth and N. Pieroth, 'Germany 1760–1815', p. 74 in eds. Hannah Barker and Simon Burrows, *Press, Politics and the Public Sphere* (Cambridge, 2002), pp. 69–92.

16   Hans-Erich Bödeker, 'Prozesse und Strukturen politischer Bewußtseinsbildung der deutschen Aufklärung', in eds., Hans-Erich Bödeker and Ulrich Hermann, *Aufklärung als Politisierung–Politisierung der Aufklärung* (Hamburg, 1987), pp. 10–31.

17   Hans-Erich Bödeker, 'The Concept of the Republic in Eighteenth-Century German Thought', p. 49, in eds., Jürgen Heideking and James A. Henretta (with the assistance of Peter Becker), *Republicanism and Liberalism in America and the German States, 1750–1850* (Cambridge, 2002), pp. 35–52.

A Crisis in Transatlantic Relations: The *Ius Gentium* and the American Revolution

The American revolutionaries drew on a set of political ideas about virtue and corruption, which had figured prominently in the opposition to the Walpolean oligarchy in England in the first half of the eighteenth century.[18] Parliament, it was argued, had become the instrument of factional interests. Government was the means by which these interests exercised control over the country and rewarded themselves and their followers with bribes, offices and pensions. The appropriation of this 'patriot' ideology by the inhabitants of Britain's overseas colonies, however, was problematic, because it was not clear whether colonists could be considered British citizens at all, who were entitled to the same traditional rights as those living in the mother country.[19] The legal status of the colonies in relation to Britain was ambiguous: together, Britain and its overseas possessions formed an empire, but this 'British empire' could be understood in at least two different ways. It could describe an extension of the realm of Britain to new territories through conquest or settlement sponsored by the sovereign. This was 'empire' in the meaning of the Act in Restraint of Appeals in 1533, which was intended to exclude papal pretensions to temporal power in England,[20] and stood for the exclusive power of the crown-in-parliament within its territories. In that case colonists were subjects of the combined sovereignty of crown and British parliament.

The 'British empire' could, however, also denote a different kind of political community, more similar perhaps to the notion of a 'perpetual confederacy', as described by the Swiss jurist Emer de Vattel in his *Law of Nations*.[21] That is, it could be an empire in the sense of a confederation of several distinct, national political entities, which acknowledged the king of England as a common head, but which were not subject to the joint sovereignty of crown and parliament. The constitutional relationship between the different parts of this empire then, however, was not clearly defined, because Britain and the colonies lacked a common constitutional law (*ius publicum*), while English common law did not apply to the relations between states. This left the *ius gentium*, the law of nations, as the legal system governing the affairs between the colonies and Britain, with the consequence that the individual colonies were, juristically, in a state of nature in relation to each other and to the mother country.

---

18   For a discussion of the use and transformation of this language in the American Revolution, cf. J. G. A. Pocock, *The Machiavellian Moment* (Princeton, 1975), chapter xv; see also Caroline Robbins, *The Eighteenth-Century Commonwealthman* (Cambridge, MA, 1961).

19   David Armitage, *Ideological Origins of the British Empire* (Cambridge, 2000), ch. 7; J. P. Greene, 'Empire and Identity from the Glorious Revolution to the American Revolution', in ed., P. J. Marshall, *The Oxford History of the British Empire, vol. II: The Eighteenth Century* (Oxford, 1998), pp. 208–30.

20   J. G. A. Pocock, 'Political Thought in the English-speaking Atlantic, 1760–1790: (i) The imperial crisis', p. 257 in: J. G. A. Pocock, ed., *The Varieties of British Political Thought, 1500–1800* (Cambridge, 1993), pp. 246–82.

21   E. de Vattel, *The Law of Nations or Principles of the Law of Nature; applied to the Conduct and Affairs of Nations and Sovereigns* (London, 1760), vol. 1, p. 11.

In his *Taxation no Tyranny* of 1775 the English writer Samuel Johnson characterised the colonies as an example of the first type of empire, an extension of England's realm overseas. He wrote that

> To secure a conquest, it was always necessary to plant a colony, and territories thus occupied and settled *were rightly considered as mere extensions or processes of empire* [my italics], as ramifications through which the circulation of one publick interest communicated with the original source of dominion, and which were kept flourishing and spreading by the radical vigour of the Mother-country.[22]

Johnson considered the other possibility, namely, that the relations of the colonies to Britain were governed by the law of nations and that the colonies therefore were in a state of nature with the mother country. The colonists, he said, had tried to make use of this argument to legitimate their revolt,[23] but in doing so they had contradicted themselves, for they also insisted that they enjoyed the traditional right of Englishmen to political representation and that this was violated by parliament's imposition of taxes on them: 'but when this is granted, their boast of original rights is at an end; they are no longer in a State of Nature'.[24] If they were subjects of a British state, their relations to the mother-country could not at the same time be governed by the laws of the pre-political state of nature.

Although Johnson assumed that the colonists were subject to the combined sovereignty of crown and parliament, he denied that this conferred on them the right to choose deputies to sit in parliament in London. When an Englishman emigrated to the colonies, it was reasonable that he no longer exercised the right to elect representatives to parliament in the mother-country: 'by crossing the Atlantic he has not nullified his right; for he has made its exertion no longer possible. By his own choice he has left a country where he had a vote and little property, for another, where he has great property, but no vote.'[25] Soon after the American Declaration of Independence in 1776 Johnson's piece was translated into German and published together with several other, topical writings in the *Amerikanisches Archiv*, a journal edited by Julius August Remer in Brunswick. Remer, like Johnson, was aware of the potential ambiguity in the relationship between the colonies and Britain: 'The dispute between the two nations', Remer wrote, could be resolved either 'in the courts of the law of nature', that is, the law of nations, or in those of English law. The latter was, however, an arbiter the colonists would never accept.[26] Remer's *Archiv*

---

22   S. Johnson, *Taxation no Tyranny* (London, 1775), p. 23.

23   'That they are entitled to Life, Liberty, and Property, and that they have never ceded to any sovereign power whatever a right to dispose of either without their consent' (ibid., p. 35).

24   Ibid.

25   Ibid., p. 38. On the arguments used in Britain to defend British sovereignty over the colonies see H. T. Dickinson, 'Britain's Imperial Sovereignty: the Ideological Case against the American Colonists', in: ed., H. T. Dickinson, *Britain and the American Revolution* (London, 1998), pp. 64–96.

26   'Die Streitfrage zwischen den beiden Nationen kann vor einem doppelten Forum entschieden warden: nämlich vor den Gerichten des Rechts der Natur und des englischen Staatsrechts. Sie allein durch das letzte entscheiden zu lassen...heißt einen Richter erwählen,

included a mixture of texts by opponents as well as supporters of the colonists, such as the Welsh dissenting minister Richard Price, but his sympathies were evidently with the Americans. His description of the conflict as one between 'two nations', rather than as a revolt by British subjects against their sovereign, already went some way towards presenting the revolt as the national secession from a transatlantic confederation, rather than a domestic uprising, which would have been more difficult to defend.

Other German supporters of the colonists also tended to adopt the view that the American revolt was not a case of sedition, but heralded the separation of one distinct political society from another. In the *De Jure Revolutionis Americanorum* of 1777, for example, Bengt Lidner, a Swedish scholar at the university of Rostock, argued that the Americans' revolution was justified by the principle 'that a society has the right to govern itself according to its advantages, or through laws, which the citizens founded, or which are created by their unforced agreement, *without influence by another state* [my italics]'.[27] A few years later, in 1782, the strongly pro-American Johann Christian Schmohl similarly argued that the Americans enjoyed the original right of a society to choose its ruler and govern itself, and therefore were justified in shaking off the sovereignty of the crown and British parliament.[28] Schmohl's support for the American colonists did not imply a critical attitude towards British domestic politics. On the contrary he was able to reconcile his support for the colonists with an Anglophile admiration for the British constitution, because he believed that the American revolt was not directed against Britain's form of domestic government, but concerned the transatlantic relationship between colonies and mother-country.[29] Civil liberty in the metropolitan centre of the British empire was compatible with political oppression on the peripheries. The classical examples of this phenomenon were the empires of Sparta and republican Rome in antiquity. As Montesquieu had pointed out in his *Spirit of the Laws*, '[l]iberty was at the centre and tyranny at the peripheries ... in the Roman world, as in Lacedaemonia, those who were free, were exceedingly free, and those who were slaves were exceedingly enslaved to the highest degree'.[30] Schmohl echoed Montesquieu's comment, when he wrote that the relationship between the British and the colonists was marked by cruelty and comparable to that between the Spartans and the Helots. 'And yet the Spartans were the bravest, noblest and greatest of all Greeks; and yet the English are among all

---

den die Amerikaner nie für kompetent erachten werden' (Remer, *Amerikanisches Archiv*, Dritter Band (Brunswick, 1778), p. 4).

27   '[Q]uod se ipsam societas, pro suis commodis, vel per leges, quos cives condiderunt, vel consensu spontaneo eorum factae sunt, sine potestate a republica aliena, gubernandi ius habet'. (B. Lidner, 'De Iure Revolutionis Americanorum [1777]', pp. 69–70 in: *id.*, *Samlade Skrifter av Bengt Lidner*, ed. H. Elovson [Stockholm, 1932], pp. 63–82).

28   J. C. Schmohl, *Über Nordamerika und Demokratie. Ein Brief aus England.*

29   Schmohl wrote his essay on *Nordamerika und Demokratie* in exile in England, where he described the Thames as the 'river of freedom' (ibid., p. 7). On Schmohl's biography and his stay in England, see Philip Merlan, 'Parva Hamanniana (II): Hamann and Schmohl', *Journal of the History of Ideas*, 10 (1949): 567–74.

30   See Montesquieu, *The Spirit of the Laws*, eds., Anne M. Cohler, Basia C. Miller and Harold S. Stone (Cambridge, 1989), Book 2, chapter 19, pp. 184–5.

Europeans the bravest, noblest and greatest.'[31] Bengt Lidner referred directly to the above passage from Montesquieu in his defence of the American colonists. Although the British boasted of their liberty, and criticised the colonists for rebelling, they, like the ancient Romans, were oblivious of their 'most savage empire', which, 'while liberty flourished in Rome, oppressed and indeed afflicted all provinces subjected to the Romans'.[32]

The case for the colonists' right to secede required proof, that the colonies constituted a society with a distinct legal identity and were not mere overseas extensions of the realm of England. Such proof had to rest largely on the historical circumstances, under which they had developed. Schmohl claimed that the colonies had not been established or sponsored by either the crown or the British parliament, but had come under their control by usurpation, and therefore had the right to be considered political societies which were separate from that of the mother country. The continual conflicts between governors and colonial representative assemblies were evidence that the sovereignty of crown and parliament had been forced on the colonists. To the extent that the colonists did make concessions to the British sovereign, these were either voluntary or coerced. In the former case they could be revoked as freely as they had been given, in the latter they were not binding in the first place.[33] Although the British government had sponsored a number of colonies in North America, all their inhabitants perished from diseases and Indian attacks, and Britain therefore had no legitimate claim to political power over the North American provinces.

Critics of the Americans therefore had to show that only British government financing and protection had allowed the colonies to prosper and, indeed, survive. They did this by drawing attention to the military defence of the colonies against the French in the Seven Years War and insisted that the colonies had been raised to their flourishing state by generous injections of British finance. It is not surprising that a number of these anti-American writings were published in Göttingen, in the territory of the Elector of Hanover and King of England. In 1776, for example, the anonymous author of a pamphlet entitled *Thoughts on the Rebellion of the English Colonies in North America* and published in Göttingen, maintained that the colonists had 'received their lands from the crown' and most of the colonies had been supported with immense costs by the mother country.[34] It was unjust and ungrateful of them to refuse to help pay off the state debt, which had been incurred for their sake.[35]

---

31 'Und doch waren die Spartaner unter allen Griechen, die tapfersten, edelsten, größesten; und doch sind die Engländer unter allen Europäern die tapfersten, edelsten, größesten' (Schmohl, *Nordamerika*, p. 21).

32 'Iactant se Brittones eandem libertatem Romanam in Anglia vigere, et vitio ergo revolutionem nuper exardescentem Americanis vertunt: ast immemores, sine ullo dubio savissimi Imperii sunt, quod cum libertas floreret Romae, Provincias omnes Romanis subiectas concussit et fere afflixit'. (Lidner, 'De Jure Revolutionis', p. 70).

33 J. C. Schmohl, *Über Nordamerika und Demokratie*, p. 13.

34 'Die Colonisten haben ihre Länderey von der Krone empfangen, und die meisten Colonien sind durch grosse von jener angewandte Kosten gegründet, und in Flor gebracht' (anon., *Gedanken über den Aufstand der englischen Colonien in dem nördlichen Amerika* (Göttingen, 1776), p. 32).

35 'Schutz und Abgaben sind unzertrennlich miteinander verknüpft' (ibid.).

The historian Christoph Heinrich Korn argued similarly in 1777 that the colonies had benefited from Britain's support. Their development was without example 'in either ancient or modern history', and the colonies owed this to the 'gentle, paternal care of the mother country'.[36]

The arguments of these authors often seem to replicate those by English critics of the colonists. Like Samuel Johnson, they regarded the colonists as British subjects, but at the same time refused them the right to elect representatives to parliament. As the anonymous author referred to above wrote, the argument of 'no taxation without representation' did not apply. The majority of the British population, like the colonists, had no right to elect members of parliament and therefore was not directly represented in it. This did not mean that they had the right to refuse to pay the taxes imposed on them by parliament. If subjection to taxes one had not consented to was slavery, then 'a few million inhabitants in England, who have no right to vote, are slaves, however proud they are of their [civil] freedom'.[37] Also, though the colonists who emigrated from Britain to America might have held the right to elect a representative for parliament, while they lived in Britain, they lost the exercise of this right as a result of leaving the mother country. The principle of 'no taxation without representation', the author argues, was first formulated, when the British Empire did not extend beyond its home island and therefore included the tacit restriction to the geographical boundaries of that period. The principle did not automatically apply to possessions acquired at a later period, and unless the crown expressly conceded the colonies the right to tax themselves, they had to accept the taxation levied on them. Similar comments were to be found in the *Historisches Journal* of 1777, edited by the Göttingen historian Johann Christoph von Gatterer,[38] and the historian Christoph Heinrich Korn also wrote that 'three quarters of the English nation itself have no representatives. Every member of parliament represents the entire nation virtually, and is obliged to act in their best interest'.[39] But if the colonies had benefited so much from the connection with Britain, why then had they decided to rebel and separate themselves from the mother country?

A common explanation was that the colonists' revolt resulted from the combination of the narrow self-interest of American merchants with the irrational fears of the rabble. The historian and geographer Sprengel said that the British measures to suppress the colonists' contraband trade 'gave the American smuggler-merchants

---

36 'Der blühende Zustand, in welchem die Kolonisten in weniger als einem Jahrhunderte gelanget sind, hat kein Beyspiel weder in der alten noch neuen Geschichte. Er ist der einzige in seiner Art. Diese schnelle Aufnahme haben die Kolonien der sanften, väterlichen Regierung ihres Mütterlichen Landes, der Großmuth ihrer Mitbürger in Europa, zu verdanken' (C. H. Korn, *Geschichte der Kriege in und ausser Europa vom Anfange des Aufstandes der Brittischen Kolonien in Nordamerika an. Dritter Theil* [Nuremberg, 1777], p. 70).

37 '[S]o sind ein paar Millionen Einwohner in England, welche kein Wahlrecht haben, Sklaven, so sehr sie auf ihre Freyheit stolz sind' (anon., *Gedanken*, pp. 36/37).

38 *Historisches Journal, von Mitgliedern des königlichen historischen Instituts zu Göttingen, herausgegeben von Joh. Christoph Gatterer. Neunter Theil* (Göttingen, 1777), pp. 39 and 81.

39 'Aber drey Viertheile der Englischen Nation selber, haben keine Repräsentanten. Jedes Parlamentsglied stellt virtualiter die ganze Nation vor, und ist verpflichtet, für ihr Bestes zu sorgen' (C. H. Korn, *Geschichte der Kriege*, pp. 75–6).

(*Schleichhändler*) a shock'.[40] The Württemberg jurist Johann Jacob Moser presented the British attempt to suppress smuggling as the main immediate cause of the revolt: 'Much of this [i.e. the British measures] was repugnant to the colonies, especially the smugglers [*Schleichhändler*]. They claimed on the contrary that the Parliament of Great Britain could not impose taxes on them, but that they had to grant these themselves.'[41] Although these 'restless and cunning minds'[42] were only a small group among the Americans, they succeeded in convincing a larger number of colonists that the British measures threatened their liberty.[43] Many colonists were particularly susceptible to this propaganda, because of their origins in the 'enthusiastic' Puritan religious sects (*Schwärmer*), which had settled in America to flee persecution in Europe. The historian Korn also drew parallels with the parliamentary revolt of the 1640s and Cromwell's Puritan followers. The religious enthusiasm of the Puritan sects was prone to turn into a blind enthusiasm for political liberty.[44] The colonists who were not religious enthusiasts were descendants of convicts transported to North America and thus likely to hold similarly 'extravagant conceptions of liberty'.[45] Sprengel also suggested that the settlers in Massachusetts were overwhelmingly religious fanatics or enthusiasts. Their religious enthusiasm easily 'made way for another, the enthusiasm for liberty [*Freiheitsschwärmerei*]'[46] and their entire history was an 'alternating series of religious and political enthusiasms'.[47] The outbreak of the revolt was thus the result of an alliance between religious-political enthusiasts and a clique of self-interested merchants. Debates over the legitimacy of the Americans' revolt never disappeared entirely, but as the secession of the thirteen colonies from Britain became an established fact, supporters and critics of the Americans turned increasingly towards comparing the new free state, its failings and successes, with those of the Old World.

---

40   M. C. Sprengel, *Briefe den gegenwärtigen Zustand von Amerika betreffend. Erste Sammlung* (Göttingen, 1777), p. 7.

41   'Vieles davon war den Colonien, absonderlich den Schleichhändlern, unanständig. Sie behaupteten in ihren Vorstellungen dagegen: das Großbrittannische Parlament könnte ihnen keine Taxe auflegen, sondern sie müßten solche selbst bewilligen' (J. J. Moser, *Nord-America nach den Friedenschlüssen vom Jahr 1783. Erster Band* [Leipzig, 1784], p. 738).

42   F. W. Taube, *Geschichte der Engländischen Handelschaft, Manufacturen, Colonien und Schiffarth in den alten, mittlern und neuen Zeiten, bis auf das laufende Jahr 1776. Mit einer zuverlässigen Nachricht von den wahren Ursachen des jetzigen Krieges in Nordamerika, und andern dergleichen Dingen* (Leipzig, 1776), pp. 3/4.

43   '[D]ie vornehmsten Schleichhändler täuschten den Pöbel mit der Gefahr ihrer Religion und Freiheit' (M. C. Sprengel, *Briefe den gegenwärtigen Zustand von Amerika betreffend. Erste Sammlung* [Göttingen, 1777], p. 21).

44   'Das Brittische Ministerium hätte betrachten sollen, wozu ein meistens aus Schwärmern bestehendes Volk fähig ist. Es wußte solches ja schon aus der verderblichen Erfahrung in England' (C. H. Korn, *Geschichte der Kriege in und ausser Europa vom Anfange des Aufstandes der Brittischen Kolonien in Nordamerika an. Erster Theil* [Nürnberg, 1776], 'Vorbericht').

45   '[A]usschweifende Begriffe von der Freyheit' (ibid., *Zweyter Theil* (1776), p. 63).

46   Sprengel, *Briefe den gegenwärtigen Zustand von Amerika betreffend. Erste Sammlung*, pp. 39–40.

47   Ibid., p. 33.

The American Revolution and the 'Dispute of the New World'[48]

In 1827 the poet Johann Wolfgang von Goethe exclaimed, 'America, you are better off' ('Amerika, Du hast es besser').[49] His praise was a belated contribution to a long-standing debate over the excellence or degeneracy of America in relation to Europe, a 'Dispute of the New World', which had been given a powerful impetus in the mid-eighteenth century by the writings of the French naturalist Buffon. In his monumental *Histoire naturelle* (1749–89) Buffon had argued that the soil and climate of North America were such that all its species were fated to decay. The New World, and South America especially, suffered from an extreme humidity, which had weakened all organic matter and made all quadrupeds smaller and less sensitive than those in Europe. On the whole Buffon excluded humans from the corruption affecting the New World, but his ideas on American decline were adopted and extended to the native American population by the German Abbé Corneille de Pauw, whose *Recherches Philosophiques sur les Americains* were published in Berlin in 1768 and appeared in a German translation the following year. De Pauw was convinced that the American continent had experienced a geological catastrophe, which had resulted in a putrid, damp climate, where quadrupeds were invariably smaller, feebler, and fewer than in Europe and monstrous in appearance. Foreign animals imported to the New World degenerated; only insects, reptiles, and poisonous plants could thrive. The unhealthy natural environment had also made the native inhabitants effete, yet insensitive, weak, careless, and inactive creatures. Europeans who settled in that part of the world were liable to become similarly degenerate. A defence of America, its climate and inhabitants, against de Pauw by the Benedictine Antoine Joseph Pernety was printed in Berlin in 1769.[50] De Pauw published a reply in 1770, which was followed by a counter-reply from Pernety in the following year.[51]

This debate over the inhabitants of America was often joined with a different debate, on 'national character', which drew on Montesquieu's *De l'Esprit des Lois* of 1748. Like De Pauw Montesquieu put forward a form of climatic determinism, stressing, for example, the difficulty of setting up free political institutions in hot, moist climates, because, he supposed, they made people lazy and servile.[52] The degree, however, to which the natural environment influenced national character was generally contentious. David Hume argued in his essay on national characters of 1748 that there were too many variations between different states within the same climate (as in the case of the ancient Greek republics) and too much uniformity in large states, such as China, which extended across several different climatic zones, for climate to be considered decisive. Hume emphasised 'moral' causes, instead, that is, 'all circumstances, which are fitted to work on the mind as motives or reasons, and which render a peculiar set of manners habitual to us. Of this kind are, the nature

---

48   The phrase 'the Dispute of the New World' is borrowed from Antonello Gerbi, *The Dispute of the New World. The History of a Polemic, 1750–1900*. Revised edition, translated by Jeremy Moyle (Pittsburgh, 1973).

49   J. W. von Goethe, 'Amerika', quoted in Gerbi, *The Dispute*, p. 359.

50   Gerbi, *The Dispute*, p. 82.

51   Ibid., pp. 88–93.

52   Montesquieu, *The Spirit of the Laws*, p. 278.

of the government, the revolutions of public affairs, the plenty or penury in which the people live, the situation of the nation with regard to its neighbours, and such like circumstances.'[53] Few German commentators shared de Pauw's or Montesquieu's extreme forms of climatic determinism. When they debated, if the New World and the national character of its inhabitants tended towards corruption or were, on the contrary, superior to the Old, they usually referred to some combination of 'moral' and natural causes, in some cases drawing on Hume's essay in doing so.

The German response to the American Revolution and the new free state was often a variation on these comparative evaluations of Old and New World, their respective climate, prosperity, natural resources, and inhabitants' 'national character'. Although Johann Christian Schmohl, for example, did not incorporate a discussion of the natural environment into his treatise on *North America and Democracy* in 1782, the comparison of the colonies with Europe was central to his defence of the Revolution. His aim, he said, was to determine 'whether the North American people are really, on the whole, as noble as I believe they are', or whether they had succumbed to moral corruption.[54] His conclusion was that the state of virtue of the North American colonists was far superior to that of Europeans. Europe had suffered moral decline, which had above all been brought about by the growth of luxury in modern commercial societies and its effect on political life and virtue, a concern he shared with many eighteenth-century political and moral theorists.[55] Schmohl believed that power in a state depended on the distribution of property. Luxury, Schmohl said, destroyed the original equality of property and introduced artificial distinctions of rank, which had no basis in nature, and which were the main cause of the rise of despotic government in Europe. The material equality among humans in the early stages of society meant that although primitive communities had natural leaders, which might even hold the title of kings, these kings were not sole legislators. The differences between them and everybody else were too slight to ground absolute legislative power,[56] and the so-called prince originally was no more than 'the leader in war, first executor of the laws given by all, and entrusted to do so by everyone; in legislation he is no more than the president, who has one vote,

---

53   David Hume, 'Of National Characters', p. 198, in: David Hume, *Essays Moral, Political and Literary*, ed. E. F. Miller. Revised edition (Indianapolis, 1987), pp. 197–215.

54   'Sie setzen die Frage, ob die Kolonien zur Aufkündigung des Gehorsams und Zusammenkörperung eines unabhängigen Staats berechtigt waren, ganz bey Seite und legen mir blos die beyden Zweifel vor, ob das Nordamerikanische Volk nach der mehrern Zahl, auch wirklich so edel sey wie ichs glaubte, und dann ob die die Veränderung ein Glück für dasselbe, und ob überhaupt ein demokratischer Freystaat derjenige sey, in welchem Menschen lange glücklich seyn können' (Schmohl, *Nordamerika*, p. 7).

55   See Istvan Hont, 'The Early Enlightenment Debate on Commerce and Luxury' *Eighteenth-Century Political Thought*, eds., M. Goldie and R. Wokler.

56   '[J]eder hat seine Stimme, der erste nicht mehr als der letzte, höchstens kann er, wenn alle Stimmen gleich sind, der Parthey, die er hält, den Ausschlag geben' (Schmohl, *Nordamerika*, p. 64).

and otherwise directs business according to the laws, assembles, counts votes and disperses [the assembly]'.[57]

European liberty and the original equality of property, however, had already begun to be eroded in ancient Rome, 'when the inequality of properties became too unregulated and enormous, and when the laws designed to preserve these [properties]' lost their force.[58] Unless the inequality of property in Europe could be reversed, which was highly improbable, its political constitution would always tend towards despotism, though Schmohl clearly believed that there were differences between the European states, among which Britain was still the least corrupt. In America the continuing material equality among its inhabitants made such despotism much less likely.[59]

Schmohl wrote before the outbreak of the French Revolution and the failure to transform the French *ancien régime* into a constitutional monarchy. The emergence of an aggressive, expansionist republican state from 1792 and of the *Terreur*, together with claims that the French Revolution had been inspired by the American, lent the question of the relationship between the America and Europe particular urgency. It was widely argued that the two Revolutions were not comparable events. In 1794, for example, in a work published in Vienna, the author Adam Pfoeter acknowledged that the effect of the American Revolution on other nations had been like an 'electric jolt' (*electrischer Schlag*), but then argued that the French Revolution was based on misguided principles, which had little to do with those of the American.[60] In 1800 the political theorist Friedrich Gentz (1764–1832) argued, that 'every parallel between these two revolutions, will serve much more to display the *contrast*, than the *resemblance* between them'.[61] In the same year the Brunswick *Hofrath* and zoographer E. A. W. Zimmermann praised Gentz's remarks, writing that the American Revolution was often considered a catalyst in the downfall of the French *ancien régime* and that 'the giddy feeling of liberty in France has been stimulated to a much higher degree by that independence of the Americans; that the outbreak of the revolution in France was accelerated by it; and that a large number of Frenchmen

---

57 'Daher der sogenannte Fürst anfangs nur Führer im Krieg, Erster, und von allen beamteter Exekutor von allen gegebener Gesetze, bey der Gesetzgebung selbst nicht mehr als Präsident ist, der selbst aber nur eine Stimme hat und sonst gesetzmäßig die Geschäffte dirigiert, zusammen berift, Stimmen sammelt, aus einander gehen läßt. Das waren einst die Fürsten in Deutschland, die Könige in Rom, in Griechenland, sind es noch unter tausend Nationen' (ibid.).

58 'Die Freyheit oder die Konkurrenz jedes Bürgers zur Gesetzgebung, gieng überall erst dann verlohren, wenn die Ungleichheit der Vermögen zu regellos und ungeheuer ward, wenn die Gesetze, die diese erhalten sollten, so wenig Kraft mehr hatten, daß der, der um ihre Erneuerung anträgt, von den reichen Tyrannen, wie Tiberius Gracchus, den Tarpejischen Fels herab in den Tiber gestürzt wird' (ibid., p. 76).

59 'Die Gleichheit der Güter erhielt (nebst Patriotismus) die gemeine Freyheit, und diese Gleichheit ist doch in Amerika in der That noch lange nicht so weit zerfallen, als in England' (Ibid, p. 35).

60 A. J. Pfoeter, *Betracht über die Quellen und Folgen der merkwürdigsten Revolutionen unseres Jahrhunderts* (Vienna, 1794), p. 284.

61 Frederick Gentz, *The French and American Revolutions Compared*, translated by J. Q. Adams, with an introduction by Russell Kirk (New York, 1955), p. 84.

looked towards America as an example for their transformation'.[62] The American free state and France, however, were not comparable, because the physical environment and national character of the North Americans were entirely different from those of the French. Therefore the American Republic could not serve as a model for the government of France.

The Americans, Zimmermann argued, were on the whole favoured with a moderate climate, which encouraged the development of a good national character.[63] He emphasised the natural prosperity of the North American free states and the abundance and variety of its wildlife, 'compared to which our entire Continent [i.e. Europe] cannot offer anything equal'.[64] The northern colonies were endowed with fertile soil and produced large quantities of high-quality wood, as well as minerals such as iron and copper. Several varieties of grain grew in the moderate zones of the free states and these 'yield such an abundant crop, that this part of America can surely be considered the grain store of the poorer countries of Europe'.[65] Their location on the Atlantic coast allowed them to make the most of their natural advantages, that is, the fertility of their soil and their wealth in mineral resources, by engaging in maritime trade, especially since the interior was well connected with the sea through the St Laurence River, the Great Lakes and the Mississippi.[66] America's population was bound to increase to such an extent that it would soon exceed that of any other state.[67]

The effect of these environmental advantages on the Americans' 'national character' was reinforced by 'moral causes', in Hume's sense of the term.[68] Religion in particular had exerted a beneficial influence on the development of the colonies. Unlike those authors who suspected dangerous religious 'enthusiasm' as a motive of the colonists' revolt, Zimmermann held a much more positive view of the Americans' religious beliefs. The colonists' peaceful settlement showed how much their Christian religion furthered mutual toleration and amicability (*Brüderlichkeit*). From the very

---

62   Zimmermann's declared aim was to show that 'der Freiheitsschwindel in Frankreich durch jene Unabhängigkeit der Amerikaner weit lebhaffter geweckt ist. Daß der Ausbruch der Revolution Frankreichs dadurch beschleunigt wurde. Daß eine sehr große Menge Franzosen auf Amerika als auf das Vorbild ihrer Umschaffung hinsahen'. E. A. W. Zimmermann, *Frankreich und die Freistaaten von Nordamerika. 2. Band* (Brunswick, 1800), pp. XXI–XXIII.

63   '[D]iese ewige Mannichfaltigkeit des Angenehmen, gebiert Gleichgültigkeit, Sättigung und Ekel' (ibid., p. 255).

64   E. A. W. Zimmermann, *Frankreich und die Freistaaten von Nordamerika. 1. Band* (Berlin, 1795), p. 82: 'Das Thierreich der Amerikanischen Staaten zeigte also überhaupt eine so brauchbare Mannichfaltigkeit, daß unser ganzer Welttheil nocht im Stande ist, genau dagegen aufgewogen zu warden.'

65   'Die Getreidearten, welche in dem Gebiete der Freistaaten mit Nutzen gebäuet werden, sind innerhalb der beiden Extremen der gemäßigten Zone eingeschlossen; daneben geben sie so reiche Ausbeute, daß man sicher diesen Theil von Amerika für das grosse Kornmagazin der dürftigeren Länder Europas ansehen darf' (ibid., p. 91).

66   'Dies sind ... die Vortheile ohne Gleichen, welche die Natur mit Vorliebe auf dieses neue Land ausgeschüttet hat. Sie hat es zu einer Höhe, zu einer Independenz über alle bekannte Reiche der Erde erhoben' (ibid., p. 137).

67   Ibid., p. 245.

68   Zimmermann here refers to Hume's essay on national characters (ibid., p. 259); cf. D. Hume, 'Of National Characters' in *Essays Moral, Political and Literary*, pp. 197–215.

beginning religion had played an important and positive role in the colonisation of North America. The very first settlements in Massachusetts and Connecticut were by dissenters, who had travelled there to enjoy religious freedom.[69] Pennsylvania, founded by the Quaker William Penn, was also the result of the desire for religious freedom,[70] and the Southern states, too, owed their existence to a large extent to the desire for freedom of conscience, since Georgia invited those persecuted for religious reasons to settle there.[71]

France was, by comparison much poorer. It was less well-endowed with natural resources than the United States: it needed to import iron, copper and lead; its resources in wood were insufficient, its own supply of livestock and of wool was meagre. Even if hitherto fallow areas were taken into cultivation, this would not be enough to meet its needs. Another problem was the geography of France. Its compact, hexagonal shape divided the country into inland, border and coastal regions. The interior provinces in particular were dependent on the others for their foreign trade and thus their economic prosperity. This created economic conflicts of interest, which restrained its material flourishing, and which, Zimmermann suggested, required an efficient despotic government to be resolved. In the new free states of America these conflicts of interest did not exist. Zimmermann was also deeply sceptical about the French 'national character'. French history revealed the French national character to be marked by irritability, excessive ambition, and frivolousness.[72]

In the 'Dispute of the New World', therefore, authors like Gentz and Zimmermann were among the pro-Americans, but their central aim was to show the inapplicability of the North American example to Europe, especially France. The American Revolution was important not so much because it provided a model for political reform, but because its creation would inevitably, in the long run, affect the condition of the European states. Zimmermann commented that the North American free state was a 'trading nation, which was greater than all of Europe, let alone France'.[73] Gentz argued that the discovery of America had been one of the greatest benefits to humanity, and that the independence of the colonies from Britain was the means to realise the full potential of this discovery. Originally the importance of the discovery of America was mistakenly identified as the 'waves of gold and silver' which 'flooded Europe'; it then was believed to consist in the opportunities for monopoly trading companies, but this was only of importance for the merchants involved, not for humanity in general; finally, the discovery and colonisation of America was considered to be the means to strengthen the international power and standing of the European mother-country. Again, this affected only the particular states that had colonies and perhaps the international balance of power, but not the general condition of humanity.[74] The true importance of the 'communication with the East and

---

69   Zimmermann, vol. II, p. 444 and 446.

70   Ibid., p. 448.

71   Ibid., p. 453.

72   Ibid., p.4.

73   Ibid., vol. 1, p. 137.

74   Friedrich von Gentz, 'Ueber den Einfluß der Entdeckung von Amerika auf den Wohlstand und die Cultur des menschlichen Geschlechts', p. 271, in: *Neue deutsche*

West Indies' for the inexorable growth of human culture and wealth was to be found elsewhere. It was not only that the new free state of America had arrived at a degree of freedom and prosperity, which was not matched by any nation of the Old World; in North America 'the simplicity of manners, the equitable distribution of material goods and the peacefulness of opinions promised an enduring constitution'. It was 'a state, which is the consolation of all unhappy and persecuted people in Europe, the hope of the disheartened friend of humanity, and perhaps at one time will be the spring of wisdom and strength for our aging part of the world [i.e., Europe]'.[75] That in itself would be remarkable. More importantly, however, Europe's own increase in wealth and culture was a product of the transatlantic connections with North America, as well as those to the East Indies, because '[t]he discovery of America and of a new route to the East Indies opened up the greatest market, that is, the greatest stimulus for human industry, which had ever existed in humanity's sphere, ever since humans emerged from the state of savagery.[76] The colonization of North America and its separation from the mother country had benefited Europe because it created a vastly expanded, circumatlantic, even global, sphere of commerce, which stimulated human industry.

Conclusion

Although Germans were deeply interested in the American Revolution, the formation of the new free state and its development, very few, if any, were looking to North America as a model for political reforms at home. Those who praised the North Americans, their freedom, prosperity, and virtue, also believed that these advantages were dependent on the former colonies' specific historical, climatic, and natural conditions, which could not be transferred to Europe. The debate over the legitimacy of the American Revolution concentrated on the transatlantic relationship to Britain, not the internal constitution of the colonies, which did not change fundamentally as a result of the Revolution. The North American free state thus might be praised or condemned, but it was not considered an example which could be followed. Its importance for debates over political reform in Europe was mainly negative: discussion of the American Revolution served to show that it could not be imitated by, for example, the French after 1789, because Old and New World were not comparable. The New World might be an alternative to the Old, but it was not a blueprint for its renewal. The solution to disaffection with the Old World for a figure like the radical pro-American Johann Christian Schmohl was not political reform at home, but emigration.

Monatsschrift 2 (1795), pp. 269–319.

75   Ibid., p. 273.

76   Ibid.,p, 273–4.

Chapter 6

Transatlantic Cervantics: Don Quixote and the Fictions of American Enlightenment

Sarah F. Wood

Carlos Fuentes, writing a foreword to *Don Quixote* in 1985, suggests that 'the modern world begins when Don Quixote de la Mancha, in 1605, leaves his village, goes out into the world, and discovers that the world does not resemble what he has read about it'.[1] For Fuentes, as for countless critics before him, Cervantes de Saavedra is the gravedigger of the Middle Ages and a progenitor of the European Renaissance, the celebrated Spaniard who transcends national boundaries to become an international icon of cultural and literary enlightenment. For eighteenth-century Britain, engaged in the intellectual debates of European Enlightenment, *Don Quixote* was a foundational text, and changing responses toward the narrative and its knight can be used as a literary touchstone for measuring the broader cultural shift from Enlightenment to Romanticism. At the start of the eighteenth century, Don Quixote was read as an addled fool, the satirical butt of Cervantes's enlightened satire; by the end of the century, he was more frequently seen as a Romantic hero in a narrative that exalted the powers of his imagination and lamented the passing of heroic chivalric ideals. At the same time, however, in response to unfolding events across the English Channel, this Spanish cultural icon was being used satirically by both radical and conservative British writers wanting to comment on the causes and consequences of the French Revolution. It was this promiscuously circulated and politically contested Quixote, rather than Cervantes's Spanish original, who crossed the Atlantic with the influx of British literary imports into America both before and after independence.

In *The Comic Imagination in American Literature*, Louis D. Rubin Jr. has argued that the 'incongruity between the ideal and the real ... lies at the heart of American experience'.[2] For Rubin, it is 'the gap between the cultural ideal and the everyday fact', the disparity between 'the language of culture and the language of sweat, the democratic ideal and the mulishness of fallen human nature' that constitutes 'the Great American Joke'.[3] Working within this paradigm, the early-republic era, working to realise the highest of ideals and experiencing the hardest of falls, would provide a fertile context for devising the greatest of American jokes. And who better to deliver the punch line than Don Quixote, the purest of idealists, whose naivety laid bare the gap between the ideal and the real, between the enlightened pledges

---

1 Carlos Fuentes, 'Foreword', in *The Adventures of Don Quixote de la Mancha*, Miguel de Cervantes Saavedra, trans. Tobias Smollett (London, 1986), xi–xiii (xi).

2 Rubin, 'Introduction: "The Great American Joke"', in *The Comic Imagination in American Literature*, ed., Louis D. Rubin Jr. (Washington, DC, 1977), pp. 3–15 (p. 5).

3 Ibid., pp. 12, 15.

of 1776—life, liberty and the pursuit of happiness—and the material limitations and political disappointments of early-republic reality. This essay, then, sets out to explore the conflicted interpretations and representations of *Don Quixote* available to early-republic authors, and to examine some of the ways in which American authors, particularly as the French Revolution progressed, responded to British representations of Spain's most famous literary export in order to explore the contradictions and limitations of Enlightenment in their own potentially fragile republic.

An accessible and entertaining exploration of the clash between the ancient and the modern, between old and new ways of ordering society, *Don Quixote* was hugely popular in eighteenth-century Britain; over the century, an astounding forty-five editions of *Don Quixote* were published in English (there were only thirty-three editions in Spanish over the same period), and the knight ran riot in British letters, in titles ranging from *The Spiritual Quixote* (1773) and *The City Quixote* (1785), to *The Philosophical Quixote* (1782) and *The Female Quixote* (1752).[4] The Quixote may not have taken the titular role in *Joseph Andrews* (1742), but Henry Fielding's title page nonetheless declared itself a history 'Written in Imitation of The *Manner* of CERVANTES, Author of *Don Quixote*'.[5] Sterne's *Tristram Shandy* (1759–67), meanwhile, contained nearly as many Quixotes as there were characters in the book, and Smollett's *Life and Adventures of Sir Launcelot Greaves* (1762) told the story of a handsome young knight who had 'set up for a modern Don Quixote', in order to wage 'perpetual war' against 'the foes of virtue and decorum'.[6]

Alongside this explosion in all things Quixotic, eighteenth-century Britain registered a remarkable shift in attitudes towards Cervantes's narrative and its knight. At the start of the eighteenth century, scholars invariably described Cervantes as an enlightened advocate for rational thought, Don Quixote as a lunatic knight, run mad in romance, and *Don Quixote* as an exemplary satire, either of well-worn romance fiction or of outdated chivalric practices. Charles Jarvis used his 'Translator's Preface' of 1742 to argue that *Don Quixote* 'was calculated to ridicule that false system of honour and gallantry, which prevailed even 'till our author's time',[7] and Gregorio Mayáns I Siscár's 'Vida de Miguel de Cervantes Saavedra', translated into English and reproduced in the same edition, likewise treated *Don Quixote* as a satire, though this time as a satire of chivalric romances rather than chivalric practices, a satire of Spanish literature as opposed to Spanish society. 'Cou'd there possibly be a stronger, or more judicious Satire against Writers of Knight-Errantry?' Siscár's 'Vida' demanded, a rhetorical question, we assume, since the biography had already acclaimed *Quixote* as the 'powerful and most effectual Remedy' that had 'purg'd the Minds of all *Europe*, and cur'd them of that inveterate radicated Fondness they

---

4   My data comes from Albert F. Calvert's tabulated 'Synopsis of the Editions of *Don Quixote*', in *The Life of Cervantes* (London and New York, 1905), p. 139.

5   Fielding, *The History of the Adventures of Joseph Andrews, and of his Friend, Mr. Abraham Adams* (2 vols, London, 1742), title page.

6   Smollett, *The Life and Adventures of Sir Launcelot Greaves*, ed. David Evans (New York and London, 1973), pp. 12, 13.

7   Jarvis, 'The Translator's Preface', in *The Life and Exploits of the Ingenious Gentleman Don Quixote de la Mancha*, Miguel de Cervantes Saavedra, trans. Charles Jarvis (2 vols, London, 1742), iii–xxiii (vii).

had for those contagious Books'.[8] Jarvis likewise commented on the efficacy of Cervantes's satire, marvelling at Cervantes's combat with 'this *giant* of *false honour*, and all these *monsters* of *false wit*', for 'no sooner did his work appear, but both were cut down at once, and for ever. The illusion of ages was dissipated, the magic dissolved, and all the enchantment vanished like smoke.'[9]

By the late-eighteenth century, though, *Don Quixote* was increasingly thought to be exalting the values of chivalric practice and romance fiction rather than excoriating the '*false honour*' of one and the '*false wit*' of the other. Readers sensed romantic leanings in the character of Cervantes—himself a martial warrior, held captive in Algiers and neglected by the Spanish court—and saw in Don Quixote the makings of a true Romantic, a just and virtuous hero, bewildered and persecuted by a degenerate age. Henry Brooke's *The Fool of Quality* (1766–70), a bestseller in its day, devoted several pages to a panegyric on Quixote, applauding the fictional Spaniard as 'the greatest hero among the moderns', the 'divinely superior' 'hero of the Mancha! who went about righting of wrongs, and redressing of injuries, lifting up the fallen, and pulling down those whom iniquity had exalted'.[10] Stuart M. Tave has charted this critical *volte-face* in *The Amiable Humorist*, describing how, 'once totally deluded, next odd but good and lovable', Don Quixote went on to become 'a man with an inner light that shone through his seemingly cracked head, an imagination that opened a more immediate glimpse of the possibilities of human greatness than a merely logical understanding could attain'.[11]

The Romantic Quixote was especially visible in the antiquarian fictions of Sir Walter Scott, whose fondness for *Don Quixote* would manifest itself in frequent citations from and allusions to the text. In *Quentin Durward* (1823), for example, the character of Louis XI gives one of his disciples the following advice: 'patience, cousin, and shuffle the cards, till our hand is a stronger one'; in the footnotes, Scott describes the metaphor as the 'same proverb … quoted by Durandarte, in the enchanted cave of Montesinos', and an anachronistic one at that, since '**the** scene of this romance is laid in the fifteenth century' and Cervantes wouldn't publish Part I of *Don Quixote* until 1605.[12] Scott's Louis XI may be among 'the first to ridicule and abandon' the principles of chivalry, throwing 'ridicule upon the extravagant and

---

8   Mayáns I Siscár, 'The Life of Michael de Cervantes Saavedra', trans. Mr. Ozell, in *Don Quixote*, trans. Charles Jarvis (2 vols, London, 1742), pp. 1–90 (pp. 62, 48).

9   Jarvis, xxiii.

10   Brooke, *The Fool of Quality; or, The History of Henry Earl of Moreland* (5 vols, London, 1766–1770; repr. New York and London, 1979), vol. 1, pp. 152, 153.

11   Tave, *The Amiable Humorist: A Study in the Comic Theory and Criticism of the Eighteenth and Early Nineteenth Centuries* (Chicago, 1960), pp. 160–61. In *The Romantic Approach to 'Don Quixote': A Critical History of the Romantic Tradition in 'Quixote' Criticism* (Cambridge, 1978), Anthony Close has likewise argued that 'there developed in eighteenth-century England, from approximately 1740 onwards, a movement of opinion anticipating the Romantic idealisation of *Don Quixote*' (p. 13). In *Don Quixote in England: The Aesthetics of Laughter* (Baltimore and London, 1998), Ronald Paulson locates the critical turning point as 1745, the year of the failed Jacobite rebellion.

12   Scott, *Quentin Durward*, ed. Susan Manning (Oxford and New York, 1992), pp. 137, 508, 3.

exclusive principles of honour and virtue', but the French monarch is by no means an enlightened slayer of benighted practices. On the contrary, while *Quentin Durward*'s narrator warmly praises the 'generosity and self-denial' of 'the spirit of chivalry', Scott's anti-chivalric monarch is 'of a character so purely selfish—so guiltless of entertaining any purpose unconnected with his ambition, covetousness, and desire of selfish enjoyment, that he almost seems an incarnation of the devil himself, permitted to do his utmost to corrupt our ideas of honour in its very source'.[13]

The devil himself had already been incarnated in Charles Lucas's anti-Jacobin novel, *The Infernal Quixote: A Tale of the Day* (1801), which opens with a Miltonic Satan, rising up and proclaiming that 'the reign of ANTICHRIST is begun.—Thanks to the daring, restless sons of France, inspired by me and mine!'[14] Preoccupied, like *Quentin Durward*, with the collapse of an *ancien régime* and the emergence of extreme political expediency, *The Infernal Quixote* would position its own Quixotic character in relation to another French sovereign, this time Louis XIV. Cut from the same diabolic cloth as Milton's Satan, Lucas's Quixote—the nefarious Marauder—personifies the morally degraded and selfishly motivated principles of revolutionary France, 'a pestilential den of degenerating equality', where the people have 'killed their King', and are now 'no better than savages.'[15] Two decades later, Lucas would explain that *The Infernal Quixote* was 'avowedly written' to 'counteract the *revolutionary* mania among the community at large',[16] yet the novel itself tells the story of an aristocratic megalomaniac who is repeatedly bested and ultimately vanquished by the brave and noble son of a lowly village carpenter, with both men experiencing a remarkable (and deserved) revolution in their social status and fortune. And while Lucas's representation of a conniving Quixote, a villain devoid of ideals, is extremely unusual—and a world apart from Cervantes's well-intentioned Spanish Don—his decision to name his villain for Quixote signals the extent to which the knight had become a recognisable rhetorical counter in the war of ideas raging around the British Isles and across the English Channel.

The History of Sir George Warrington; or, The Political Quixote (1797) offered readers another example of an English aristocrat looking to the French republic for his moral code and political manifesto.[17] The young hero of this tale, a likeable but impressionable Northumberland baronet, is 'duped' by 'Paine's Rights of Man' into espousing the philanthropic principles of the French revolution. Moderating voices repeatedly warn him that 'a state of equality is a state of envy, anarchy, and

---

13   Ibid., pp. 3, 5.

14   Lucas, *The Infernal Quixote: A Tale of the Day*, ed. by M. O. Grenby (Peterborough, Ont., 2004), iv.

15   Ibid., pp. 168–9.

16   'Appendix A: From Charles Lucas, *Gwelygordd; or, the Child of Sin. A Tale of Welsh Origin* (1820)', *Infernal Quixote*, p. 413.

17   The title page of *George Warrington* announced it to be written by Charlotte Lennox, but Jerry C. Beasley has argued that 'after *Euphemia*, Charlotte Lennox wrote no more. Other works of fiction have been mistakenly attributed to her, including *The History of George Warrington; or, The Political Quixote* (1797), which an unscrupulous bookseller published as "By the Author of the Female Quixote"' ('Charlotte Lennox', *DLB*, 39 (Ann Arbor, Michigan: Gale, 1985), pp. 306–12 [p. 312]).

confusion', and that 'Liberty, beyond what Englishmen already enjoy, is an airy vision, and equality a wild chimera', but not until the third and final volume, when Sir George gets round to reading the 'newspapers of the day', does he finally repent of his Jacobin ways.[18] Most unlike the infernal Marauder, and much more like the Quixotes we are used to seeing in British fiction, Sir George is not malicious, merely a misguided philanthropist, and his story is represented as both a political and a sentimental journey, with revolutionary politics and scheming women ultimately vanquished by conservative values and marriage to the virtuous Louisa Moreland. Quixotic figures such as George Warrington, Emma Courtney in Mary Hays's *Memoirs of Emma Courtney* (1796) or Bridgetina Botherim in Elizabeth Hamilton's *Memoirs of Modern Philosophers* (1800), were over-enlightened and deeply politicised, the fictional products of a polarised and feverish political atmosphere.

In *Romance and Revolution: Shelley and the Politics of a Genre*, David Duff has argued that the 'language of romance, whether used for literary purposes or in other contexts, was peculiarly unstable and ambivalent' during the 1790s, 'always susceptible to inversion, its positive associations quickly reducible to negative ones'.[19] This was certainly the case with Don Quixote, who quickly became a double agent deployed by both sides in the war of ideas. Used by conservatives to satirise the democratic utopianism of the radicals, and by radicals to satirise the aristocratic obsolescence of conservatives, Quixote became a literary touchstone in the conflict between progress and tradition, reason and religion, democracy and aristocracy.

Edmund Burke's *Reflections on the Revolution in France* (1790) clearly demonstrated the susceptibility to inversion of the language of romance. Horrified by the violence of the French Revolution, and in particular by the Jacobins' treatment of Marie Antoinette, Burke invoked the spirit of romance in order to lament the fall of the monarch:

> Little did I dream that I should have lived to see such disasters fallen upon her in a nation of gallant men, in a nation of men of honour, and of cavaliers. I thought ten thousand swords must have leaped from their scabbards to avenge even a look that threatened her with insult. But the age of chivalry is gone. That of sophisters, economists, and calculators, has succeeded; and the glory of Europe is extinguished for ever.[20]

There were over seventy responses to Burke's *Reflections*: most were hostile, many pilloried the romance imagery in his work, and several of these made use of Don Quixote in their satire. Published by William Holland, 'The Knight of the Woful [*sic*] Countenance Going to Extirpate the National Assembly' (see Figure 6.1) was one of several engravings to align the Irish conservative with Cervantes's Spanish hidalgo.[21]

---

18   *George Warrington* (3 vols, London, 1797), pp. 32, 188, 196, 62.

19   Duff, *Romance and Revolution* (Cambridge, 1994), p. 12.

20   Burke, *Reflections*, intro. A. J. Grieve (London and New York, 1953), p. 73.

21   The British Museum Catalogue guesses that the print is made by an 'H. W.', possibly William Holland, or another artist, H. Wigstead. See also Isaac Cruikshank, 'The Aristocratic Crusade, or Chivalry revived by Don Quixote de St. Omer and his friend Sancho' (31 January, 1791), and 'Don Dismallo, After an Absence of Sixteen Years, Embracing his Beautiful Vision!' (18 November, 1790).

Figure 6.1   'The Knight of the Woful [*sic*] Countenance going to extirpate the
             National Assembly', engraving, 15 November 1790 © The Trustees
             of the British Museum. Used with permission

In this picture, a ludicrous-looking Burke emerges from his publisher's house, wearing a suit of armour and a miniature of Marie Antoinette. Mounted upon an ass with the head of Pope Pius VI (an allusion to Burke's alleged association with the Jesuits of St Omer), this Knight of Woeful Countenance grasps his lance in one hand and a 'Shield of Aristocracy and Despotism' in the other. *Reflections* lies before him on the ass, and though the knight may consider himself to be a mirror of chivalry, his muse and mistress is clearly a mirror of tyranny. The oval medallion of Marie Antoinette is positioned alongside the 'Shield of Aristocracy and Despotism', with the monarch's profile looking straight ahead at the shield's scenes of torture and incarceration. A visual reflection and enlargement of the oval miniature portrait, the shield suggests that the queen is both the source and symbol of 'Aristocracy and Despotism', and of the atrocities committed in their name.

In his *Rights of Man: Being an Answer to Mr Burke's Attack on the French Revolution* (1791–92), Thomas Paine likewise seized upon the image of Quixote to savage the Old World nostalgia and political conservatism of his opponent:

> When we see a man dramatically lamenting in a publication intended to be believed, that *'The age of chivalry is gone!'* that *'The glory of Europe is extinguished for ever!'* that *'The unbought grace of life'* (if any one knows what it is), *'the cheap defence of nations, the nurse of manly sentiment and heroic enterprise, is gone!'* and all this because the Quixote age of chivalry nonsense is gone, what opinion can we form of his judgement, or what regard can we pay to his facts? In the rhapsody of his imagination he has discovered a world of windmills, and his sorrows are, that there are no Quixotes to attack them. But if the age of aristocracy, like that of chivalry, should fall, (and they had originally some connexion), Mr Burke, the trumpeter of the Order, may continue his parody to the end, and finish with exclaiming, *'Othello's occupation's gone!'*[22]

Exposing Burke's recourse to romance as a conservative ploy to resist political change, Paine uses Don Quixote to deflate and belittle 'the trumpeter of the Order'. Seen through the revolutionary eyes of Thomas Paine, Burke's elegy for the waning age of aristocracy exposes an irrational mind, a flawed judgement, and an extravagant imagination, all leaving him vulnerable to charges of Quixotism. Thomas Paine may have dedicated *Rights of Man* to 'GEORGE WASHINGTON, President of the United States of America',[23] but as the French Revolution turned increasingly ugly, and American politicians split along French and British lines, Paine would become a particular bugbear of American conservatives, cropping up time and again in political satires and works of fiction to evoke the dangerous excesses of Enlightenment in the new republic.

*

George Washington acquired his first copy of *Don Quixote* on September 17, 1787, purchased by the President on the very day he signed the US Constitution and, according to Stanley T. Williams in *The Spanish Background of American Literature*,

---

22   Paine, *Rights of Man* and *Common Sense*, intro. Michael Foot (London, 1994), p. 20.
23   Ibid. [p. 3].

'the great, the all-conquering Cervantes ... was everywhere' in the new republic.[24] Works such as Hugh Henry Brackenridge's *Modern Chivalry* (1792–1815), Royall Tyler's *The Algerine Captive* (1797), Tabitha Gilman Tenney's *Female Quixotism* (1801) and Washington Irving's *A History of New York* (1809) recognised the peculiar ambivalence of Quixote and used him as a complex rhetorical counter in their arguments over the relative merits and pitfalls of equality as opposed to hierarchy, new-fangled ideas as opposed to traditional values, cosmopolitanism as opposed to isolationism, and French revolution as opposed to British aristocracy.

Female Quixotism, written by the wife of three-times Federalist senator, Samuel Tenney, is amenable—on certain levels at least—to a decidedly anti-Jacobin reading. Tenney's Quixotic heroine, Dorcas(ina) Sheldon, already disadvantaged by a literary diet of European novels, has to contend with a series of unscrupulous suitors who try and trick her into marriage to get their hands on the family silver. Dorcasina's romantic reading habits and romanticised self-image make her particularly susceptible to being 'duped', and as often as not the conmen are self-serving rabble-rousers, tarred with one Jacobin brush or another. Dorcasina's final 'suitor', Seymore the school-master, already possesses 'an amiable wife and several fine children' in South Carolina, and used to be 'a man of fortune' until 'some business call[ed] him to France', where he 'thoroughly imbibed all the demoralizing, and atheistical principles of that corrupt people'. Having 'squandered his time and money in gaming houses and brothels', he runs up debts and is 'obliged to flee, leaving his family overwhelmed with distress'.[25] 'Mr M.' meanwhile, a local gentleman 'who has children grown up, and who has been one of the best fathers and husbands', has likewise undergone a dramatic change of character since reading a book 'by one Tom Paine'. He now 'keeps a Madam' who 'goes drest like any queen; while he hardly allows his wife and daughters enough to keep them decent' (FQ, 316). Horrified by the tale of Mr M., Dorcasina launches into a sweeping isolationist diatribe, excoriating 'those pernicious sentiments, the growth of other climes', that 'have found their way to this once happy country', and praying that Heaven may 'prevent the further progress of Jacobinism, atheism, and illuminatism; they all seem to be links of the same chain' (FQ, 316).

Dorcasina's impromptu political oration takes place in the final pages of the book, immediately after she has finally confronted the treachery of Seymore and confessed the folly of her own, deluded behaviour. It is only the second time in the narrative that Dorcasina has shown an interest in the political welfare of her country (the American Revolution passes by unnoticed); the first time is in the opening pages of the novel, before she has even been introduced to her first potential suitor. Imagining the prospect of marriage to a Virginian slave owner, Dorcasina 'indulged herself in the agreeable, humane, but romantic idea, that, being the wife of Lysander, she should become the benefactress of his slaves':

---

24   Williams, *The Spanish Background of American Literature* (2 vols, New Haven, CT, 1955), vol. 1, p. 44.

25   Tabitha Gilman Tenney, *Female Quixotism: Exhibited in the Romantic Opinions and Extravagant Adventures of Dorcasina Sheldon*, ed. Jean Nienkamp and Andrea Collins; foreword Cathy N. Davidson (New York and Oxford, 1992), p. 297. Future references are prefixed by FQ and referred to in parentheses.

She even extended her benevolent reveries beyond the plantation of her future husband, and, wrapt in the glow of enthusiasm, saw his neighbours imitating his example, and others imitating them, till the spirit of justice and humanity should extend to the utmost limits of the United States, and all the blacks be emancipated from bondage, from New-Hampshire even to Georgia. (FQ, 9)

By extending Dorcasina's romantic daydreams of Lysander to include romantic 'illusions' (FQ, 9) of emancipated slaves, the narrative suggests that its heroine's romanticised marital expectations are inextricable from her romanticised and, by implication, her equally ludicrous political ideas of racial equality. Dorcasina's exacting demand that her suitors should fall obediently at her feet inverts established gender hierarchies in the same way that slave emancipation would overturn institutionalised racial hierarchies. The narrative, then, is framed by two, very different, political perspectives, and just as Dorcasina's perceived political 'enthusiasm' provides the starting point for all the personal misjudgements and mistakes to come, her conversion to political conservatism in the final pages of the narrative reinforces and authenticates her conversion to common sense.

Dorcasina's realisation is a double-edged one though, for the disillusionment she experiences is not so much with the books she reads as with the life she is expected to lead. She acknowledges the fictional status of the novels she adores, but continues to read them nonetheless, experiencing 'the same relish, the same enthusiasm as ever', and dividing her indictments pretty evenly between the 'pernicious volumes' that 'inspire illusory expectations' (FQ, 325) of American life, and the disappointing reality of a US republic that fails to fulfil the expectations it has raised in its female citizens. Dorcasina's experiences bear more than a passing resemblance to those of Mary Hays's eponymous heroine in *Memoirs of Emma Courtney* (1796). Written by a confidante and disciple of radical philosopher, William Frend, this was the disquieting, semi-autobiographical story of a British female Quixote raised on a diet of Enlightenment philosophy and 'ten to fourteen novels' every week.[26] A 'reasoning maniac',[27] who uses rational argument to justify her romantic behaviour, Emma spends many years pursuing the man she adores, Augustus Harley, only to discover that he already has a wife and child. Ultimately acknowledging that her views have been 'equally false and romantic' and facing a lonely middle age, Mary Hays's heroine might be expected to blame her books for the wasted life she has led; instead, she blames a 'lurking poison' in 'the constitutions of society', arguing that 'while the institutions of society war against nature and happiness, the mind of energy, struggling to emancipate itself, will entangle itself in error'.[28] As Federalists and Republicans wrangled bitterly over the legacy of the American constitution and the future of the new republic, and as writers repeatedly used Don Quixote to

---

26   Hays, *Memoirs of Emma Courtney*, ed. Eleanor Ty (New York and Oxford, 2000), p. 18.

27   Ibid., p. 142. Elizabeth Hamilton's anti-Jacobin novel, *Memoirs of Modern Philosophers* (1800), models its heroine, Bridgetina Botherim, on the radical ideas and miserable love life of Mary Hays. Bridgetina takes Godwin's precepts literally and her exaggerated belief in the perfectibility of mankind turns her into an object of ridicule.

28   Ibid., pp. 158, 195, 158–9.

expostulate on the dangers of political extremism at either end of the spectrum, there would be no shortage of 'reasoning maniacs' in American fiction.

The longest, and most philosophically complex, of the early republic's Quixotic fictions was Hugh Henry Brackenridge's meandering *Modern Chivalry* (1792–1815), which opened, like its Spanish prototype, with a Quixotic protagonist snapping shut his books and stepping out into a strange and disorienting world. Brackenridge introduces the character of Captain Farrago as though he were Pennsylvania's answer to Uncle Toby, the Quixotic captain of *Tristram Shandy*. Toby's unsuspecting simplicity, endearing whimsicality and child-like ignorance of the world constitute the defining characteristics of a particular kind of Quixote, increasingly popular in eighteenth-century English fiction, and defined by Stuart Tave as 'the amiable humorist'.[29] Embodied in figures such as Fielding's Parson Adams and Goldsmith's man in black, this kind of literary Quixote was usually a gentleman of more mature years, and more often than not a confirmed bachelor. The opening sentence of *Modern Chivalry*'s first chapter forms Farrago in the same mould, as H. H. Brackenridge informs us that the fifty-three year old Captain is 'in some things whimsical, owing perhaps to his greater knowledge of books than of the world; but, in some degree, also, to his having never married, being what they call an old batchelor [*sic*], a characteristic of which is, usually, singularity and whim'.[30]

The narrator returns to this image in the closing pages of the book, concluding his story of the Captain—now known simply as 'the governor'—with a chapter devoted to the causes of Farrago's bachelordom, and the prediction that 'if we ever get our Don Quixotte married, it is ten to one, but it will be to a spinster' (MC, 798). *Modern Chivalry* is thus book-ended with the sentimentalised sketch of a good-natured Quixote, formative first and last impressions, which suffuse Farrago with the rosy glow of the amiable humorist and de-politicise his dubious rise to power in Part II of the text.

As was the case with his Spanish predecessor, the 'old school' books that Farrago reads have failed to prepare him for the harsh realities of backwoods life (MC, 53); instead, they have filled him with unrealistic expectations of western progress, with idealistic delusions of a civilised and stable frontier. Faced with all kinds of absurd democratic excesses, the Captain can—and does—lecture the people until he is blue in the face, but his recourse to reason, to Roman notions and Greek philosophers, most commonly falls on deaf ears. Long on sermons but short on action, Farrago appears both pompous and ridiculous, his harangues irrelevant and his 'old school' presence inflammatory along the western frontier.

---

29   Tave, pp. 140–63.

30   Brackenridge, *Modern Chivalry*, ed. Claude M. Newlin (New York and London, 1968), p. 6. Future references are prefixed by MC and referred to in parentheses. Individual volumes of *Modern Chivalry* were published in 1792 (Part I, vol. 1), 1792 (Part I, vol. 2), 1793 (Part I, vol. 3), 1797 (Part I, vol. 4), 1804 (Part II, [vol. 1]), 1805 (Part II, vol. 2), 1815 (Part II, vol. 4). Published in Pittsburgh in 1793, Part I, vol. 3 was the first literary work to be published west of the Allegheny Mountains. The first collected edition of *Modern Chivalry* was published in Richmond and Philadelphia in 1815.

Published in 1804, Part II of *Modern Chivalry* (which was in fact the fifth instalment of the work) suggests a deliberate break or juncture in a seemingly aimless and endless work. Its opening words reinforce the sense of discontinuity with what has gone before: 'Here is a great gap. Not a word said about the travels of the Captain, from the packing up of Teague, and sending him off to France, until after the termination of the French revolution, and the armistice or convention of Amiens' (MC, 329). Published in the year Napoleon became the Emperor of the French, and positioning itself within the context of French politics, Part II explicitly occludes the French Revolution, moving readers straight from aristocracy to empire in the turn of a page. Furthermore, the political force that Thomas Jefferson described as Bonaparte's 'unprincipled and maniac tyranny' provides more than a political framework and a narrative starting-point for Part II of *Modern Chivalry*; it also suggests an interpretative framework for reading the rise and reign of Captain Farrago, Brackenridge's own imperious frontier governor.[31]

With critics concentrating on earlier episodes, Part II has often failed to attract its share of critical attention; in *Writing and Postcolonialism in the Early Republic,* Edward Watts decides to discuss only Part I in his chapter on *Modern Chivalry*, dismissing the second part as 'overlong, repetitious, and, at times, almost unreadable'.[32] But to underestimate Part II is to overlook Farrago's astonishing transition from ineffectual outsider to state governor, as Brackenridge grafts onto American soil the failure of French republicanism and the emergence of French imperialism, imagining a scenario where republican democracy becomes so absurdly unworkable along the western frontier that an ambitious soldier—this time Captain Farrago—is able to create the most imperial of regimes with frightening ease.

Setting out on his travels all over again in Part II, Farrago does things differently this time round: he no longer rides aimlessly 'about the world' to 'see how things were going on here and there' (MC, 6); this time he pushes concertedly westward, marching through 'the back settlement' and 'the Lack-learning settlement', and arriving at 'the new settlement' in a matter of four chapters (MC, 517; 523; 538). And this time, the Captain is accompanied by a 'caravan' of frontier characters: 'the blind lawyer and fidler [*sic*]; Clonmel the ballad singer; the latin [*sic*] schoolmaster; O'Fin, an Irishman; Tom the Tinker, and others' (MC, 510). Only the Captain is mounted, we learn; the rest are 'on foot', a motley bunch of subservient ragamuffins who nonetheless prove an effective infantry when Farrago reaches his final destination, the most westerly of the narrative's '*western settlements*' (MC, 437). Upon arrival, Farrago dispenses with his usual sermons and recourse to classical knowledge. Instead, he gags the Latin schoolmaster, mobilises the brute force of his impromptu army, and subdues the people through fear. Armed with truncheons, clubs and logs, they encounter 'no resistance', for as the narrator remarks, the 'wattles and hearts of oak have a great tendency to procure submission' (MC, 636; 637).

Having invaded and colonised the new settlement, Farrago is 'elected governor of the new state' and it isn't long before he takes the title of 'his excellency' and

---

31   Jefferson, *Writings*, ed. Merrill D. Peterson (New York, 1984), p. 1361.
32   Watts, *Writing and Postcolonialism in the Early Republic* (Charlottesville and London, 1998), p. 48.

starts holding 'levees' in the style of European royalty (MC, 555; 659). So it is that the self-professed republican of Part I shamelessly adopts the power-seeking, power-keeping strategies of Old World imperialism. The political philosophy of Montesquieu had cemented the popular theory that 'only a small homogeneous society whose interests were essentially similar could properly sustain a republican government';[33] as Farrago accompanies his westward advance with an ideological retreat from republicanism, the imperial tenor of his governorship betrays an underlying fear that territorial expansion will bring about the downfall of republicanism. No longer the comical, ineffectual outsider, Farrago is now compared to the French Emperor, another soldier turned statesman responsible for the overthrow of a nascent republic. Before long, we are told, 'the words aristocracy were muttered', 'the people began to talk of his resembling Bonaparte', and 'there were those who threw out hints that he had an understanding with that emperor' (MC, 660; 636; 637). Even the Captain begins to grow 'uneasy under this usurped authority'—uneasy enough to deny that he speaks French, that is, though not uneasy enough to relinquish his position of power (MC, 636). And while he claims to have spoken French by accident, imitating the unfamiliar sounds of a horse-carrier in 'the most perfect simplicity of mind' (MC, 637), readers will recall the 'several weeks' that he spent with a French aristocrat at the end of Part I, deconstructing the arguments of 'Rights of Man' and conversing 'chiefly in the French language, which the Captain spoke very well' (MC, 312; 311). Nor is this the first time that the Captain's professed 'simplicity' has come under suspicion. An unnamed member of the settlement, identified only by his brown wig, has already suggested that Farrago's eccentricity 'might be a disguise to conceal his views; a masque of simplicity the better to introduce monarchy' (MC, 508). Of course, there is no reason to give this particular voice from the crowd either more or less credence than any other voice raised in the text—the narrator's included—for *Modern Chivalry* is defiantly polyphonic, its numerous crowd scenes enabling bit-part players to deliver some of the best lines in the book, while those who speak loudest and longest (notably Captain Farrago and the book's narrator, named on the title page as H. H. Brackenridge) swing unpredictably between sense and nonsense, insight and stupidity.

While it is plausible to read *Modern Chivalry*, like *Female Quixotism*, as a cautionary tale, one that reads post-Revolutionary France as a bewitching and insinuating 'glass' in which America can 'read her own distorted likeness'[34] and gaze upon her own potential fate, locating any reliable viewpoint or authoritative voice proves impossible in *Modern Chivalry*, with its polemical tone and its shifting ironic stance. As Christopher Looby has remarked, 'Brackenridge modeled his narrative closely on Cervantes', and 'the elusiveness of his purposes—their endless ironic displacement—is fundamentally true to Cervantes'.[35] We see precisely such displacement during the episode where Farrago

---

33   Gordon S. Wood, *The Creation of the American Republic, 1776–1787* (Chapel Hill, 1969), p. 356.

34   Bill Christophersen, *The Apparition in the Glass: Charles Brockden Brown's American Gothic* (London, 1993), p. 12.

35   Christopher Looby, *Voicing America: Language, Literary Form, and the Origins of the United States* (Chicago and London, 1996), pp. 242–3.

meets his biographer, the 'mad poet who had been engaged in travestying his travels' (MC, 386). The author has become a character in his own text, and a crazy one at that, holed up in an asylum for his own security, an anthropological curiosity who finds himself observed and judged by his own fictional creation. Turning the tables on 'H. H. Brackenridge', the educated and enlightened narrator who is so fond of making his own 'observations' and recording his own 'reflections', the episode re-casts him as a 'reasoning maniac' and throws a question mark over the sanity, never mind the seriousness, of his lengthy disquisitions.

*

For the most part, British authors were eager to strip Quixote of his Spanish traits and assimilate him into British society. Fielding's *Don Quixote in England* (1734), the most literal of the literary imports, sees the 'original' Don arrived in England in search of the 'plenteous stock of monsters' that reputedly inhabit the island.[36] His acculturation is seamless: no sooner has the knight set up house in a provincial inn than he is invited to stand for parliament, to become a representative of the English people, while his squire declares himself 'so fond of the English roast beef and strong beer, that I don't intend ever to set my foot in Spain again'.[37] Sir George Warrington and Smollett's Sir Launcelot Greaves both embody the tendency of English fiction to acculturate and domesticate the Quixote, to transform the bag of bones who wanders the highways of La Mancha from a man on the road to a gentleman on the road to marriage, an amiable, high-born and benevolent member of the English establishment. There are significant exceptions, however: Hays's female Quixote, Emma Courtney, an ardent disciple of radical philosophy and romantic fiction, repents of her radical ways but remains a spinster nonetheless, ending her days 'as if in an immense desert, a solitary outcast from society'.[38]

Emma's singular fate is more in line with the transatlantic Quixotes of early-republic fiction: Tenney's Dorcasina, Brackenridge's Farrago, Royall Tyler's Updike Underhill and Washington Irving's Peter Stuyvesant are all unmarried when their stories come to a close. Time and again, American Quixotes stand alone and on the edge; with neither family nor profession to confer upon them a meaningful place in society, they are counter-cultural figures who most frequently inhabit the geographical and ideological margins of American society. And while British authors for the most part do their best to uphold the dignity and authority of their Quixotic characters, Brackenridge, Tyler, Tenney and Irving reveal a catalogue of faltering heroes and glorious failures, whose alienated and externalised perspectives on the society they inhabit recalls Montesquieu's *Persian Letters* (1721) or Irving's own 'Letters from Mustapha Rub-A-Dub Keli Khan' (1807–8), so disoriented are they by their experiences in the new republic and so effectively do their experiences de-bunk the myth of Enlightenment progress.

---

36   Fielding, *Don Quixote in England*, in *Plays and Poems, IV*, in *The Complete Works of Henry Fielding* (16 vols, London, 1903), vol. 11, pp. 5–71 (p. 67).

37   Fielding, *Don Quixote in England*, p. 25.

38   Hays, p. 163.

The Algerine Captive, a fictional autobiography of failed Yankee teacher-turned-doctor, Updike Underhill, provides the most striking instance of Quixotic alienation and critique. Disillusioned with the harsh realities of life in a New England school, Updike re-trains as a doctor, '*mounteth his Nag*' '*and setteth out full speed*' in quest of '*Practice, Fame, and Fortune*'.[39] When Benjamin Franklin makes a cameo appearance in Chapter 23, Tyler's ambitious young narrator 'anticipate[s] much pleasure' from an interview with 'one, who, from small beginnings, by the sole exertion of native genius and indefatigable industry, had raised himself to the pinnacle of politics and letters; a man who, from an humble printer's boy, had elevated himself to be the desirable companion of the great ones of the earth' (AC, I, 129–30). But Benjamin Franklin—a by-word for self-improvement and a transatlantic icon of Enlightenment progress—is most pointedly all that Updike tries and fails to be, with Updike's own American experience giving the lie to the rhetoric of Franklin's *Information to Those who would Remove to America* (1784). Referring in particular to 'the professions of divinity, law, and physic', Franklin's pamphlet assures an English readership that strangers 'are by no means excluded from exercising those professions; and the quick increase of inhabitants every where gives them a chance of employ, which they have in common with the natives'.[40] According to this proselytising pamphlet, everybody is welcome in America 'because there is room enough for them all'.[41] But while Franklin's *Autobiography* bears out such optimism with its author's own success story, Updike's autobiography disproves and discredits Franklin's *Information*. Despite his 'own acquirements and the celebrity of [his] preceptor' (AC, I, 105), Tyler's newly qualified doctor encounters an overcrowded, inhospitable America, where medical jobs are few and far between. One New England township already boasts '*a learned, a cheap, a safe, and a musical Doctor*' (AC, I, 107), and in 'sea-ports' up and down the coast, 'the business was engrossed by men of established practice and eminence' (AC, I, 141). Nor does 'the interior country' present a more likely proposition, for Updike writes that here, the people 'could not distinguish or encourage merit. The gains were small, and tardily collected' (AC, I, 141). In debt and out of work, Updike Underhill feels compelled to take the post of surgeon on a slaving ship bound for Africa. In short, while the self-made Franklin writes pamphlets encouraging removal to America, Tyler's financially undone doctor is forced to remove from America, squeezed out of the USA by a dearth of opportunity and a growing sense of personal failure.

The talismanic names of Franklin, Witherspoon, Moyes, Raynal and Buffon resonate through Volume One of *The Algerine Captive*, creating an atmosphere charged with the energies and possibilities of Enlightenment. Yet Updike's America turns out to be a hostile environment for the realisation of Enlightenment principles. When Updike '*inspects the Museum at Harvard College*' he finds only a few

---

39   Tyler, *The Algerine Captive; or, The Life and Adventures of Doctor Updike Underhill, Six Years a Prisoner Among the Algerines*, ed. Jack B. Moore (2 vols, London, 1802; repr. Gainesville, FL, 1967), vol. 1, p. 104. Future references are prefixed by AC and referred to in parentheses.

40   Franklin, *Information to Those who would Remove to America* (London, 1794), p. 6.

41   Ibid., p. 10.

'wretched bauble specimens' (AC, I, 102–3), and wherever he goes, he '*encountereth Folly, Ignorance, Impudence, Imbecillity* [sic]*, and Quacks*' (AC, I, 107). Education is undervalued and frequently inappropriate, while scholarship is mocked and invariably misunderstood. Medical practice is dominated by self-serving impostors who easily play on the superstitious prejudices of their patients, and the brutal realities of the slave-journey originate here, with the skills of surgeon only valued insofar as they augment and assist the 'infamous cruel commerce' of chattel slavery (AC, I, 166). In order to realise his professional potential, witness enlightened debate and experience universal benevolence, Updike has to journey across the Atlantic, and not to London either—here he finds only a drunken and opinionated Paine making a less than distinguished cameo appearance—but to the allegedly benighted kingdom of Algiers. It is here, during his stint as an American slave, that he finds sympathetic friends from within the Muslim community and builds a lucrative medical practice. 'The first amputation' he performs attracts a crowd of 'principal physicians', and Tyler's ambitious young surgeon recalls how 'my friend the mollah came to congratulate me on my success, and spread my reputation wherever he visited' (AC, II, 75–6). In New England, Updike observes ironically that a successful doctor might aspire at most to bestow the 'great fortune' of 'one hundred pounds' at the time of his death (AC, I, 105–6); as a doctor in North Africa, the learned slave is soon able to raise a ransom of one *thousand* dollars, and believes that had he 'conformed to their faith, beyond a doubt [he] might have acquired immense riches' (AC, II, 84). Indeed, by Chapter 13, Updike declares that 'my circumstances were now so greatly ameliorated, that if I could have been assured of returning to my native country in a few years, I should have esteemed them eligible' (AC, II, 74).

Nor was Tyler the only American author using an Algerine captivity to reflect upon the double standards of the new republic. In her preface to *Slaves In Algiers* (1794), Susanna Haswell Rowson attempts to de-politicise her play by omitting any reference to international conflict and instead positioning the piece within the realm of Quixotic literature. '*Some part of the plot is taken from the Story of the Captive, related by Cervantes, in his inimitable Romance of Don Quixote, the rest is entirely the offspring of fancy*', she insists, declaring that her '*chief aim has been, to offer to the Public a Dramatic Entertainment, which, while it might excite a smile, or call forth the tear of sensibility, might contain no one sentiment, in the least prejudicial, to the moral or political principles of the government under which I live.*'[42] But Rowson's somewhat heavy-handed disclaimer returns to haunt the closing moments of the play: renouncing 'the law of retaliation' and refusing to enslave her former master (the Dey of Algiers), Rowson's liberated American heroine makes a declaration of universal independence: 'By the Christian law, no man should be a slave,' she proclaims. 'Let us assert our own prerogative, be free ourselves, but let us not throw on another's neck, the chains we scorn to wear.' Furthermore, 'Tho' a woman', Rowson is determined to 'plead the Rights of Man', and *Slaves in Algiers* is as strong a critique of female disempowerment as it is of black slavery.[43]

---

42 Rowson, *Slaves in Algiers; or, A Struggle for Freedom* (Philadelphia, 1794), ii.
43 Rowson, pp. 70 [2].

In *The Algerine Captive*, Updike's journey is a geographical one, to the margins of the known African world; in Irving's *A History of New York*, pseudonymous author Diedrich Knickerbocker takes his readers back in time, to the margins of known American history, when New York was New Amsterdam and representatives of the Dutch East India Company governed the colony. And while both narratives revolve around international conflict—between America and Algiers in the case of *The Algerine Captive* and between the British and the Dutch in *A History of New York*—neither care to discuss the American Revolution. For observers at the time and commentators since, the War of Independence was a defining moment of Enlightenment progress, securing America's release from its self-incurred tutelage, to paraphrase Immanuel Kant's definition of Enlightenment. But while histories, novels, plays, and paintings of the period repeatedly conjure up the ghost of the Revolution to instruct the rising generation in the ways of republicanism, *The Algerine Captive* and *A History of New York* stubbornly refuse to remember the event, occluding overt references to the War and effectively initiating an unspoken and devious strategy of selective amnesia. Despite turning eighteen during the War of Independence, and despite the military pedigree of the Underhill line—the family 'heir loom' is even 'a long-barrelled gun', which 'had perhaps killed Indians on Long Island' (AC, I, 80)—Updike doesn't even consider a career in the army. In 1782, he is busy courting Boston belles with 'Greek heroics' (AC, I, 75), and by 1785 he has completed his medical studies without so much as mentioning the Revolution.

Diedrich Knickerbocker likewise overlooks the War of Independence, rescuing long-forgotten figures from the 'insatiable maw of oblivion' while newer, fresher memories, bleeding still like unhealed wounds, go unacknowledged in his text.[44] When occasional references to the Revolution do crop up in Irving's *History*, they are invariably oblique and belittling. The Independent Columbian Hotel, where Diedrich writes his narrative, offers one such example. It may proclaim American independence, but the nationalistic grandeur of its name belies a rather shabbier reality. Seth Handaside's establishment is such 'a very small house' that he is 'a little puzzled' where to put his guest; his is a down town hotel that offers no sanctuary from the unpleasant landmarks of an overcrowded and under-sanitised city. The Dutchman's room commands 'a very pleasant view of the new grounds on the Collect, together with the rear of the Poor house and Bridewell and the full front of the Hospital' (HNY, 373), suggesting that the outlook for the newly independent America—from Diedrich's vantage-point at least—was not so promising.

Allusions to 1776, when they do appear, are marked by an uneasy ambivalence in the text, for Diedrich Knickerbocker is decidedly inconsistent where his satirical targets are concerned, and he juxtaposes a longing to venerate with an irrepressible desire to humiliate the patriarchs. Peter the Headstrong, for example, is described by Diedrich as a 'lion hearted, generous spirited, obstinate, old "seventy six" of a governor' (HNY, 567). The sentiment is ostensibly a generous one, but by drawing our attention to the 'quotedness' of the term, the inverted commas raise a skeptical

---

44   Irving, *A History of New York From the Beginning of the World to the End of the Dutch Dynasty*, in *History, Tales and Sketches*, ed. James W. Tuttleton (Cambridge, 1983), pp. 363–720 (p. 381). Future references are prefixed by HNY and referred to in parentheses.

eyebrow at the figure of speech that has become a cliché, an uncritical approbation of figures from the founding era. Diedrich is usually more than happy to omit inverted commas in order to ventriloquise the words and ideas of others, but both here in Book V and again in Book VI, he uses inverted commas to de-mythologise Revolutionary leaders, distancing himself from the 'enlightened mob' who indulge in an uncritical hero-worship of the founding fathers:

> Nor must I neglect to mention a number of superannuated, wrong headed old burghers, who had come over when boys, in the crew of the *Goede Vrouw,* and were held up as infallible oracles by the enlightened mob. To suppose a man who had helped to discover a country, did not know how it ought to be governed was preposterous in the extreme. It would have been deemed as much a heresy, as at the present day to question the political talents, and universal infallibility of our old 'heroes of '76'—and to doubt that he who had fought for a government, however stupid he might naturally be, was not competent to fill any station under it. (HNY, 670)

Also published in 1809, Joel Barlow's July the Fourth 'Oration' discoursed upon the merits of 'the illustrious relics' who had fought for American independence, declaring that those 'whitened locks that still wave among us are titles to our veneration'.[45] Washington Irving was not so sure. His acerbic indictment of the old 'heroes of '76' voices an increasing sense of resentment as Revolutionary leaders continued to cling tenaciously to power in the nineteenth century. According to Jefferson's characteristically precise calculations, the tenure of a generation lasted only for nineteen years, a duration that would see the patriots of '76 stepping aside as early as 1795.[46] But even as Irving was writing *A History of New York*, James Madison was elected to the presidency and another father, this time the so-called 'Father of the Constitution', was continuing where Jefferson had left off. On one level, at least, *A History of New York* dares to suggest that the founding fathers have lived too long, stunting the growth of the new republic and prolonging the filial dependence of the post-Revolutionary generation.

During the politically and culturally formative years of the early republic, Don Quixote proves himself an indispensable figure when it comes to critiquing the unrealisable ideals of America's founding fathers. In 1784, Immanuel Kant had suggested that 'the motto of enlightenment' was 'have courage to use your own reason!'[47] There are many ways in which American authors effectively use the figure of Quixote as a vehicle for contributing to enlightened debate about the constitutional dilemmas and political contradictions of the nascent republic, reminding their readers that the 'modern' American world does not resemble what they have read about it. Yet what Quixotic fictions most delight in representing is enlightened debate run riot: Quixotic commentators repeatedly contradict or appear to forget their own opinions; they take their arguments beyond reasonable lengths and to

---

45   *The Works of Joel Barlow*, eds William K. Bottorff and Arthur L. Ford (2 vols, Gainesville, FL, 1970), vol. 1, p. 526.

46   Jefferson, *Writings*, p. 961.

47   Kant, 'What is Enlightenment?' in *The Enlightenment: A Sourcebook and Reader*, ed. Paul Hyland (London and New York, 2003), pp. 54–8 (p. 54).

illogical extremes, inverting the sense—though not the spirit—of Kant's 'motto of enlightenment', having the courage to abuse their own reason in order to critique ideological certitude and resist dialectical closure.

Chapter 7

Placing *The Power of Sympathy*: Transatlantic Sentiments and the 'First American Novel'

James Chandler*

Some novels are born great, some achieve greatness, and others have greatness thrust upon them. William Hill Brown's *The Power of Sympathy*—a rather slight, youthful, and derivative performance—is not a part of any 'great tradition' or canon of 'great books'. Whatever status it has in literary history stems mainly from the circumstances of its early reception, when it came to be recognised as the first novel to be published after the ratification of the US Constitution. The timing of its appearance has been its main claim to fame. Nonetheless, for the topic of transatlantic enlightenment, Hill's novel is worth a closer look. As a novel of sentiment, it speaks directly to what the editors of this volume have described as its central problem. This is, they say, the challenge of reconciling the two diverging recent views of enlightenment: on the one hand, a set of enlightenments understood as locally bounded phenomena (French, Scottish, American); on the other hand, enlightenment as a broadly transatlantic phenomenon, with features displayed in common around much of the so-called Atlantic Rim. 'Sentiment' itself—like its close cousin 'opinion'—developed into an eighteenth-century concept that to a degree reflected this double valence. Sentiments, like opinions, are local, personal. But sentiment, like opinion, is sharable throughout nations and publics, even between nations and publics. *The Power of Sympathy* self-consciously stages its narrative performance not only in respect to the British sentimental novel but also in respect to the British sentimental novel's *relation* to its continental counterpart. This is a part of the novel's claim on our attention here.

Beyond this question of the geography of enlightenment, however, there is the important fact that *The Power of Sympathy* was published on a date that places it at two *historical* thresholds, that of the US Constitution and the French Revolution. This means that in addition to negotiating the problem of enlightenment's cultural contexts, Brown's novel can be seen to bridge the differences between enlightenment and romanticism. Here again, the novel's self-conscious relation to the sentimental movement is a matter of signal importance, for there is no movement that more insistently complicates too-ready distinctions between 'enlightened' and 'romantic' than the one we associate with the sympathetic imagination of Adam Smith and the idiosyncratic sensibility of Laurence Sterne.

 * I would like to thank Susan Manning and Eric Slauter for extremely helpful suggestions to improve this essay, and my graduate student assistants Mollie Godfrey and Andrew Yale for their help in readying it for publication.

New Literary Histories

It wasn't so long ago that the history of the novel in English for the eighteenth and nineteenth centuries was written as a drama in three acts. These were of equal duration, but unequal importance. The first six or seven decades of the eighteenth century—the period of Defoe, Swift, Richardson, Fielding and Sterne—was the age of the novel's heroic inventors. The last six or seven decades of the nineteenth century—the period of Dickens, Thackeray, the Brontës, Eliot, Gaskell and Hardy— was the period of the novel's mature achievement. The middle period—from, say, the death of Sterne in 1768 to the publication of *The Pickwick Papers* in 1837—took shape as something of an embarrassing lull in the story. True, this period produced an indisputably great novelist, Jane Austen. True, too, it also produced Sir Walter Scott, also surely a great novelist, though his work later came to seem juvenile, and eventually Modernism's very emblem of obsolescence.[1] Otherwise, apart from the anomaly of Mary Shelley's *Frankenstein* (itself accorded academic respect only recently), the standard view was that the novel-reading world that Scott came to dominate in his time had itself been consumed in questionable genres such as the gothic novel, the regional tale, the didactic narrative, and of course the sentimental novel (itself the legacy of Laurence Sterne, the last great inventor-hero of Act 1). Literary history of the period from 1770 to 1830 was preoccupied—and saw that age, the so-called Romantic age, as preoccupied—with poetry, especially lyric poetry, and with the way in which poetry was accorded pride of place in the realm by its own poets and critics.

The last couple of decades in literary studies have rewritten that drama, dramatically. Some standard conceptions of the Romantic age as a period have come under challenge, among them the notion that lyric poets—especially that six poets, all male, all English, in exactly two generations—should represent its practices and values. The study of the novel in this period has seen a veritable explosion of interest—in many kinds of writers and in many kinds of fiction—and the result has been a rebalancing of critical attention in the history of the novel more broadly.

The Gothic novel was perhaps the first to be rehabilitated, but that effort was soon followed by intensive revaluation of the other subgenres. Take the case of Maria Edgeworth, a novelist who used the regional, the didactic, and the sentimental in her work. Her four remarkable tales of Ireland around the time of the Union— written between 1798 and 1816—have won enormous new respect in many quarters. Edgeworth's novels are suddenly back in print in readily available editions. Further, according the status of 'intellectual' to writers like Edgeworth meant that their own intellectual contexts needed proper recovery. In Edgeworth's case, a recovery of her connection to the Scots intellectual tradition has been especially important. A similar story of critical and historical recovery could be told about Edgeworth's Irish rival, Lady Morgan, about her Scottish counterparts, John Galt, James Hogg, and Scott himself. And it could be told about a number of women writers suddenly

---

1   As we see in Virginia Woolf's *To The Lighthouse*, where Mrs. Ramsay understands that her husband is reading Scott's *The Antiquary* as a way of coming to terms with his own professional extinction.

back on the map: Elizabeth Inchbald and Mary Hays, for example. I would say that no single mode or subgenre has gained more from the revaluation of the last twenty years than the sentimental novel, about which there is now, it seems, a small academic industry.

All of this will be relatively familiar to historians of British literature who work in these periods. Just as familiar to Americanists will be the claim that something similar happened in US literary history for that period. The early American novel had long laboured under a double embarrassment. It was considered jejune, inchoate—too young and unformed to be of much use or value. It was also considered derivative of already dubious British fiction writing in the period. Even as late as the early Hawthorne, we have the case of a writer whose first novel, *Fanshawe* (1828) appeared to be such a slavish imitation of Scott, even to Hawthorne himself, that Hawthorne attempted to buy up the first run to keep the book off the market. A somewhat earlier, but still as serious and mature a figure as James Fenimore Cooper, writing thirty years into the Republic, was dismissed by many early readers (though not by Balzac) and certainly by some later readers, as a failed transplantation of Scott's new breed of historical novel to North America. Before Cooper? There was Charles Brockden Brown, who for some could boast no greater claim than bringing Ann Radcliffe's gothic of the 'explained supernatural' to the banks of the Schuykill River in Philadelphia. And beyond that, a host of obscure sentimental narratives that had been out of print since the nineteenth century.

Today, however, thanks to some of the same kinds of changes that led to the reconfiguration of British fiction, this situation has also changed dramatically. Even American fiction of the 1790s now is a subject of serious investigation. In addition to Cathy Davidson's 'Early American Women Writers' project, many titles are now out in standard paperback format. Charles Brockden Brown's novels are very much back in print. And the sentimental novel in America is enjoying the same kind of attention as has lately been lavished on its British counterpart. Among the so-called sentimental 'seduction novels' of the 1790s alone, Penguin published Susanna Rowson's *Charlotte Temple* and *Lucy Temple* in a single edition in 1991. And they have more recently issued a combined edition that includes Hannah Webster Foster's *The Coquette*.

My subject here is the other novel that Penguin recently reissued with Foster's *The Coquette*: William Hill Brown's *The Power of Sympathy*. I single this one out for several related reasons. The first—as mentioned at the outset— is that it has something of a special claim in literary history, having long been recognised as 'the first American novel'. It is now quite standard for scholarly commentators to accord it this distinction, and critical recognition of it as such can be traced back to the late-nineteenth century. Nor is the claim merely a retroactive one. The book's first publisher, Isaiah Thomas, advertised it as 'the first American novel' when it appeared.[2] Yet in spite of the boast, or perhaps because of it, the novel constitutes itself in relation to European writings, especially British writings. It thus affords a chance to examine transatlantic connections in a particularly marked case, and

---

2   Cathy N. Davidson, *Revolution and the Word: The Rise of the Novel in America* (New York, 1986), p. 90.

it might—though this remains a matter of speculation—be taken to exemplify an emergent, distinctively American brand of sentimental narrative, one feature of which is tonal lability. While derivative of Sterne, it anticipates the curiosities we find three decades later in a writer like Washington Irving.

Set in America, *The Power of Sympathy* is in fact a novel in which we find one of the earliest published instances of the term 'transatlantic' itself. The first listing in the *OED* is by John Wilkes in 1779, and the first *American* listing is by Thomas Jefferson in *Notes on the State of Virginia* (1785). In Brown's novel, the context is a letter from the widow Mrs. Eliza Holmes, one of three dispensers of wisdom in the book, to her protégée Myra Harrington. Apropos of the culture of the British Blue-Stockings, Mrs. Holmes opines:

> I am sensible of the ridicule sometimes levelled at those who are called learned ladies… . This ridicule is evidently a *transatlantick* idea, and must have been imbibed from the source of some *English* Novel or Magazine.[3]

There is an ambiguity in the notion of the 'transatlantic idea'. In *Notes on the State of Virginia*, Jefferson uses 'trans-Atlantick' in contradistinction to 'cis-Atlantick'.[4] But the distinction is not quite symmetrical. For Mrs. Holmes, the phrase clearly means an idea from the other side. But since her very citing of it means that it has made the crossing, it is to be distinguished not only from the cis-Atlantick but also from those ideas that do not make the crossing, that merely are, in this case, 'English'.

It is a problem that emerges naturally in an age preoccupied with the new Sternean subgenre of the *Sentimental Journey*, the journey in sentiment. Jefferson himself carried Sterne's book with him on his own travels and cited it often. He also, in my view, understood it well. To his friend Robert Skipwith he wrote on August 3, 1771: 'We neither know nor care whether Laurence Sterne really went to France, whether he was there accosted by the poor Franciscan, at first rebuked him unkindly, and gave him a peace offering; or whether the whole be not a fiction. In either case we are equally sorrowful at the rebuke, and secretly resolve we will never do so; we are pleased with the subsequent atonement, and view with emulation a soul candidly acknowledging its fault, and making a just reparation.'[5] Extending Jefferson's point, we may say that the very idea of the sentimental journey, with its implicit notion of virtual movement by means of imaginative sympathy, is closely connected with the elusive titular theme of Brown's book. What and how and why does sympathy's 'power' enable it to 'move'?

One may now situate the problem of Brown's novel in relation to the conjunction of fields addressed by this collection. On the one hand, the special relevance of this

---

3   William Hill Brown, *The Power of Sympathy* [1789] (New York, 1996), p.56. Further references to this work given in text.

4   Thomas Jefferson, *Notes on the State of Virginia* (London, 1787), p. 107.

5   Julian P. Boyd, *et al.*, eds, *The Papers of Thomas Jefferson* (33 vols to date, Princeton, 1950), 1:79. For a fuller discussion of the reception of Sterne's work in America, see Lodwick Hartley, 'The Dying Soldier and the Love-lorn Virgin: Notes on Sterne's Early Reception in America', in *The Winged Skull: Papers from the Laurence Sterne Bicentenary Conference*, eds. Arthur H. Cash and John M. Stedmond (Kent, 1971), pp. 159–69.

analysis for Transatlantic Studies as an emergent cultural field lies in the way in which the 'first American novel' might be said to define both its generic status as novel and its cultural status as 'American' in relation to 'transatlantic ideas'. On the other hand, the relevance of this to ongoing work in Scottish enlightenment studies lies in the particular transatlantic idea that the book enshrines in its title. Stuart Tave's still valuable study of the theory and practice of humour in the eighteenth century nicely notes this later connection. While notions of the sympathetic imagination had been broached and bruited in the seventeenth century, it was, he says, 'under the leadership of the Scottish philosophers of the eighteenth century, Hume and especially Adam Smith and his successors, that sympathy became an essential force in both ethical action and aesthetic creation'.[6] It is now critically accepted that sympathy underwent serious conceptual development in the hands of Scottish theorists of the moral sentiments. I like Tave's formulation, though, because of his specific suggestion that with the Scots, sympathy becomes 'an essential force'. (In his recent book *American Sympathy*, Caleb Crain gestures in the same direction: 'For a century and a half [presumably from the early eighteenth to the late nineteenth centuries] sympathy had the force of a biological fact.'[7] As I'll be suggesting, though, Brown's book, which Crain strangely neglects, metaphorises this force in a wide range of ways other than the biological).

The phrase 'The Power of Sympathy' is resonant throughout the novel, and its full connotative range is strongly registered by nearly all the book's letter-writing characters. It is registered explicitly in specific comments and implicitly in bizarre shifts of tone, and disorienting moments of ambiguity and ambivalence. It is a puzzling book, and it certainly poses more questions than can be settled here. Still, finding the right way to ask questions of this new body of work on both sides of the Atlantic seems to be in order at this moment in literary studies, and finding new ways of addressing 'identification' may be especially germane for issues of 'cultural identity' in this period of the aftermath of the Anglo-Scottish Union—and, subsequently, the American War of Independence.

What, then, does it mean to think of sympathy as a certain force or power? What are the implications for human agency in thinking of sympathy this way? What does the notion of sympathy as a power have to do with the central role of 'reflection' in the sentimental school of thought, and in the novels that emerged alongside it? These are questions that Brown's book puts before us. They are questions, it might be argued, that have special relevance for the land of Harriet Beecher Stowe, who cited Sterne as a model for *Uncle Tom's Cabin*, and, more relevant to Brown, for Thomas Jefferson, who, as Garry Wills has shown, couched his Declaration of Independence in sentimental terms derived from the Scottish Enlightenment.[8] Not only was Sterne Jefferson's favorite novelist; his favorite poet was James Macpherson's Ossian.

---

6   Stuart M. Tave, *The Amiable Humorist* (Chicago, 1960), pp. 202–3.

7   Caleb Crain, *American Sympathy: Men, Friendship, and Literature in the New Nation* (New Haven, 2001), p. 4.

8   Garry Wills, *Inventing America: Jefferson's Declaration of Independence* (New York, 1978), pp. 259–319.

The First American Novel

The Power of Sympathy is an epistolary novel, and for his cast of letter-writing characters, Brown gives us two sets of young lovers but doesn't tell us much about them. At the start of the book, Mr. Worthy is already engaged to Myra Harrington. Her brother, a friend of Worthy's, has a romantic interest in her friend Harriot Fawcet. (The onomastics—'Harriot'/'Harrington'—seem meant to work as a mnemonic aide.) They write most of their letters from Boston. Apart from the two pairs of lovers, there is another trio of characters who live at and write from the rural retreat of Belleview. These are the Rev. and Mrs. Holmes, and their son's widow, Eliza Holmes, the author of the letter about the Blue-Stockings I quoted above.

The main line of the story can be briefly sketched. The novel opens with a letter written by young Harrington to Worthy, to the effect that he has met a young 'charmer' he means to seduce. Dissuaded by Worthy and discouraged by Harriot herself, Harrington pursues a more chaste courtship with Harriot, to whom he eventually proposes marriage, in spite of his father's vague protests. On the eve of their nuptials, Harrington receives an anonymous letter saying that he must not marry Harriot because she is in fact his sister—half-sister, as it turns out. At this point we are given, as an interpolation, the last of the several seduction vignettes, which proves to be the only vignette directly relevant to the plot. This vignette, the so-called 'History of Maria', tells the story of how, years earlier, the Hon. Mr Harrington, young Harrington's father, a married man, seduced and abandoned Maria Fawcet, Harriet's mother, who was left to wander the roads of New England. After Maria was found and taken in by Rev Holmes and his wife, he appealed for explanation and redress to the Hon. Mr Harrington, who wrote back a letter acknowledging his guilt but disowning responsibility for the victims. Maria Fawcet lived on only a short while, in a state of extreme confusion, and after she died, the Holmeses placed her infant daughter Harriot in the care of a guardian, one Mrs Francis. Back in the novel's present tense, both Harriot and young Harrington themselves lapse into fatal states of confusion on hearing the news of their close kinship. Harriot dies within weeks of the revelation. Harrington, over the course of many letters to Worthy, and very much in the manner of Goethe's Werther, repeatedly threatens to take his own life. Worthy remains inexplicably absent for this critical period, and when he finally reaches Boston, he is unable to see Harrington before the latter has shot himself, having left behind a copy of *The Sorrows of Young Werther* at his bedside.

As this summary suggests, the plot is not exactly Fieldingesque in its construction. Yet the novel has complicating and interesting dimensions. Indeed its real action occurs less at the level of plot than at what might loosely be called that of 'sentimental psychology'. After the lovers find out that they are related as siblings, for example, very little actually happens apart from the death of Harriot by grief and of Harrington by suicide. Their emotional response to the discovery, however, is dilated upon in extensive detail. Thus, in her long letter to Harrington after hearing the news, Harriot plays out an obsessive preoccupation with what now seems to be the double-sidedness of their connection:

Must I then forget the endearments of the lover, and call you by the name of brother? But does our friendship remain upon this foundation? Is this all that unites us? And has there subsisted nothing more tender—a sentiment more voluntary in our hearts? My feelings affirm that there has. At the hour of our first interview I felt the passion kindle in my breast: Insensible of my own weakness, I indulged its increasing violence and delighted in the flame that fired my reason and my senses. Do you remember our walks, our conversations, our diversions? (p. 86)

Two pages into the letter, she is still rehearsing old scenes with ever more alarming anxieties about their new meaning:

When you pressed my cheek with the kiss of love, of fraternal affection, what meant its conscious glow? What meant the ebullition of my veins, the disorder of my nerves, the intoxication of my brain, the blood that mantled in my heart? My hand trembled, and every object seemed to swim before my doubtful view—Amidst the struggle of passion, how could I pronounce the word—how could I call you by the title of brother. True—I tried to articulate the sound, but it died upon my tongue, and I sank motionless into your arms. (p. 87)

It was not necessary, in terms of the plot, to have Harriot write a letter at this point, let alone one with this kind of detail. As commentators have pointed out, much of the narration in the novel is indirect. It seems fair to suppose that the collapse of Harriot could have been handled in the same way. Or if she must be given a letter, even a letter to Harrington, it might well have been made more decorous, even as it suggested her unravelling.

Some such decorous perspective on the events is actually present in the novel, and it is articulated by Worthy in a later letter to Harrington, when Harrington, too, is indulging his imagination about how things went so badly wrong. Worthy's preachy response to his friend concludes with this admonition:

Let us watch over all we do with an eye of scrutiny—the world will not examine the causes that give birth to our actions—they do not weigh the motives of them—they do not consider those things which influence our conduct—but as that conduct is more or less advantageous to society, they deem it madness or wisdom, or folly or prudence— Remember this. (pp. 94–5)

Such a comment only intensifies the question of why the psychological detail in the late letters of Harriot and Harrington remains salient. But the puzzle does not stop here. Worthy, as I have noted, is another advice-giver among the novel's letter writers. A passage like this one is a good example of how the comments of these advice-givers seem problematic precisely in their utterly banal reasonableness. Davidson, the most astute reader this novel has had, probably goes further than anyone in raising the question of the real virtue and value accorded these characters. I tend to agree with her. To be sure, we should be scrupulous about our actions in respect to their being advantageous or otherwise to society. To be sure, it is bootless to get caught up in morbid speculation about what might have been. At the same time, there is something rather chilly about Worthy's response here, and it is not helped by the fact of his unexplained failure to get himself to Boston in time to help his desperate friend in his moment of crisis. Davidson's crisp formulation of the paradox—that Worthy is at once the most authoritative character and the one most subject to satire—grasps something that is not merely localised to his case.

Indeed, the novel itself seems to give the lie to Worthy's worldly sententiousness in its own preoccupation with the workings of emotion. There seems to be no place in Worthy's comment for the very 'power of sympathy' that not only fascinates the novel start to finish, but that also actually fascinates Worthy himself in other moments.

For example, earlier, after he arrives at Belleview from New York, Worthy writes to Myra, with whom he had once visited the place, in glowing terms about the surrounding rural scenes: 'they impress the mind with ideas similar to what we feel in beholding one whom we tenderly esteem', he says. But he then reports that, on making this same observation to Eliza Holmes, she provides him with a deeper analysis: "These are the very scenes", said she, "which your beloved Myra used to praise and admire, and for which you, by a secret sympathy, entertain the same predilection" (p. 30). After Eliza points out that Worthy has also betrayed his attraction to a piece of Myra's embroidery, Worthy acknowledges that the object had interested him but insists he had forgotten it had been done by Myra. He then reports his reflections on turning back to it after this realisation:

> I considered the work as coming from your hand, and was delighted the more with it. A piece of steel that has been rubbed with a loadstone, retains the power of attracting small bodies of iron: So the beauties of this embroidery, springing from your hands, continue to draw my attention, and fill the mind with ideas of the artist. (p. 31)

Since the force of the secret sympathy that draws his attention is likened to a loadstone's operation on iron fillings, this comment does not seem to be about Mesmer's *animal* magnetism, nor about biology more broadly. This makes it seem inanimate. Yet when this force is made less secret, more conscious, it has even more effect. The whole sequence shows a strong interest in what Worthy later denies we should be interested in at all: the 'motives' that lead us to action. And certainly, with its emphasis on the power of beauty, the secret force in question is not reducible to the kind of utilitarian calculus that Worthy advances.

Language of the sort that Worthy and Myra Harrington employ in this scene is used elsewhere by other characters. Indeed, Worthy is here unwittingly echoing an earlier letter in which Harrington had explained how he reformed his intention to seduce Harriot:

> Of all those indescribable things which influence the mind, and which are most apt to persuade—none is so powerful an orator—so feelingly eloquent as beauty—I bow to the all-conquering force of Harriot's eloquence—and what is the consequence?—I am now determined to continue my addresses on a principle the most just, and the most honourable.

> How amiable is that beauty which has its foundation in goodness! (p. 14)

In the phrase, 'that beauty which has its foundation in goodness', the clause might be restrictive or non-restrictive. But if it is restrictive, as it seems to be from the grammar and punctuation, then there is a kind of beauty that does not have its foundation in goodness, and that is presumably less amiable, less conducive to justice, but no less powerful. How then can the power of beauty, as such, be our guide?

In pursuit of clarity on this issue, we might survey all the different kinds of forces and powers that seem to be at work in the book: not just the 'force of eloquence' and 'power of beauty' here, but also the 'force of words' (pp. 31–2), the 'power of imagination' (p. 37), the 'power of charming' (p. 75), 'the power of nature', 'the force of sympathy', and so on. Such an exercise, however, would reveal an array of powers, a *field* of forces, that do not neatly self-categorise in moral terms. How is this field structured or defined in the book? To rework the book's own metaphor: how is it that in claiming 'sympathy' for its moral compass, the novel scatters sympathetic power everywhere, not just in the world's fixed and central pole of orientation?

To make this question even more pointed, we can add a remarkable fact, one duly noted in the criticism about this novel: by the end of the book, the titular force, the 'power of sympathy', has been identified by the novel's characters as at once the cause that enables us to feel for the plight of Harrington and Harriot, *and* the cause of their attraction to each other in the first place. Two different characters in the novel make this connection explicit. Caleb Crain has suggested that 'there is something mysterious about sympathy'—the very idea, as it were. But nowhere is sympathy a more mysterious element than in 'the first American novel'.[9]

The Power of Sympathy as Metafiction

For a long time, what little twentieth-century scholarship there was on *The Power of Sympathy* focused mainly on the question of its authorship. Milton Ellis, whose 1933 article in the journal *American Literature* did much to solidify Brown's claim to authorship, nonetheless went on to say that the novel was 'deservedly forgotten, since it had little except its priority to recommend it'.[10] (With champions like this, who needs detractors?)

The tide turned a bit thirty years ago with an interpretative essay by Robert Arner that argued while Brown did not manage 'to deal satisfactorily with the contradictory power of the emotions as a force equally of damnation and of salvation', the novel was still 'considerably more complex than is commonly thought', since its contradictions 'arise in part from the literary traditions in which the work originated in conflict with the distrust of emotion which Brown seems to have derived from his New England surroundings'.[11]

Arner's attempt at critical generosity probably helped *The Power of Sympathy* to gain readers. What I find less than fully satisfactory about his reading is that it deals

---

9   Crain, *American Sympathy*, p. 2.

10   Milton Ellis, 'The Author of the First American Novel', *American Literature* 4 (1933): 361.

11   Robert D. Arner, 'Sentiment and Sensibility: The Role of Emotion and William Hill Brown's *The Power of Sympathy*', *Studies in American Fiction* 1 (1973): 125, 131.

with the book's 'literary traditions' as if they were merely 'sources' of 'influence'. In other words, it is the kind of reading that makes sense for a slightly later and immensely more popular novel like Susanna Rowson's *Charlotte Temple* (1794), whose texture remains relatively clear of pointed literary echo and allusion.

This, however, is decidedly not the case with *The Power of Sympathy*, whose relation to the tradition of sentimental fiction is anything but unself-conscious. We are not just talking about 'influences' somehow registered in the text, in other words, but about marked allusions. This is a novel in which novel writing and novel reading are debated, and in which specific authors are referenced in a variety of explicit ways. It certainly, in my judgement, lends this book a complexity of interest not available in, say, *Charlotte Temple*. Further, the author who is given greatest prominence in the book is Laurence Sterne, himself a master of allusive reflexivity.

Sterne is, in fact, first invoked by the very character who comments on transatlantic ideas about learned ladies, Eliza Holmes. After Myra Harrington addresses her as a 'Serious sentimentalist' (p. 13), Mrs. Holmes replies to Myra in a characteristically advice-giving mode:

> A great proportion of our happiness depends on our own choice—it offers itself to our taste, but it is the heart that gives it a relish—what at one time, for instance, we think to be humour, is at another disgustful or insipid—so, unless we carry our appetite with us to the treat, we shall vainly wish to make ourselves happy. 'Was I in a desart', says Sterne, 'I would find wherewith in it to call forth my affections—If I could do no better, I would fasten them on some sweet myrtle, or seek some melancholy cypress to connect myself to—I would court their shade and greet them kindly for their protection—If their leaves withered, I would teach myself to mourn, and when they rejoiced, I would rejoice along with them.' (p. 15)

To say that the heart gives relish to the happiness that is offered to our taste is not exactly to say that our happiness largely depends on our own choice. The heart, after all, is not normally thought to be an organ of decision making. Moreover, there seems to be something slightly out of keeping with the upbeat message in this advice given at the conclusion to this letter, where Mrs. Holmes becomes complacent, even misanthropic, in her declaration of retirement from the 'misjudging race' of humanity. This is one reason that, like Worthy, Davidson sees Holmes's character as a mixed affair.

Mrs. Holmes's next epistolary performance, a long two-part letter to Myra, reports a conversation at Belleview about novel reading. The participants, as it happens, are the three didacticists, along with Mrs and Ms Bourn. The main question is the effect of novels on young ladies, and in answer to it, Rev Holmes, who *seems* to carry great moral authority in the novel, pronounces on the influence of bad novels on female readers: 'Novels', he says, 'not regulated on the chaste principles of true friendship, rational love, and connubial duty, appear to me totally unfit to form the minds of women, of friends, or of wives' (p. 21). In response to this unequivocal answer, Mrs Bourn raises a question of her own: 'what rule can be hit upon to make study always terminate to advantage?' This question is not answered, and does not even seem to be grasped by the Rev himself. This surprising sense of balance between the Rev and the otherwise unprepossessing Mrs Bourn is left hanging precariously, though it actually seems to be tipped in Mrs Bourn's favour by Worthy's comments.

The rather unexpected alliance or alignment between Mrs Bourn and Worthy is confirmed later, when the conversation turns Shandean, in more senses than one, and a copy of one of Sterne's books becomes the object of general attention:

> My good father-in-law being so strenuous in proving the eligibility of reading satire, had spun out, what he called his *new idea*, to such a metaphysical nicety, that he unhappily diminished the number of his hearers; for Mrs. Bourn, to whom he directed his discourse, had taken down a book and was reading to herself....
>
> A considerable silence ensued, which Worthy first broke, by asking Mrs. Bourn what book she had in her hand. Every one's attention was alarmed at this important enquiry. Mrs. Bourn, with little difficulty, found the title page, and began to read, '*A Sentimental Journey through France and Italy, by Mr. Yorick*'.
>
> 'I do not like the *title*,' said Miss Bourn.
>
> 'Why, my dear!' apostrophized the mother, 'you are mistaken—it is a very famous book'.
>
> 'Why, my dear!' retorted the daughter, 'It is sentimental—I abominate every thing that is sentimental—it is so unfashionable too'.
>
> 'I never knew before', said Mr. Holmes, 'that wit was subject to the caprice of fashion'.
>
> 'Why "Squire Billy"', returned Miss, 'who is just arrived from the centre of politeness and fashion, says the bettermost genii never read any sentimental books—so you see sentiment is out of date'. (pp. 27–28)

By going out of his way to place the critique of Sterne and the sentimental in the mouth of so unthoughtful and lightweight a character as young Miss Bourn, Brown seems to make an implicit argument in its behalf. And thus, when Brown has Worthy rise to the defense of Sterne and, implicitly, Sterne's influence in the novel, it seems worth taking seriously, in spite of the mock Shandean mode in which he conducts it:

> 'Sentiment out of date!' cries Worthy...taking the book from her mother...'—alas! Poor Yorick'—may thy pages never be soiled by the fingers of prejudice'. He continued this address to the book, as they went out, in the same Shandean tone—'These antisentimentalists would banish thee from the society of all books. Unto what a pitiful size are the race of *readers* dwindled!' (p. 28)

Worthy, we have seen, is himself suspect on other grounds. But what really is the burden of this speech, on Worthy's part or on Brown's? And what is the meaning of this modulation into Sterne's style? What is at stake in this descriptive and performative engagement with Sterne on the part of the characters most given to preaching and most vulnerable to satire? Is there something that we are not seeing and hearing in this passage despite our having eyes and ears?

Certainly Sterne had his enemies in New England. A contributor to the *New England Quarterly* for 1802 supposed that 'few writers have done more injury to morals than Sterne … . Formerly, if a man felt a passion for the wife or mistress of a friend, he was conscious at least, that if he persisted in the pursuit, he was acting wrong; and if the Novel Writer invented such a character, it was to hold him out as an object of detestation and punishment. Now this is so varnished over with delicate attachment and generous sensibility, that the most shocking acts of perfidy and seduction are committed not only without remorse, but with self-complacency …'.[12] But in the ensuing conversation between Eliza and Worthy about the general discussion, the objection to Sterne against which they wish to defend him is rather different. And the playing out of the exchange is performatively weird. This is Eliza's account of it:

> I could not but remark, as we went on, that Miss Bourn had spoken the sentiments of many of her sex;—'and whence', said I to Worthy, 'arises this detestation of books in *some* of us females, and why are *they* enemies to anything that may be called sentiment and conversation: I grant it often happens there is such rapidity of *speeches* that one may be at a loss to distinguish the speakers; but why is there such a calm silence, should an unfortunate sentiment inadvertently—'

> 'I will tell you,' interrupted he, 'You all read, and it is from the books which engage your attention, that you generally imbibe your ideas of the principal subjects discussed in company—now, the books which employ your hours of study, happen to be Novels; and the subjects contained in these Novels are commonly confined to *dress*, *balls*, *visiting*, and the like *edifying* topics; does it not follow that these must be the subjects of your conversation?' (pp. 28–9)

It is hard to know how much to credit the novel's self-consciousness about its relation to the novelistic conventions it makes its own subject here. Worthy's comment, though couched in a rhetoric of reasonableness and logic ('does it not follow …'), is a complete *non sequitur* in respect to the comment it interrupts, partly because it interrupts the comment without seeing it through to its point. One imagines that Eliza's point, when completed, was going to be something like this: A question about why some female readers (like Miss Bourn) oppose sentimental novels is qualified by the acknowledgment that sometimes such novels produce a confusing array of speakers in a conversation, such that they all sound alike. This acknowledgment seems meant to explain some of the resistance one finds to the sentimental novel. Yet this consideration is itself qualified by the further question, in line with the first, about why an inadvertent and unfortunate sentiment should be met with so little in the way of verbal response within the world of a novel. This unfinished thought is difficult to complete coherently, and yet Worthy's comments do not seem to approach a possible interpretation of it. What is the relation between the incoherence of dialogue as posited, on the one hand, and staged, on the other, in this scene?

I would like to turn now to one final set piece scene framed in relation to Sterne's work. In letter 36, the last that Harrington will write before the revelation about his being brother to Harriot, he produces his own impersonation of Sterne's Yorick. It is a long passage, but it needs to be cited in full so that it stands revealed in all of its

---

12 Arner, 'Sentiment', p. 121.

symptomatic peculiarity, so that one can see its complex relation to the complexity of sentimental modes and norms:

> I have just left Harriot—but how have I left her? In tears. I wish I had not gone. Mrs. Francis had intrusted Harriot with some trifling commission—It was not done—she had not had time to perform it. Harriot was reprimanded—Yes! By Heaven—this Mrs. Francis had the insolence to reprimand Harriot in my presence—I was mortified—I walked to the window—my heart was on fire—my blood boiled in my veins—it is impossible to form an idea of the disorder of my nerves—Harriot's were equally agitated—Mrs. Francis saw our confusion and retired— she left me so completely out of temper that I was forced to follow her example. I kissed away the tear from the cheek of Harriot and withdrew to my chamber.
>
> Here let me forget what has passed—my irritability will not permit it—my feelings are too easily set in motion to enjoy long quietness—my nerves are delicately strung; they are now out of tune, and it is a hard matter to harmonize them.
>
> I **feel** *that I have a soul*—and every man of sensibility feels it within himself. I will relate a circumstance I met with in my late travels through South Carolina—I was always susceptible of *touches of nature*.
>
> I had often remarked a female slave pass by my window to a spring to fetch water. She had something in her air superiour to those of her situation—a fire that the damps of slavery had not extinguished.
>
> As I was one day walking behind her, the wind blew her tattered handkerchief from her neck and exposed it to my sight—I asked her the cause of the scar on her shoulder—She answered composedly, and with an earnestness that proved she was not ashamed to declare it—'It is the mark of the whip', said she, and went on with the history of it, without my desiring her to proceed—'my boy, of about ten years old, was unlucky enough to break a glass tumbler—this crime was immediately inquired into—I trembled for the gate of my child, and was thought to be guilty. I did not deny the charge, and was tied up. My former good character availed nothing. Under every affliction, we may receive consolation; and during the smart of the whip, I rejoiced—because I shielded with my body the lash from my child; and I rendered thanks to the best of beings that I was allowed to suffer for him.'
>
> '**Heroically** spoken!' said I, 'may he whom you call the best of beings continue you in the same sentiments—may thy soul be ever disposed to **sympathize** with thy children, and with thy brethren and sisters in calamity—then shall thou feel every circumstance of thy life afford thee satisfaction; and repining and melancholy shall fly from thy bosom—all thy labours will become easy—all thy burdens light, and the yoke of slavery will never gall thy neck.'
>
> I was sensibly relieved as I pronounced these words, and I felt my heart glow with feelings of exquisite delight, as I anticipated the happy time when the sighs of the slave shall no longer expire in the air of freedom. What delightful sensations are those in which the heart is interested! In which it stoops to enter into the little concerns of the most remote ramification of Nature! Let the vain, the giddy, and the proud pass on without deigning to notice them—let them cheat themselves of happiness—these are circumstances which are important only to a sentimental traveller.

Hail *Sensibility*! Sweetener of the joys of life! Heaven has implanted thee in the breasts of his children—to soothe the sorrow of the afflicted—to mitigate the wounds of the stranger who falleth in our way. *Thou* regardest with an eye of pity, those whom *wealth* and *ambition* treat in terms of reproach. Away, ye seekers of power—ye boasters of wealth—ye are the *Levite* and the *Pharisee*, who restrain the hand of charity from the indigent, and turn with indignation from the wayworn son of misery:—But *Sensibility* is the good *Samaritan*, who taketh him by the hand, and consoleth him, and poureth wine and oil into his wounds. Thou art a pleasant companion—a grateful friend—and a *neighbour* to those who are destitute of shelter.—

From thee! Author of Nature! From thee, thou inexhaustible spring of love supreme, floweth this tide of affection and **sympathy**—thou whose tender care extendeth to the least of thy creation—and whose eye is not inattentive even though a sparrow fall to the ground. (pp. 61–2)

This is elegant writing at the level of style, and Isaiah Thomas would include such passages in a 'Beauties of' selection for the *Massachusetts Magazine*, precisely on the model of the many 'Beauties of Sterne' books of the period.[13] But how are we to understand the effusion—the confusion—of Young Harrington's letter, its bizarre turns of sentiment from recollected insult to recollected injury to blessing to self-congratulation? Harrington pointedly echoes a phrase in Sterne's *Sentimental Journey*: 'Sentimental traveller' is the category Yorick identifies himself with in the celebrated taxonomy of travellers with which he begins. And many other crucial allusions to Sterne are present, if only one knew how they added up.[14]

We find some help in another recent book on early American sentimentalism, Julia Stern's *The Plight of Feeling*, a major book-length study of US fiction of the 1790s. *The Power of Sympathy* is not one of her major case studies but it does receive some attention in the set-up of the argument, and this passage in particular is discussed in some detail. Her conclusion is in the mode of critique:

This so-called cathartic revelation about the powers of the sympathetic imagination, the whimsical notion that the slave mother can transcend her degraded station through mental exercise, lightens the burdens of Harrington's heart. Meanwhile, the object of his 'compassion' remains sunk in exactly the situation in which she began.[15]

I would not call this reading incorrect, though we might say it is *merely* correct. Stern recognises that this scene is crucial to Brown's novel—Maria, after all, is the name of Brown's victim, too, as we discover in a late interpolated narrative. Stern suggests that the passage is based on Laurence Sterne's treatment of 'The Captive' in the famous starling chapter of *Sentimental Journey*, and she is satisfied to tar

---

13   'The Beauties of the Power of Sympathy', *Massachusetts Magazine*, 1 (1789): 50–53; this passage appears on p. 51.

14   'I feel that I have a soul', for example, echoes Yorick's 'I am positive I have a soul' (p. 114) in the latter's reflections on the encounter with Maria of Moulines, on which Brown's passage is modeled (see below).

15   Julia A. Stern, *The Plight of Feeling: Sympathy and Dissent in the Early American Novel* (Chicago, 1997), pp. 25–6.

them both with the same brush: 'As such', she sums up, 'the scene borrows from the perverse economies of sympathy that structure Sterne's meditation on "The Captive", an episode that has equally little to do with the real sufferings of abject others and everything to do with shoring up the narrator's emotional self-satisfaction and self-congratulation. Such moments offer not disinterested windows into the plight of embodied others but mirrors into the narcissistic absorption of disembodied selves' (p. 26). Harsh words, and probably deserved. But I think there is a dimension of both texts that is missing in such a comment and that might make a difference.

Conclusion: Sympathy and the Structure of Sentiment

The first thing to clarify is that, while 'The Captive' is certainly relevant to Harrington's effusion, the passage in *Sentimental Journey* that it more pointedly echoes is Yorick's encounter with Maria at Moulines. This is an episode that would be collected with the volumes called 'Beauties of Sterne', and lavishly illustrated in later editions of the *Sentimental Journey*. It is an episode that certainly resonated transatlantically: it had its impact on Thomas Jefferson, who alluded to it more than once in letters to Maria Cosway, the woman he called 'my good Maria: not her under the poplar with the dog and string at her girdle'.[16] It is the episode that Sterne concludes with the famous effusion that begins:

—Dear sensibility! Source inexhausted of all that's precious in our joys, or costly in our sorrows! Thou chainest thy martyr down upon his bed of straw—and 'tis thou who lifts him up to Heaven—eternal fountain of our feelings!—'tis here I trace thee—and this is the divinity which stirs within me … all comes from thee, great—great SENSORIUM of the world! which vibrates, if a hair of our heads but falls upon the ground, in the remotest desert of thy creation. (*SJ*, p. 117)

Educated readers in Jefferson's America, where in 1788 William Dunlop's *The Father: Or American Shandy-ism* played to enthusiastic audiences in New York, could not miss the echoes to this passage in Harrington's effusion. If this kind of allusion calls for something beyond Arden's influence study, it may also call for something beyond Julia Stern's parallelism.

To suggest how, we must first recall that Sterne's 'Maria' vignette in *Sentimental Journey*, while the target of Brown's allusion, is itself allusive to the final pages of Sterne's *Tristram Shandy*. In a nine-volume novel, this vignette stands out for its extreme exploitation of sentiment. The postillon tells Tristram the sad story of the woman he beholds piping solitary in the field, a story about how Maria's banns were forbidden by clerical intrigue. Tristram describes her poignantly: 'she was in a thin white jacket with her hair, all but two tresses, drawn up into a silk net, with a few olive leaves twisted a little fantastically to one side—she was beautiful; and if ever I felt the full force of an honest heartache, it was the moment I saw her—'.[17] But as

---

16   Thomas Jefferson, *Jefferson in Love: The Love Letters Between Thomas Jefferson & Maria Cosway*, ed. John P. Kaminski (Madison, WI: Madison House, 1999), p. 109.

17   Laurence Sterne, *Tristram Shandy*, ed. James Aiken Work (New York, 1940), p. 630.

the pathos builds toward a climax, Sterne produces a surprising turn. The postillon speaks a simple blessing on her, and then comes the strange moment:

> As the postillon spoke this, Maria made a cadence so melancholy, so tender and querulous, that I sprung out of the chaise to help her, and found myself sitting betwixt her and her goat before I relapsed from my enthusiasm. Maria look'd wistfully for some time at me, and then at her goat—and then at me—and then at her goat again, and so on, alternately—
>
> Well, Maria, said I softly—What resemblance do you find? (p. 630)

Such a moment seems to me somehow beyond the reach of Julia Stern's critique, seems even to mock the very charge of narcissism. Nor does Sterne fail to register this rupture or to turn it into an occasion for a mock solemn oath:

> I do entreat the candid reader to believe me, that it was from the humblest conviction of what a Beast man is,—that I ask'd the question; and that I would not have let fallen an unseasonable pleasantry in the veritable presence of Misery, to be entitled to all the wit that ever Rabelais scatter'd—and yet I own my heart smote me, and that I so smarted at the very idea of it, that I swore I would set up for Wisdom and utter grave sentences the rest of my days—and never—never attempt again to commit mirth with man, woman, or child, the longest day I had to live.
>
> As for writing nonsense to them—I believe, there was a reserve—but that I leave to the world. (p. 631)

So not only is the Maria episode, with its famous paean to 'Sensibility', the point of contact between Sterne's two great works of fiction, it is also the scene of the greatest lability of tone, moving from the utmost pathos to comic absurdity in the twinkling of an eye, mixing apology for the bêtise with levity about the regret he claims to feel about it.

Is it possible that Brown, with the extreme self-reflexivity of his literary reference to Sterne, can be read as mobilising this entire ensemble of reference when he uses Sterne to frame the strange series of shifts in Harrington's behaviour? Did Brown find in Sterne a recognition—rather than a suppression—of the labile power of sympathy? I mean the power of sympathy as worked out in Smith's influential work *Theory of Moral Sentiments*. Like the contemporary philosopher Christine Korsgaard, I take this elaboration to involve the method she calls 'reflective endorsement'. It 'has its natural home', she says, 'in theories [like those of the sentimentalists] that reject realism and ground morality in human nature', seeing 'moral value … [as] a projection of human sentiments'.[18] It is the theory that offers the impartial spectator as at once a condition and a consequence of our natural reflective capacities.

Now Brown, unlike Maria Edgeworth, tell us that his characters are conversant with Adam Smith. Still, evidence that Brown's novel invokes such views is not hard to find. More than one reference is made to our 'internal monitor … that sits in

---

18   Christine Korsgaard, *The Sources of Normativity* (Cambridge, 1996), p. 19.

judgment ... and gives her verdict of approbation or dislike'(72).[19] There are, to be sure, other possible sources for this kind of language in the eighteenth century. The phrase 'the God within the mind' in the letter from the elder Harrington that also includes the phrase 'internal monitor' is probably from Pope's *Essay on Man* (2:190). And the phrase 'internal monitor' itself can be found in several British and Irish texts published in the wake of Hume's and Smith's work on the general point of view and the impartial spectator. At the same time, it is known that Smith's treatise, at least, was widely available at the time in Brown's Boston.[20] Further, the characters in *The Power of Sympathy*, in their various exchanges, show that they have a good sense of the relevant issues. Eliza Holmes, for example, neatly summarises Korsgaard's line on Smith and Hume when she writes to Myra: 'We may lay it down as a principle, that that conduct which will bear the test of reflection ... is virtuous' (p. 73).

There is, however, a problem internal to the notion of reflection itself in this tradition. I mean the deep analogy it posits between interpersonal reflection as developed through sympathetic spectatorship in social interaction (Smith's starting point in the *Theory of Moral Sentiments*) and reflection as played out in the internal dynamics of the theory of ideas (Hume's starting point in the *Treatise of Human Nature*). By the latter, I mean the sense of reflection at stake in what Hume calls 'an impression of reflection'—the feeling we get when an idea—itself the relic of a feeling—returns on the mind in memory or imagination.[21] The problem is not, as Julia Stern suggests, an issue of narcissism—of projecting an inside out or seeing the outside as a reflection of ourselves. The problem is that both internal and external relations are constituted according to the same reflective model with each presuming the other. Reflection cannot have transcendent power to regulate the power of sympathy if it proves to share its dynamic, if it amounts to the same 'structure of feeling' (to take Raymond Williams's term back to its late-eighteenth-century origins).

To approach the question from a slightly different angle, one might say that Brown's emphasis on the *power* of sympathy suggests that he may have been attuned to the debate within Scottish-enlightenment moral philosophy between a "contagion" and a "projection" model of sympathy—the difference between feeling what another feels and what we would feel in like situation. Hume and Smith tend to represent these positions respectively, though each has elements of both sides, much to the vexation of their commentators.[22] The more the contagious element in sympathy is

---

19   William Hill Brown, *The Power of Sympathy* [1789] (New York, 1996), p. 72. See Adam Smith, *The Theory of Moral Sentiments* (Indianapolis, 1976), p. 114.

20   According to Eric Slauter, no fewer than four Boston booksellers advertised Smith's *Theory of Moral Sentiments* between its publication and the publication of Brown's novel, and while some booksellers may have ordered and stocked the title especially for Harvard students, Condy and Mein both advertised the book in Boston newspapers, probably a sign that they imagined an audience for the book beyond the college (personal correspondence).

21   David Hume, *A Treatise of Human Nature* (Oxford, 1975), pp. 7–11.

22   For a comment on the ambiguities implicit in Smith's account as to the degree in which the 'contagion' model of sympathy might trouble the strict 'projection' model, see Joseph Cropsey, *Polity and Economy*, 2nd ed. (South Bend, 2001), p. 14.   For an effort to sort out these ambiguities, and to respond to those who see Smith's theory 'infected'

emphasised, the less the regulatory function can be counted on. The contagious force of sympathy seems in Brown's tale to be strong, and to have adverse and irreversible consequences.

I do not claim that William Hill Brown would necessarily have been fully conversant with the details of Smith's arguments.[23] But I suspect that Thomas Jefferson would have been, just as he understood the new genre of the sentimental journey as a reflective form in which a linguistically structured series of shifts in point of view constitutes the real travel—across the Channel, the River Tweed, the Irish Sea, or the Atlantic Ocean.[24] Beside Sterne's *Sentimental Journey*, the other book materially 'present' in *The Power of Sympathy* is *The Sorrows of Young Werther*, the book by Harrington's death bed, the book whose last letters are mimicked in Harrington's own. At Werther's own bedside there was also a book, Macpherson's Ossian, which Harrington quotes near the time of his death. As Ossian stands behind Brown's Goethe, so Smith stands behind his Laurence Sterne.

My effort here has been to point to features of Smith's *Theory of Moral Sentiments*, as the most authoritative account of 'the power of sympathy' in its day, in order to explain something about the relation of Brown's novel to the Sternean sentimental contexts it so dramatically and explicitly invokes. I have tried to suggest that in the marked *epistemological ambiguity* about the power of sympathy in Brown's novel— an ambiguity that ultimately derives from Smith's *Theory*—corresponds closely to an equally marked *ethical ambivalence* about that power. This ambivalence is in turn registered in Brown's way of echoing and even amplifying the egregious tonal lability of the very passages in Sterne's book to which Brown's offers a kind of transatlantic sequel. Sympathy's power may be a virtue, but the question is left hanging as to whether this is virtue in the sense of goodness or virtue in the sense of capacity or force. It is a tension that would remain unresolved on both sides of the Atlantic for decades to come.

---

by the contagion model, see Samuel Fleischacker, *On Adam Smith's Wealth of Nations: A Philosophical Companion* (Princeton,2004), pp. 9–10.

23   Elizabeth Barnes invokes the Smithian context for Hill's novel in an account that stresses its relation to the developing positions of Thomas Paine, in 'Affecting Relations: Pedagogy, Patriarchy, and the Politics of Sympathy', *American Literary History,* 8 (Winter, 1996): 597–614. See also Paul Downes's account of *The Power of Sympathy* as a post-seduction novel in 'Fiction and Democracy', in Shirly Samuels, ed., *A Companion to American Fiction, 1780–1865* (Oxford, 2004), pp. 20–30. A number of literary and cultural histories have picked up the story of the American sentimental after Brown's novel—i.e., in the first decades of the new Republic and beyond. See, for example, Jane Tompkins, *Sensational Designs: The Cultural Work of American Fiction, 1790–1860* (Oxford, 1985); Ann Douglas, *The Feminization of American Culture* (New York, 1977) which offers extended discussion of the 'sentimentalization' of 'status' and of 'creed and culture'; and the essays collected in *Sentimental Men: Masculinity and the Politics of Affect in American Culture*, eds Mary Chapman and Glenn Hendler (Berkeley and Los Angeles, 1999).

24   See Jefferson's full exchange with Robert Skipwith on the moral utility of fiction, *Papers of Thomas Jefferson*, 1:74–83.

Chapter 8

Adam Smith and the Crisis of the American Union

Peter S. Onuf *

Within a few years of its publication in 1776, Adam Smith's *Wealth of Nations* became the textbook for the new—now 'classical'-economics that would ultimately transform the political economies of the 'civilised' world. The Scottish philosopher's assault on the premises of mercantilist statecraft affirmed and elaborated the Enlightenment's apotheosis of free, unfettered commerce, offering his readers a compelling vision of a progressive, prosperous, and peaceful new world.

Nowhere was Smith more enthusiastically received than in the new United States of America. Appealing to the enlightened opinion of a 'candid' world, provincial American patriots linked their opposition to the tyranny and despotism of British mercantilist regulation with the best interests of mankind as a whole. By dismantling the most powerful empire in the Atlantic world, the Americans struck a decisive blow for free trade. 'The most sacred rights of mankind' were at stake in the American struggle against mercantilism, Smith wrote on the eve of independence.[1] Dismantling the colonial monopoly would vindicate American rights, but it would also benefit the entire trading world, including Britain. The truths Smith taught seemed axiomatic and self-evident to Revolutionaries who, with George Washington, looked toward that 'not very remote' time 'when the benefits of a liberal and free commerce will, pretty generally, succeed to the devastations and horrors of war'.[2] American enthusiasm for Smith was confirmed over subsequent decades with the publication of new editions and textbooks and commentaries that popularised the master's teaching. A half century after its publication, Thomas Cooper of South Carolina could write that 'no person yet has carefully perused' *The Wealth of Nations*, 'without becoming a convert to his leading doctrines'.[3]

Yet the vogue for Smith did not preempt conflicting prescriptions for American commercial policy. To the contrary, the American reception of Smith in the decades

* Portions of this essay have been previously published in Nicholas Onuf and Peter Onuf, *Nations, Markets, and War: Modern History and the American Civil War* (Charlottesville: University of Virginia Press, 2006).

1   Adam Smith, *An Inquiry into the Nature and Causes of the Wealth of Nations* [hereafter *WN*], eds. R. H. Campbell and A. S. Skinner (2 vols., Oxford, 1976), vol. 2, p. 582.

2   George Washington to the Marquis de Lafayette, Mt. Vernon, Aug.15, 1786, ed. John C. Fitzpatrick, *The Writings of George Washington,* (38 vols., Washington, D.C., 1931–44), vol. 28, p. 518.

3   Thomas Cooper, *Lectures on the Elements of Political Economy*, 2nd ed. (1830) (New York, 1971). On Smith's reception see Joseph Dorfman, *The Economic Mind in American Civilization* (New York, 1961), vol. 2.

leading up to the Civil War showed that his legacy could cut in opposite directions. Increasingly bitter debates between free traders and advocates of protective tariffs reflected conflicting prescriptions for securing the new nation's vital interests—and even its independence—in a trading system dominated by Britain. These conflicts were in turn exacerbated by fundamental and deepening disagreement over the nature of the new American regime. Did Americans constitute a single people or nation? If the United States was, in the words of James Madison, 'partly federal, and partly national', how would the distinction be applied and sustained in practice?[4] These controversial questions would only be resolved in a devastating war. While they remained in suspense, advocates of opposing positions—free traders and protectionists, defenders of states' rights and 'nationalists'—all invoked Smith's authority. In the process, they showed that *The Wealth of Nations* could be read in profoundly different ways. These divergent readings would play a critical role in the sectional crisis that led to the destruction of the union in the American Civil War.

Reading *The Wealth of Nations*

Confusion about the proper interpretation of Smith begins with the title of his masterpiece. Was the primary goal of Smith's assault on mercantilism to promote the 'wealth' of *all* 'nations', or was he more interested in promoting the prosperity and well-being of the *British* nation? Of course, Smith could have seen these goals as ultimately compatible, but the immediate effect of extending the ambit of market freedom in Britain—the most advanced commercial society in the civilised world— would be to *enhance* its comparative advantage with respect to less enlightened regimes. Competitors might emulate the British example and thus participate in its growing prosperity. But it was not clear that economies at a less advanced stage of development could participate in an international division of labour on equal terms.

Smith couched his historical account of Britain's rise as a market society in terms of the obstacles that impeded its optimal development. Smith's account of the home market was too empirical, too grounded in the complexities of Britain's particular situation, to be fully satisfactory to succeeding generations of classical economists. They took upon themselves the task of discovering and elaborating Smith's 'theory' of market society.[5] In doing so, they would conceptualise the homogeneous space where the modern laws of economics play out. What for Smith had been a particular, historically situated *home* market now took on the character of *the* market. To make sense out of Smith, to enlist him as the founder of their discipline, classical, free trade economists thus had to suppress the historical dimension of *The Wealth of Nations*. Their polemical opponents, the 'national' or 'historical' economists who

---

4   Jacob E. Cooke, ed., *The Federalist* (Middletown, Conn., 1961), no. 39 (Madison), p. 257.

5   'One of the criticisms of Smith, in the period of reconstruction of political economy in the 1790s and 1800s, was indeed that he was too little concerned with the simple principles of the thing, or too much concerned with all the details of economic life.' Emma Rothschild, *Economic Sentiments: Adam Smith, Condorcet, and the Enlightenment* (Cambridge, Mass., 2001), p. 237.

advocated regulation of foreign trade and protection of manufactures, moved in the opposite direction, foregrounding contingent historical conditions that justified limits on market freedom and deferring the free trade millennium until a far distant future.[6]

The Wealth of Nations proved to be such a crucial, influential text because it supported widely divergent readings. Read forward, in the conventional fashion, Smith's treatise moves from theory to history, concluding with policy prescriptions for the American crisis that were clearly no longer relevant—if they ever had been. Read backward, however, a radically different argument emerges. From this historical perspective, Smith's condemnation of British policy in the American crisis sets forth a general principle of fundamental significance. Smith had no illusions about influencing present policy, but instead sought to articulate the relationship between the nation-state and the market it protected and fostered. Preceding discussions of mercantilist economics and of the development of the home market fleshed out Smith's historical understanding of this relationship, providing the appropriate context for his more familiar and influential formulations about markets, the division of labour, and the natural impulses of economic man in his opening pages.

Smith's fundamental insight, which he announced at the beginning of his masterpiece, is that the division of labour—the functional specialisation of 'productive powers'—is the engine of human progress. The increasing division of labour promotes exchange, which in turn promotes the division of labour. 'As it is the power of exchanging that gives occasion to the division of labour', he wrote in Book I, chapter 3, 'so the extent of this division must always be limited by the extent of that power, or, in other words, by the extent of the market.'[7] Without the division of labour, itself the result of a natural propensity to exchange what we produce for our own benefit, societies cannot advance and civilisation is impossible.[8]

Smith's conception of the division of labour is inextricably linked to a conception of historical progress. Some nations stood at a higher stage of 'civilisation' than others and would therefore gain more from the rapid extension of the world market. This was the case, Smith showed, in the history of the European conquest of the New World. 'By opening a new and inexhaustible market to all the commodities of Europe', he wrote, 'the discovery of America … gave occasion to new divisions of labour and improvements of art, which in the narrow circle of the ancient commerce, could never have taken place for want of a market to take off the greater part of their

---

6   Edward Mead Earle, 'Adam Smith, Alexander Hamilton, Friedrich List: The Economic Foundations of Military Power', in ed., Edward Mead Earle, *Makers of Modern Strategy: Military Thought from Machiavelli to Hitler* (Princeton, 1943), pp. 117–54; Istvan Hont, 'Free Trade and the Economic Limits to National Markets: Neo-Machiavellian Political Economy Reconsidered', in ed., John Dunn, *The Economic Limits to Modern Politics* (Cambridge, U.K., 1990), pp. 41–120; Bernard Semmel, *The Liberal Ideal and the Demons of Empire: Theories of Imperialism from Adam Smith to Lenin* (Baltimore, 1993); Keith Tribe, *Strategies of Economic Order: German Economic Discourse* (Cambridge, UK, 1995).

7   *WN*, vol. 1, p. 31.

8   The thrust of Smith's argument is apparent in title of Book I of *WN*: 'Of the Causes of Improvement in the Productive Powers of Labour, and of the Order according to which its Produce is naturally distributed among the different Ranks of the People.'

produce.' In theory, this 'new set of exchanges ... should naturally have proved as advantageous to the new, as it certainly did to the old continent'.[9] Unfortunately, the Europeans' military preponderance—a function of their more highly developed economies—made the conquest of less civilised peoples and the expropriation of their wealth irresistible.

By tracing advanced commercial societies through stages of development that reflected the progressive perfection of market society, Smith could also explain differences among nations across space.[10] Smith's 'natural liberty' made the most sense in exchange among societies at the same stage of development, though the history of British commercial relations with France and other European nations suggested that trade would always be subject to the kinds of political interference Smith himself grudgingly endorsed. Nations at different stages of development were much more likely to resort to force, both because more advanced societies could not resist exploiting their preponderant power and because the very survival of weaker, less developed nations depended on forceful resistance to encroachments on their rights.

Smith urged policy-makers in societies at an advanced stage of development to keep the domains of economics and politics as distinct as possible, promoting the wealth of nations through reciprocally beneficial market exchanges. But weak societies on the periphery of the expanding European market had to move in the opposite direction, building up effective war-making states even if European nations might begin to dismantle theirs. The goal was for 'the inhabitants of all the different quarters of the world ... [to] arrive at that equality of courage and force which, by inspiring mutual fear, can alone overawe the injustice of independent nations into some sort of respect for the rights of one another'. Smith recognised that the beneficial effects of a global market depended on the prior achievement of a rough political equality, or balance of power, among the nations of every 'quarter' of the world. This did not mean that less developed nations should avoid contact with the world, for the extension of market relations promoted the economic development— the movement through history—that alone could equalise power. Indeed, 'nothing seems more likely to establish this equality of force than that mutual communication of knowledge and of all sorts of improvements which an extensive commerce from all countries to all countries naturally, or rather necessarily, carries along with it'. The anti-mercantilist Smith thus advocated something very much like mercantilism as he urged less developed nations to manage foreign trade relations in ways that would promote national power and enable them to redress European 'injustices'.[11]

---

9   Ibid., vol. 1, p. 448.

10   On the four-stage 'conjectural history' of the Scottish Enlightenment, see Ronald L. Meek, *Social Science and the Ignoble Savage* (Cambridge, UK, 1976). On Smith's 'Historical Theory', see Andrew S. Skinner, *A System of Social Science: Papers Relating to Adam Smith*, 2nd ed. (Oxford, 1996), pp. 76–105. For a good recent discussion of conceptions of history and progress in the Scottish Enlightenment, see Joyce E. Chaplin, *An Anxious Pursuit: Agricultural Innovation and Modernity in the Lower South* (Chapel Hill, 1993), pp. 26–37.

11   *WN*, vol. 2, pp. 626–7.

Union and Nation

The reception of Adam Smith in antebellum America was determined by the ambiguous character of the federal union and conflicting assessments of its changing geopolitical circumstances. Smith's anti-mercantilist strictures were naturally appealing both to staple producers who would benefit from international free trade as well as to libertarian opponents of a powerful federal state. Free traders focused on the axioms of the new 'science' of political economy, discounting historical commentary that dominated the latter portions of Smith's text. The nation-state faded from view in the bright light of theory: for dogmatic free traders, only the most rigorously limited state—and only the most self-effacing 'statesman'—could avoid the onus of old regime, mercantilist corruption. American free traders enthusiastically embraced this anti-historical reading of Smith, conflating his polemic against mercantilism with the revolutionary struggle against British imperial despotism. Focusing narrowly on theoretical and technical issues, Thomas Cooper, Thomas Roderick Dew, and other American free trade economists proved the most eager and receptive students of the orthodox British school of political economists.[12]

The formation of the union gave rise to broadly shared sentiments of American nationhood, but it also enabled the states to act like nations—to promote the distinct interests and command the loyalties of their peoples—during times of constitutional crisis. The memory of the founders was constantly invoked when Americans mobilised for war or sectional differences threatened the union.[13] Yet centrifugal, disunionist tendencies were also justified by memories of the Revolutionary fathers who had resisted British efforts to impose a despotic central authority over the colonies. Americans came together in opposition to despotism, in order to preserve corporate as well as individual rights, and threats to break up the union were always cast in defensive terms: other Americans were all too likely to betray the union, as loyalists had during the revolution. At such moments, Americans could easily see each other as foreigners who would use the machinery of the federal government to reduce them to neo-colonial subjection. In this anti-imperial, libertarian spirit, patriotic Americans risked the union they claimed to cherish.[14] In doing so, of course, they would betray the revolutionaries' vision of a peaceful, expanding union of free republics with an increasingly integrated and interdependent continental market.[15]

The experience and ideological legacy of the Revolution gave rise to a dialectic of union and disunion, crisis and compromise, that was institutionalised in the very

---

12   See particularly Cooper, *Lectures on the Elements of Political Economy*; Thomas Roderick Dew, *Lectures on the Restrictive System Delivered to the Senior Political Class of William and Mary College* (Richmond, 1829): Henry Vethake, *The Principles of Political Economy*, 2nd ed (1844; New York, 1971).

13   Peter B. Knupfer, *The Union As It Is: Constitutional Unionism and Sectional Compromise, 1787–1861* (Chapel Hill, 1991).

14   Peter S. Onuf, 'Federalism, Republicanism, and the Origins of American Sectionalism', in Edward L. Ayers *et al.*, *All Over the Map: Rethinking American Regions* (Baltimore, 1996), pp. 11–37.

15   Cathy D. Matson and Peter S. Onuf, *A Union of Interests: Political and Economic Thought in Revolutionary America* (Lawrence, Kans., 1990).

structure of the federal Constitution. But it was debates over national commercial policy and over political economy generally that made differences among the states and regions of the federal republic increasingly salient. After the inconclusive conclusion of the War of 1812, controversy over a federal tariff that would protect American manufactures constituted the most divisive issue in American politics for the next three decades, setting the stage for and shaping responses to subsequent divisions over the expansion of slavery into new western territories and states that would ultimately destroy the union.[16]

Henry Clay's 'American System' sought to implement the internal improvements and balanced, interdependent development that would transform widely scattered and loosely connected economic interests into the kind of national market Smith advocated in *The Wealth of Nations*. Particular regions might not benefit immediately from these developmental policies—indeed, staple-producing regions that already enjoyed optimally lucrative trade relations in the Atlantic economy would shoulder a disproportionate share of the costs of development—but all would share in the future prosperity of the national economy. Clay and his fellow protectionists argued that American independence could only be secured by developing the home market and that the failure to achieve true economic independence would guarantee a permanently subordinate, dependent position in the Atlantic economy and state system.

War and the threat of war spurred developmental programmes. In the wake of the federal government's inept performance during the War of 1812, ambitious young nationalists were determined that the union would be better prepared for the next war. There was no reason, in the light of recent history, to expect that the frustratingly inconclusive 'peace' negotiated at Ghent in 1814 would be long-lasting. The British were unwilling to make any concessions on the neutral rights questions that had drawn Americans into the war and thereby jeopardise the maritime hegemony that guaranteed the peace of Europe. No one was prepared to assume that Europe— and the Atlantic world generally—would remain at peace, and Americans' sense of vulnerability was further compounded by the uncertain future of European empires in their hemisphere, particularly with the spread of independence movements in Spanish America.[17]

Nationalists promoted the development of a self-sufficient continental economy that could both survive disruptions of foreign trade and give the United States a stronger bargaining position in negotiating for favourable terms when peace returned. Free trade might remain the great desideratum for an overwhelmingly agricultural economy that depended on finding the most lucrative markets for its staple products,

---

16 For a good survey history of these developments see Forrest McDonald, *States' Rights and the Union: Imperium in Imperio, 1776–1876* (Lawrence, Kans., 2000). On the tariff see F. W. Taussig, *The Tariff History of the United States*, 7th ed. (New York, 1923) and J. J. Pincus, 'Tariff Policies', in ed., Jack P. Greene, *Encyclopedia of American Political History* (3 vols., New York, 1984), vol. 3, pp. 1259–70.

17 James E. Lewis, Jr., *The American Union and the Problem of Neighborhood: The United States and the Collapse of the Spanish Empire, 1783–1829* (Chapel Hill, 1998); Lewis, *John Quincy Adams: Policymaker for the Union* (Wilmington, Del., 2001).

but development-oriented nationalists were convinced that the federal government must continue to pursue 'neo-mercantilist' policies until the happy day when the powers of the earth finally recognised their own true interests.[18] If the United States hoped to vindicate their independence they had to be able to engage with their European counterparts on equal terms.

The National Republican programme foundered on the ambiguous empirical question of when 'war' gave way to 'peace', and over how durable that peace would be. According to one free trader, writing in 1834, protectionists assumed, with Thomas Hobbes, 'that the natural state of man is WAR'. But American history belied the Hobbesian dogma, 'for we have been at war only four or five years out of the fifty-one that have elapsed since the treaty of peace which established our independence'. Protectionists perversely insisted that 'we ought to foster manufactures, by high protecting duties in peace, to have them cheap and plentiful in war. In other words, that in order to diminish possible difficulties for five years, we should endure a most oppressive and unequal taxation for fifty!'[19] In 1816, few American statesmen would have calculated such a proportion, for a Hobbesian state of war was their norm, whether or not the United States was formally engaged in war. (Periodic depredations on American shipping in the 'peaceful' years between 1783 and 1812 constituted a compelling image of a natural state of war that Americans could not hope to avoid.) By 1834, war could be seen as the exception to the rule of peace and National Republican machinations took on a sinister cast: the supposed threat of war was merely a pretext for consolidating power in the federal government in the hands of manufacturers and their corrupt allies. If there was any danger of war for Americans, its source was in this very project of sectional aggrandizement and in the determination of Andrew Jackson to run roughshod over the rights of South Carolina and other states as they sought to resist the federal juggernaut.

If there was no external threat of war, if the Atlantic system had in fact entered into a long period of peace and stability, the case for federally-directed internal improvement and economic development was much harder to make. The key question was whether an 'artificial' realignment of the national economy would harmonise interests, strengthen the union, and promote American prosperity, or whether it would simply establish a hierarchy of advantage, with some sections and sectors gaining the upper hand over their rivals. Free traders could invoke Adam Smith's authority to argue that government interventions retarded growth, thus subverting the prosperity that in the long run made a nation powerful. 'By our natural growth alone, and without government's intermeddling to force labour and capital into channels which they would not spontaneously take—we shall be ready for any future contest.'[20]

The astonishing growth of the cotton trade led southern free traders to take a more benign view of the former metropolis, arguing for a natural complementarity

---

18   John E. Crowley, *The Privileges of Independence: Neomercantilism and the American Revolution* (Baltimore, 1993); Vernon G. Setser, *The Commercial Reciprocity Policy of the United States* (Philadelphia, 1937).

19   'M', 'Suiting Facts to Theory', in Raguet, ed., *The Examiner,* Feb. 5, 1834, vol. 1, p. 216.

20   Ibid.

of interests in the Atlantic economy. American cotton producers believed they enjoyed an effective monopoly and therefore an equal, if not privileged, position in trade relations with their British customers, an assessment reflected in the notion that cotton was 'king'.[21] By contrast, the federal government, dominated as it was by the antagonistic interests of manufacturers, threatened to obstruct this 'natural' complementarity of Anglo-American interests and to take on the role of a despotic, metropolitan, and foreign government. For free traders, dependency could always be explained in political terms: southern staple producers would be subjected to a degraded, neocolonial condition if the federal government interfered with their free access to foreign markets. Such calculations led to a remarkable transformation in southern attitudes, as the Anglophobia of the revolutionary generation was transformed into something very close to Anglophilia. The danger of metropolitan tyranny was relocated on the American side of the Atlantic.[22]

Southern free traders invoked Adam Smith's authority as they sought to roll back a neo-mercantilist regime of protective tariffs. Their hostility to protection reflected the underdevelopment of an interdependent national economy based on mutually advantageous interregional exchange that Smith had promoted in Britain and that National Republicans sought to foster in the United States. From the free traders' perspective, a protective tariff constituted redistributive taxation, siphoning wealth from southern planters for the benefit of northern manufacturers. Struggles over taxation underscored the 'disparity of circumstances and situation between the Northern and Southern States', one free trade writer asserted, so producing 'considerable alienation of feeling'. Efforts to equalise the regions, to counter natural advantages 'arising from differences in soil and climate, are evidently beyond the control of legislative interference'. The protective system artificially increased the 'wealth and population' of the North, giving 'that portion of the Union ... additional influence in the national councils'. The federal government's interference in the economy retarded growth by penalising the most productive sectors and subsidising the less productive through this 'indirect taxation'.[23] The protectionists' misguided efforts to promote balanced development and an interdependent national economy

---

21   I am indebted here to Brian Schoen, 'The Fragile Fabric of Union: The Cotton South, Federal Politics, and the Atlantic World, 1783–1861' (Ph.D. diss., Virginia, 2003).

22   Paul Conkin, *Prophets of Prosperity: America's First Political Economists* (Bloomington, 1980); Joseph J. Persky, *The Burden of Dependency: Colonial Themes in Southern Economic Thought* (Baltimore, 1992). On antebellum economic thought see also Allen Kaufman, *Capitalism, Slavery, and Republican Values: Antebellum Political Economists, 1819–1848* (Austin, 1982). On southern Anglophilia, see the suggestive comments of Edward L. Ayers, 'What We Talk about When We Talk about the South', in Ayers *et al.*, *All Over the Map*, p. 76.

23   'FREE TRADE', from 'Men and Manners in America', by the Author of 'Cyril Thornton', in Raguet, ed., *The Examiner,* 13 Nov. 1833, vol. 1, p. 116. See the discussion in Jesse T. Carpenter, *The South as a Conscious Minority, 1789–1861: A Study in Political Thought*, with a new introduction by John McCardell (1930; Columbia, S.C., 1990), pp. 29–30. For an insightful discussion of John C. Calhoun's political economy see James Read, *Concurrent Majority, Statesmanship, and Slavery: The Political and Constitutional Theory of John C. Calhoun* (forthcoming).

would forfeit the comparative advantage that American staple producers enjoyed in the Atlantic trading system.

Bitter debates over national economic policy underscored the perceived distinction between political and economic spheres. Free traders contrasted predatory political opportunists, who sought to control the federal government in order to redistribute wealth, with their putative victims, the staple producers who generated that wealth. South Carolinian George McDuffie quantified the grievance in his famous 'forty-bale' theory: for every 100 bales of cotton southern planters sent to Britain, northerners deflected the profits of forty to themselves through the protective system.[24] Opponents of the protective system thus became increasingly sensitive to the costs of the union, even as its benefits faded from view. Such calculations demystified the union itself, which was increasingly conceived in instrumental terms.

In seeking to exploit broad nationalist sentiment to strengthen the bonds of union, post-war reformers instead energised the forces of particularism. The Republicans' compact theory, interpreting the federal Constitution as a super-treaty among sovereign states, provided the conceptual framework for the migration of loyalties, from the whole union to its constituent parts.[25] Contests over the expansion of slavery in the Missouri controversy (1819–21) and over tariff policy, culminating in the Nullification Crisis (1831–33), led to a progressive 'alienation of feelings' among the states. Under such circumstances, the equation of 'union' with 'nation' became increasingly tenuous. Defenders of states' rights would no longer concede the high ground to their opponents. 'We are in danger of losing our liberties', editor Condy Raguet wrote in 1834, 'because we are afraid to call things by their right names. The truth is, that a State is a nation, and a nation is a State,—They are convertible terms, and one signifies nothing more nor less than the other, as is proved by the fact that in the Declaration of Independence, the term "State" is applied to Great Britain as well as to the Colonies.' If national identities could survive political obliteration, as did 'the English nation, the Scotch nation, the Irish nation' when the United Kingdom was formed, the American states sustained their 'separate nationality' in a much fuller degree in their union, for the federal Constitution guaranteed that each member state would continue to enjoy 'the rights and attributes of a sovereign nation'. Raguet deflated the idea of 'nation', which he made 'convertible' with 'state', but by the same logic gave the 'state' a new aura of legitimacy, as the political expression of a distinct, self-governing people or 'nation'. 'Self-government'—the right of a 'sovereign nation' to determine its own destiny—trumped the kind of 'peace' or union that a despotic metropolitan government could enforce on subject provinces.[26]

Free traders insisted that the union was *not* a nation. Thomas Cooper charged that 'the moral entity—the grammatical being called a NATION, has been clothed in attributes that have no real existence except in the imagination of those who metamorphose a word into a thing'.[27] By imagining that the nation had some kind of

---

24   Persky, *Burden of Dependency*, p. 59 and *passim*; William W. Freehling, *Prelude to Civil War: The Nullification Controversy in South Carolina, 1816–1836* (New York, 1965).

25   Andrew C. Lenner, *The Federal Principle in American Politics* (Madison, 2000).

26   'States or Nations' in Raguet, ed., *The Examiner,* Oct. 15, 1834, vol. 2, p. 91.

27   Cooper, *Lectures on the Elements of Political Economy*, p. 28.

transcendent corporate identity, neo-mercantilist protectionists justified interference in international trade that threatened to impoverish the South and provoke commercial conflicts that would lead to war. Protectionist talk about the home market was a dangerous snare and delusion. The free-traders' Smith instead celebrated the benefits of foreign trade: 'a more extensive market' provided a vent for domestic surpluses and promoted the development of a nation's 'productive powers'.[28] The mercantilists' policy of 'beggaring all their neighbours' was obviously misguided: 'a nation that would enrich itself by foreign trade is certainly most likely to do so when its neighbours are all rich, industrious, and commercial nations'.[29] The logical conclusion was that governments should never interfere with market exchanges that increased the wealth of all nations.

Home Market

At first, protectionists found themselves at a rhetorical and ideological disadvantage in countering the free traders' reading of Smith. But Smith's conception of historical development eventually gave protectionist economists leverage against the free traders, enabling them to underscore the primacy of the home market and therefore to prescribe a more constructive, progressive role for the nation-state. *The Wealth of Nations* provided a broad historical narrative that illuminated inequalities among nations at different stages of development and emphasised the role of the state in securing vital national rights and interests. The heavily historical works of Friedrich List, Henry Carey, and other exponents of 'national', or protectionist economics advanced a form of dependency theory, insisting that free trade could only confer equal benefits where trading partners engaged on equal terms: as they looked across the Atlantic, they saw not only the threat of future war, but the continuing reality of British domination of trade relations: national economic development was the necessary corrective.[30]

Protectionists seized on Smith's acknowledgment that the 'inland or home trade' was 'the most important of all, the trade in which an equal capital affords the greatest revenue, and creates the greatest employment to the people of the country, was considered as subsidiary only to foreign trade'.[31] By contrast, according to one Whig writer's gloss of Smith, 'commerce with distant nations' yielded much smaller 'returns to the labor and capital deployed'.[32] The home trade was 'a steadier, safer,

---

28   *WN,* vol. 1, p. 447.

29   *WN,* vol. 1, pp. 493, 495.

30   Friedrich List, *National System of Political Economy,* trans. G. A. Matile, including the Notes of the French Translation by Henri Richelot, with a Preliminary Essay and Notes by Stephen Colwell (1841; Philadelphia, 1856; rept. New York, 1974); Henry C. Carey, *The Past, the Present, and the Future* (Philadelphia, 1848); Carey, *The Slave Trade: Domestic and Foreign: Why It Exists, and How It May Be Extinguished* (London and Philadelphia, 1853); Calvin Colton, *Public Economy of the United States* (New York, 1848).

31   *WN,* vol. 1, 435; cited and discussed in 'What Constitutes Real Freedom of Trade?', in *American Whig Review* 6 (Nov. 1850), p. 465.

32   'What Constitutes Real Freedom of Trade?', *American Whig Review* 6 (Oct. 1850), p. 366.

and, on the whole, more eligible branch of business than the foreign', added another writer who also cited Smith.[33] The home market was preferable on various grounds. Capitalists could monitor their stock continuously and did not have to fear losses in foreign wars. Protectionists thus approvingly quoted Smith's celebration of the superior virtue and patriotism of the 'small proprietor', 'of all improvers the most industrious, the most intelligent, and the most successful'.[34] Smith's agrarian bias—a bias toward the home market—was apparent in his juxtaposition of the farmer to the merchant who, 'it has been said very properly, is not necessarily the citizen of any particular country'. Capital was safer at home; it also generated more wealth as it circulated in the home market. 'In an immense country, with every variety of soil, and climate, and geological structures', one part of the country 'could produce what another part cannot', and all would enjoy 'the vast advantage of having a market nearer and surer'.[35] In time of war, a nation with a well-developed home market would be better able to vindicate its independence against external threats.

Free traders routinely invoked Smith's authority as they sought to dismantle international trade barriers. But Smith was less interested in promoting foreign trade than in illuminating the pernicious implications of mercantilistic regulation in the domestic economy. Mercantilists were certainly misguided when they interfered with free foreign trade, but their biggest mistake was to take foreign trade too seriously, to imagine that a favourable international balance of trade was crucial to a nation's prosperity. Smith instead insisted that the fullest possible extension of the market *within* the nation was the first great desideratum, for the wealth of a nation depended on the full development of its own productive resources. Smith's preference for the home market was a function of his conception of the progress of particular national economies that would ultimately lead to a unified world market.

Smith's most forceful denunciation of mercantilism and its injustices came in the concluding passages of *The Wealth of Nations*, in his famous commentary on the contemporaneous American crisis. His major concern here was with perfecting and extending Britain's national market—and with equalising tax burdens throughout the empire—, not with instituting an international regime of free trade. The best outcome of the crisis would be a full incorporation of the colonies in the British home market; next best would be the most cordial, freest possible trade relations with an independent United States. In other words, nation came first, and world followed, a sequence that tracked Smith's historical understanding of the stages of societal development.[36]

Smith's preference for the home market not only called into question the relative importance of foreign trade but also the value of free trade itself under particular

33   Review of various publications on the 'American System', *North American Review* 32 (Jan. 1831), p. 145.

34   *WN*, vol. 1, p. 423, quoted in 'What Constitutes Real Freedom of Trade?', *American Whig Review* 6 (Oct. 1850), p. 366.

35   'The Infancy of American Manufactures: A Brief Chapter of Our National History', *American Whig Review* 1 (Jan. 1845), p. 55.

36   Winch, *Riches and Poverty*, pp. 156–65; Skinner, *A System of Social Science*, pp. 209–30; Eliga H. Gould, *The Persistence of Empire: British Political Culture in the Age of the American Revolution* (Chapel Hill, 2000), pp. 140–45.

historical circumstances. The 'inland or home trade', he wrote in Book IV, was 'the most important of all, the trade in which an equal capital affords the greatest revenue, and creates the greatest employment to the people of the country, was considered as subsidiary only to foreign trade'.[37]

For Smith, the main impediments to national economic development were the legally sanctioned monopolies. Corporate interests employed them to exploit their countrymen; mercantilist regulations projected them into the arena of foreign trade. Increasing the ambit of 'natural liberty' at home and abroad was obviously the key to national prosperity. Given Britain's dominant position in the commercial world, Smith had no reason to fear that freer foreign trade would wreak significant damage on any major sector of the domestic economy. Dissolving barriers between national and world markets would serve Britain's interests.[38]

This was not necessarily the case in the new United States. In a country of continental dimensions, the extension of the home market could support a sufficiently elaborate division of labour to promote a rapid pace of economic development.[39] But extension could proceed too rapidly, particularly when an underdeveloped economy was drawn into the orbit of a more advanced commercial economy. Market expansion thus had to be combined with a sufficient concentration of population and productive resources in order to foster optimal development. Smith did not worry about the concentration of capital at 'home', because it seemed to him a natural phenomenon: 'home is in this manner the center, if I may say so, round which the capitals of the inhabitants of every country are continually circulating'.[40] Centrifugal tendencies were more pronounced at the periphery, however, and the concentration of productive resources therefore much more problematic. Would weaker, less developed economies ever develop a home market, given the tendency of capital to return to its 'home' in the most advanced commercial societies?

The unequal distribution of wealth and power within and among nations represented the operation of the division of labour across time and space. Smith dismissed the physiocrats' contention that agriculture was the source of all value. A growing population gave rise to manufactures, increasing productivity and concentrating wealth in towns: 'the inhabitants of a town, though they frequently possess no lands of their own, yet draw to themselves by their industry such

---

37   *WN*, vol. 1, p. 435.

38   Bernard Semmel, *The Rise of Free Trade Imperialism; Classical Political Economy, The Empire of Free Trade and Imperialism 1750–1850* (Cambridge, UK, 1970). As George Fitzhugh astutely noted in 1854, Smith's 'country ... was an over-match for the rest of the world. International free trade would benefit his country as much as social free trade would benefit his friends. This was his world, and had it been the only world his philosophy would have been true. But there was another and much larger world, whose misfortunes, under his system, were to make the fortunes of his friends and his country'. Fitzhugh, *Sociology for the South: or, The Failure of Free Society* (1854; New York, 1965), p. 12.

39   'In an immense country, with every variety of soil, and climate, and geological structures', one part of the country 'could produce what another part cannot', and all would enjoy 'the vast advantage of having a market nearer and surer'. 'The Infancy of American Manufactures: A Brief Chapter of Our National History', *American Whig Review* 1 (Jan. 1845), p. 55.

40   *WN*, vol. 1, p. 455.

a quantity of the rude produce of the lands of other people as supplies them, not only with the materials of their work, but with the fund of their subsistence'. The same pattern had taken place in Europe, and was now taking place in the world as a whole: 'what a town always is with regard to the country in its neighbourhood, one independent state or country may frequently be with regard to other independent states or countries'.[41]

In the fullness of time, inequalities among nations would diminish as they converged at the highest stage of development. Inveterately suspicious of the motives and measures of politicians, Smith warned that improvement should not be forced and that a 'landed nation' would only squander its capital stock if it sought 'to raise up artificers, manufacturers, and merchants ... prematurely, and before it was perfectly ripe for them'.[42] This, of course, was a favourite passage of free traders who opposed protectionist efforts to foster 'infant industries'.[43] Historically, Smith wrote, government-sponsored monopolies had given 'traders and artificers in the town an advantage over the landlords, farmers, and labourers in the country', breaking 'down that natural equality which would otherwise take place in the commerce which is carried on between them'.[44] As he acknowledged, 'natural equality' did not mean an equal distribution of wealth. And notwithstanding the tendency of townsmen to combine and conspire against agriculturalists in the countryside, Smith recognised that towns promoted economic development and the progress of civilisation. Indeed, Smith's conception of the nation itself hinged on the domestication of mercantile capital: 'no part of it can be said to belong to any particular country, till it has been spread as it were over the face of that country, either in buildings or in the lasting improvement of lands'.[45]

Revolution and Civil War

Adam Smith provided American free traders with a vision of the world as a market, liberated from the fetters of mercantilist regimes and the never-ending cycle of wars they provoked. Yet he also offered protectionists a countervailing conception of the nation-as-market that justified regulation of foreign trade and state-sponsored developmental policies in order that would secure commercial as well as political independence in a trading system dominated by Britain. These contradictory readings were equally plausible. Together they illuminated the protean ambiguity in the text of *The Wealth of Nations* and in the Western liberal tradition generally that has shaped the history of the modern world.

Smith's commentary on the American Revolutionary crisis anticipated the choices Americans faced on the eve of their Civil War. In 1776 Britain's rulers could either incorporate the colonies into an expanded British nation or recognise their

---

41 Ibid.
42 Ibid., vol. 2, p. 672.
43 Douglas Irwin, *Against the Tide: An Intellectual History of Free Trade* (Princeton, 1996).
44 *WN*, vol. 1, p. 142.
45 Ibid., vol. 1, p. 426.

independence: Smith insisted that the mercantilists' vision of a 'great empire', an *unequal* union in which dependent provinces submitted to a dominant metropolis, was no longer sustainable. Misguided efforts to restore imperial rule would only protract a senseless and devastating war. In 1861 the new Lincoln administration confronted an independence movement in the deep South that self-consciously invoked the Revolutionary legacy. Would Lincoln seek to preserve a collapsing union by force, at the certain risk of another—perhaps even more devastating—war, or should he acknowledge the South's revolutionary right to national self-determination?

The parallels between the Revolution and Civil War were of course compelling to Southerners. But it was by no means clear to Northerners that the cases were analogous or that Smith's counsel to Lord North's ministry was now relevant. The question pivoted on whether or not the United States by had 1861 already come to constitute the kind of nation Smith recommended in the earlier crisis of Anglo-American union. For Smith in 1776 a greater British nation that incorporated the colonies was a visionary prospect, the road *not* taken. For Lincoln, the disciple of Henry Clay and other great nation-makers, the American nation was an achievement and legacy, a beacon of 'hope to the world for all future time', that must be preserved at all costs.[46] The union was a nation and insurrection therefore must be suppressed. But if, as Southerners claimed, the union was the negation of nationhood—a form of despotic rule that thwarted the legitimate aspirations of Southern people to determine their own destiny—its dissolution would instead initiate a bright new chapter in the history of freedom.

The nation, Smith taught, should be a regime of equal benefits and burdens, a domain within which enterprising individuals could enjoy the fullest possible exercise of their 'natural liberty'.[47] When Smith addressed the American crisis in Book V of *The Wealth of Nations* (on 'the Revenue of the Sovereign or Commonwealth'), his attention focused on the problematic boundaries of Britain's national market. Were the colonies part of the 'nation' and would they participate fully in its market regime? Would the Americans pay their fair share of the costs of civil government? In an enlightened nation where monopoly privileges had been abolished, the costs of defending the nation's sovereignty would be borne equally by all taxpayers.

The nation thus defined the boundaries of the internal, home market, and it was only within that bounded domain that a regime of free trade was possible. The 'freedom of interior commerce', Smith explained, was 'the effect of the uniformity of the system of taxation' and 'perhaps one of the principal causes of the prosperity of Great Britain'.[48] Freedom was linked with taxation because Britain and other European nations operated within a diplomatic system that pivoted on a balance of political and military power. Britain's power depended on incorporating distant provinces into both the state and a growing internal market. 'The extension of the custom-house laws of Great Britain to Ireland and the plantations, provided it

---

46   Speech in Independence Hall, Philadelphia, Pa., Feb. 22, 1861, in ed., Roy Basler, *The Collected Works of Abraham Lincoln* (9 vols., New Brunswick, N.J., 1953–55), vol. 4, pp. 240–41.

47   *WN*, vol. 2, p. 687.

48   Ibid., vol. 2, p. 900.

was accompanied, as in justice it ought to be, with an extension of the freedom of trade, would be in the highest degree advantageous to both.' Free trade 'between all the different parts of the British empire' and a system of uniform taxation would create 'an immense internal market for every part of the produce of all its different provinces'.[49]

Britain's comparative advantage in Europe was a function of the superior development of its home market. By contrast, the British overseas empire was riddled with mercantilistic regulations that impeded market freedom and economic development. Mercantilists were enthralled by the vision of 'a great empire on the west side of the Atlantic', an empire that 'has hitherto existed in imagination only'.[50] They were dazzled by the apparent advantages of monopolising the colony trade, failing to recognise the distorting effects of its artificially high profits on 'that natural balance which would otherwise have taken place among all the different branches of British industry'.[51] Privileged interests both at home and in the colonies flourished at the expense of the nation as a whole.

Colonial taxpayers, spared most of the costs of imperial administration, were among the immediate beneficiaries of this corrupt mercantilist regime. Nevertheless, the denial of their market freedom—that is, of full integration in the British national market—would stunt their future prospects. Given the colonies' 'present state of improvement', imperial regulations of colonial trade may 'have not hitherto been very hurtful'. This would no longer be true, however, as the colonies moved rapidly to a higher stage of development. It would then become apparent that it was 'a manifest violation of the most sacred rights of mankind', Smith concluded, 'to prohibit a great people...from making all that they can of every part of their own produce, or from employing their stock and industry in the way that they judge most advantageous to themselves'.[52]

Smith's most highly charged and judgemental language rhetorically marked the boundaries of the nation-as-market. At some glorious distant day, market and world might coincide—a prospect that Smith's students dwelled on much more than Smith himself—but in the present state of historical development, the nation played a critical, progressive role in expanding the ambit of market freedom. The British nation stood at an epochal conjuncture in the imperial crisis leading up to the American Revolution. It could either extend its boundaries westward, to Ireland and the 'plantations', by incorporating subject peoples fully into the national market. Or it could renounce its jurisdiction (in the colonies, at least), and acknowledge American independence.

Incorporation would subject these peoples to a 'uniform' system of taxation, and thus remove the 'badges of slavery' that mercantilist regulations had 'imposed upon them'.[53] Independence for the American colonies would allow Britain to negotiate a treaty of commerce with them that 'would effectually secure a free trade, more

---

49   Ibid., vol. 2, p. 935.
50   Ibid., vol. 2, p, 946.
51   Ibid., vol. 2, pp.604–5.
52   Ibid., vol. 2, p. 582.
53   Ibid.

advantageous to the great body of the people, though less so to the merchants, than the monopoly which she at present enjoys'.[54] Incorporation was the better choice, because free trade would then not be hostage to political negotiations in a context of persisting international rivalries. If incorporation was no longer possible, however, an early peace on favourable terms was clearly preferable to a devastating war, the reverse image of the economist's vision of free trade, peace, and prosperity.

In 1861 Southerners rejected the kind of incorporation Smith sought for the Americans in 1776, seeking instead to withdraw from an illegitimate union that jeopardised their most vital interests, most notably the institution of slavery. Yet, ironically, it was the classical economist Smith, the visionary advocate of a world-wide division of labour, who taught Southerners 'to calculate the value of our union' and so call into question the very reality of American nationhood.[55] Northern protectionists in turn challenged the free traders' appropriation of Smith, discovering new dimensions in the master's great text that the 'theorists' had ignored. The Whig economist Henry Carey thus distinguished Smith from his professed disciples: 'after an interval of many years, upon a reperusal of *The Wealth of Nations*, I found that the essential object of that great work had been to teach the people of Great Britain, that the system, against which it has been the object of protection among ourselves to guard, was not less manifestly destructive of themselves than it was violative 'of the most sacred rights of mankind' at large'.[56] Carey's Smith was the champion of a developing home market, a patriot committed to securing and perfecting the nation against all threats, internal and external. Disunion, the fragmentation and destruction of a national market, was in this Smithian—and Lincolnian—perspective a retrograde movement, a potentially catastrophic retreat from the progressive extension and perfection of market relations that constituted the logic of modern history. Secession was inexorably regressive. 'Why,' Lincoln asked, 'may not any portion of a new confederacy, a year or two hence, arbitrarily secede again, precisely as portions of the present Union now claim to secede from it?'[57]

Southerners answered Lincoln's question by invoking their own claims to nationhood. Southerners were united by the common interests, institutions, and principles of an homogenous, civilised and separate people. In making these claims, they turned away from the cosmopolitan Smith who had led them out of the union. As they sought to redefine their place in the world, Southerners instead embraced the nationalist logic that protectionists' reading of Smith's *Wealth of Nations* had revealed. They would risk everything in a great war to vindicate their independence and secure their nation's wealth from Northern depredations.

---

54   Ibid., vol. 2, p. 617.

55   Speech of Thomas Cooper, July 27, 1827, in *Niles Weekly Register*, 33 (Sept. 8, 1827), reprinted in ed., William W. Freehling, *The Nullification Era: A Documentary Record* (New York, 1967), 25.

56   Henry C. Carey, *The Prospect: Agricultural, Manufacturing, Commercial, and Financial. At the Opening of the Year 1851* (Philadelphia, 1851), 5.

57   Lincoln's First Inaugural Address, March 4, 1861, Basler ed., *Works of Lincoln*, 4:268.

Chapter 9

The Enlightenment at Sea in the Atlantic World

Paul A. Gilje

Writing shortly before his death in 1891, Herman Melville placed his last novel in the 1790s, during a period of political and ideological upheaval. *Billy Budd* is a story of impressment and harsh naval justice. But like much of Melville's work there is a strain of sardonic humour and a playfulness with the meaning of words. Billy Budd is taken off a merchant ship whose owner, inspired by Thomas Paine, christened the vessel *Rights-of-Man*. Billy joins a British warship named ominously the HMS *Bellipotent*. As the longboat carrying Billy to the British navy passed under the stern of the merchantman, the 'officer and oarsmen were noting—some bitterly and others with a grin—the name emblazoned there'. At this moment 'the new recruit jumped up from the bow' of the boat, and silently and sorrowfully waved his hat to his ex shipmates. 'Then, making a salutation as to the ship herself', Billy declared 'And good-bye to you too, old *Rights-of-Man*'. Melville exonerates Billy of any satirical intent, stating that to this honest tar, 'To deal in double meanings and insinuations of any sort was quite foreign to his nature'. But Melville's pen leaves no doubt that the boat's crew and the officer understood the double meaning. Would the sailors have gotten the joke? Is Billy's gesture unlikely and just the invention of Herman Melville, or had ideas from the Enlightenment, including the rights of man, seeped into the forecastle?[1]

To understand the Enlightenment at sea, we must first outline a few generalizations about the Age of Reason concerning equality, reform, and social criticism. Then, we will examine the relationship between common men, especially common seamen, and the Enlightenment. Finally, we will turn to the words and ideas of common seamen to answer the question posed by Melville's Billy Budd and to determine if the Anglo-American mariner, the sailors holding the oars in the *Bellipotent*'s boat, would have understood Melville's joke.

Embedded in the Enlightenment were contradictions. On the one hand, the emphasis on natural social relations seemed to herald a new age of equality; on the other, most of the writers and thinkers of the Enlightenment saw themselves as natural aristocrats. Before 1750 it was easy enough for a philosophe both to call for a republican simplicity and to assume the superiority of gentlemen. The age of revolution made it increasingly difficult to sustain this dichotomy. When the Virginia planter Thomas Jefferson scribbled the phrase 'We hold these truths to be self evident, that all men are created equal', he was eloquently putting into words

---

1   Melville, *Billy Budd and Other Stories*, ed. Harold Beaver (New York, 1967), pp. 322–28.

an idea that most enlightened philosphes would agree with; but he also unleashed powerful forces that neither he, nor any other natural aristocrat could fully control. The ideal of equality had a life of its own, and was picked up and used by many different groups. In the United States it led to the spread of universal white manhood suffrage in the early-nineteenth century, a movement for the abolition of slavery, and the first stirring of the demand for equal rights for women. In France it created tremendous political upheaval driven by the slogan of liberty, equality, and fraternity. In the United Kingdom, the ideal of equality spawned a movement for constitutional reform that was stifled during the French and Napoleonic Wars, but ultimately led to electoral overhaul in the nineteenth century.[2]

Besides altering the political landscape, the Enlightenment also led to another type of reform—a reform of manners. Here, too, there were contradictions. Starting with the gentlemanly ideal, which should have been the exclusive province of the aristocracy, ideas of polite behaviour spread across society and helped to create the bourgeois, or middle class, world of the nineteenth century. Enlightened thinkers, beginning with John Locke, held that man was perfectible and should be responsible for his own behaviour. Released from the all controlling hand of providence, men were free agents who chose their own path and molded their own conduct. This development had profound implications. Refinement became an obtainable goal for any one who sought to achieve it. Through education and personal discipline proper behaviour could be learned. Enlightened thinkers therefore sought reform by establishing schools and other institutions to instill civility. In places like provincial Philadelphia, young artisans banded together for self improvement in the 'junto' of Benjamin Franklin fame. Franklin, the lightening tamer, became the embodiment of the Enlightenment as he sought to refashion himself from hard working mechanic to leisured gentleman and eighteenth-century philosopher. By applying the laws of reason to nature mankind could approach perfection.[3]

While it is possible to see the enlightened vision of a new world with some clarity, the closer one looks, the muddier the details become. Maybe, if everyman obtained the right level of gentility and taste, a truly egalitarian order was possible. But under what circumstances could that world exist? Much of the Enlightenment was an elaborate social critique of current regimes. Both the high minded philosophes and the underground literary culture described by Robert Darnton satirised false distinctions in society. Even the lower orders were not spared the venom of the philosophe's pen. The poor were often seen as wasteful. Hogarth's depictions of the street, drinking, and the low life of the underclass are legion. At heart most philosophes distrusted the common people, believing, in the words of Arthur Young,

---

2   See for example R. R. Palmer, *The Age of the Democratic Revolution: A Political History of Europe and America, 1760–1800* (Princeton, N.J., 1959–1964); E. P. Thompson, *The Making of the English Working Class* (New York, 1963); Gordon S. Wood, *The Radicalism of the American Revolution* (New York, 1992).

3   Richard L. Bushman, *Refinement of America: Persons, Houses, Cities* (New York, 1992); Gordon S. Wood, *The Americanization of Benjamin Franklin* (New York, 2004).

that 'Everyone but an idiot knows that the lower class must be kept poor or they will never be industrious'.[4]

Searching for the right circumstances to create a universe of equality brings us to the relationship between common men and the Enlightenment. Putting aside the criticism of the lower orders, many enlightened thinkers thought highly of some common men. Thomas Jefferson provides an excellent window into how an eighteenth-century philosophe might view the common men of the Atlantic world. In 1785, while Jefferson was in Paris, he wrote to John Jay dividing common men into three groups: farmers, artisans and mariners. Each represented three different components of the political economy: agriculture, manufacturing and commerce. Jefferson extolled the virtues of the farmer, believing that farmers were the 'peculiar deposit for substantial virtue' and that 'those who labour in the earth' were 'the chosen people of God'. Jefferson held that 'Corruption of morals in the mass of cultivators is a phenomenon of which no age no nation has furnished an example'. Jefferson thought the least of artisans. He admitted that carpenters, masons, and smiths were important and even necessary to sustain agriculture. But he declared that 'while we have land to labour ... let us never wish to see our citizens occupied at a work-bench, or twirling a distaff'.[5] Jefferson also knew that a carpenter earned more money in a week than a farm labourer made in a month.[6] That knowledge did not faze him. As he later explained to 'the labor of the husbandman' would be added the 'the spontaneous energies of the earth on which it was employed: for one grain of wheat committed to the earth, she renders twenty, thirty, and even fifty fold, whereas to the labor of the manufacturer nothing is added. Pounds of flax, in his hands, yield, on the contrary, but pennyweights of lace'.[7] Jefferson's concerns lay deeper than this political economy and science. He feared that artisans were dependent upon others for employment and that they could therefore easily be corrupted and contaminate the political system. In one of Jefferson's most memorable passages (which sounds as if it could have been inspired by Hogarth) he wrote: 'The mobs of great cities add just so much to the support of pure government, as sores do to the strength of the human body. It is the manners and spirit of a people which preserve a republic in vigour. A degeneracy in these is a canker which soon eats to the heart of its laws and constitution.'[8]

When he compared mariners and artisans, Jefferson thought sailors were the more 'valuable citizens'. This observation is surprising because the popular image of sailors in many ways was the antithesis of the rational and refined world of the

---

4   Quoted in Roy Porter, *The Creation of the Modern World: The Untold Story of the British Enlightenment* (New York, 2000), p. 377; Robert Darnton, *The Literary Underground of the Old Regime* (Cambridge, Mass., 1982).

5   Thomas Jefferson to John Jay, Aug. 23, 1785, Thomas Jefferson Papers Series I, General Correspondence. 1651–1827, Digital Archives, Library of Congress, Image 193.

6   Julian P. Boyd., *et al.*, eds, *The Papers of Thomas Jefferson* (33 vols. to date, Princeton, 1950–), Vol 7, pp. 32–55.

7   Thomas Jefferson to Benjamin Austin, Jan. 9, 1816, Thomas Jefferson Papers Series I, General Correspondence. 1651–1827, Digital Archives, Library of Congress, Image 737.

8   These quotations are from Jefferson's *Notes on the State of Virginia*. See Merrill D. Peterson, *The Portable Thomas Jefferson* (New York, 1975), p. 217.

Enlightenment. If any single group represented degeneracy in great cities, it was the sailor. Ashore, the stereotypical mariner was anything but refined; he was often drunk, unruly, and spent his money with abandon. In fact sailors espoused an ideal of 'liberty' emphasising personal licence which appeared to be the very opposite of the concern for order of the aristocracy of the eighteenth century and the moral responsibility of the middle class in the nineteenth century. As John Ross Browne explained, 'a sailor let loose from a ship is no better than a wild man. He is free; he feels what it is to be free. For a little while, at least, he is no dog to be cursed and ordered about by a ruffianly master. It is like an escape from bondage.'[9] American Joshua Penny expressed similar sentiments in describing his behavior while on his first 'liberty' in 1800 after having been pressed into the British navy, 'We went to London, with too much money not to loose a little. I had lived so long without the privilege of spending any thing, that I, too, was a gentleman while my money lasted'. Penny added 'No man spends his money more to his own notion than a sailor'.[10] The sailor on 'liberty' may have aped gentlemanly behaviour by riding in carriages and dressing in fine clothes above his station, but this conduct was more of an absurd parody, than an expansion of manners that so marked the developing middle class.[11]

Jefferson looked beyond these factors, and approached the common seamen with the calculating eye of an eighteenth-century man of science. Jefferson studied maritime enterprise, writing an insightful pamphlet on whaling in the 1780s while ambassador to France, and producing well-researched state papers on the fisheries and commerce as secretary of state in the 1790s.[12] Throughout much of his public career, Jefferson had to think about sailors, seeking to protect them from Barbary Pirates and dealing with the impressment of Americans into the British navy. Jefferson had three reasons for favouring sailors over artisans. First, it was the skill and expertise of mariners that brought manufactured goods from Europe and allowed the export of commodities that enabled farmers to be independent. If commerce was a necessary evil to sustain agriculture and free the United States from manufacturing, then the honest tars responsible for that commerce were a blessing that needed to be encouraged. As Jefferson explained: 'The loss of seamen, unnoticed, would be followed by other losses in a long train. If we have no seamen, our ships will be useless, consequently our Ship timber, Iron and hemp: our Ship building will be at an end, ship carpenters go over to other nations, our young men have no call to the Sea, our produce, carried in foreign bottoms, be saddled with freight and insurance' and ultimately we would become dependent and dragged into foreign wars. Moreover, losing shipping would 'have ruined or banished whole classes of useful and industrious Citizens.'[13]

---

9   John Ross Browne, *Etchings of a Whaling Cruise*, ed., John Seelye, (Cambridge, 1968; orig. pub. New York, 1846), p. 275.

10   Joshua Penny, *The Life and Adventures of Joshua Penny* ... (New York, 1815), p. 39.

11   Paul A. Gilje, *Liberty on the Waterfront: American Maritime Culture in the Age of Revolution* (Philadelphia, 2004).

12   For these reports and writings see eds., Boyd *et al.*, *The Papers of Thomas Jefferson*, Vol. 14.

13   *Ibid.*, Vol. 19, p. 219.

Second, fishing and whaling reaped the harvests of the seas. This activity was thus closely akin to agriculture. The people of Nantucket, for example, turned to whaling because 'Their country, from its barrenness, yielding no subsistence, they were obliged to seek it in the sea which surrounded them'. These hardy yeoman farmers of the sea 'instead of wages, had a share in what was taken. This induced them to fish with fewer hands, so that each had a greater dividend in the profit. It made them more vigilant in seeking their game, bolder in pursuing it, and parsimonious in all their expenses.'[14] Finally, sailors were the first line of defence of the nation. Merchant shipping and fishing would be the nurseries of mariners that could man the privateers and navy that would help counter the power of any European king who made war on the United States.[15]

Jefferson's view of the common seaman, therefore, represented his enlightened approach to political economy. If he was to sustain his vision of a virtuous republic, built upon the ideas of the age of reason, then he had to support American involvement in the commerce of the Atlantic, and he had to nurture and sustain a class of 'valuable citizens', men who earned their living from the sea.

Other men inspired by the Enlightenment began to think of ways of improving—read correcting—the behaviour of maritime workers through reform and Christianity to create truly 'valuable citizens' and replicas of the middle class. If man could be perfected, then even the seaman could change his character and become virtuous and upright. This movement was trans-Atlantic, beginning in Great Britain in the late-eighteenth century with John Thornton's efforts to aid British sailors and soldiers. It was continued during the French and Napoleonic Wars by waterfront missionaries who flew a Bethel flag, organised the Naval and Military Bible Society, and preached a message of self-discipline in an attempt to guide the seamen's behaviour along the proper path. A few Americans followed the British example before the War of 1812. After that conflict, and into the 1820s and 1830s, the movement really grew within the United States. In short, for these middle-class reformers, Jefferson's recognition of the contribution of the sailor was not enough; something had to be done to bring refinement to the waterfront.[16]

Considering the sailor as an important cog in the machine of commerce and as a proper object of Christian charity, provides some context for understanding the Enlightenment at sea and offers insight into how some enlightened thinkers viewed

---

14   *Ibid.*, Vol. 14, p. 243.

15   *Ibid.*, Vol. 14, p. 390.

16   *The Naval Chaplain, Exhibiting A View of American Efforts to Benefit Seamen* (Boston, 1831); Boston Society for the Religious and Moral Improvement of Seamen, *Address to Masters of Vessels on the Objects of the Boston Society for the Religious Improvement of Seamen* (Boston, 1812); and ibid., *The First Annual Report of the Executive Committee of the Boston Society for the Religious and Moral Improvement of Seamen* (Boston, 1813). See also George Sidney Webster, *The Seaman's Friend: A Sketch of the American Seaman's Friend Society, By Its Secretary* (New York, 1932); Roald Kverndal, *Seamen's Missions: Their Origin and Early Growth: A Contribution to the History of the Church Maritime* (Pasadena, 1986), pp. 417–34; Harold D. Langley, *Social Reform in the United States Navy, 1798–1862* (Annapolis, 1980), pp. 50–51; and Paul A. Gilje, *Liberty on the Waterfront*, (Philadelphia, 2004), pp. 195–227.

the common seaman, but it does not answer the question we began with: would Jack Tar have understood Melville's joke? Did the Enlightenment not only stretch across the Atlantic, but also *upon* the Atlantic, reaching into the forecastle and the world of the common seamen? To answer this question we need to explore the relationship between the social critique of the Enlightenment and the egalitarian currents intrinsic to Anglo-American maritime culture, examine what sailors read, and see if common seamen expressed ideas that we can connect to the Enlightenment. Although most of the evidence in this essay comes from American sources, the analysis rings true for the Anglo-American Atlantic world.

There is little question that the enlightened thinkers sustained a critique of eighteenth-century society. The French philosophes lambasted the *ancien régime*, providing the ideological kindling that broke out in the conflagration of the French Revolution. In Britain, Roy Porter writes, during 'the last third of the eighteenth century criticism cresendo'd against the political oppressiveness, social corruption, and moral licentiousness of blue blood'.[17] Thomas Holcroft declared that a 'peer of the realm' was 'but man educated in vice, nurtured in prejudice from his earliest childhood, and daily breathing the same infectious air he first respired!'[18] Thomas Paine's radicalism was bred in this spirit and he carried his resentments across the Atlantic to the American Revolution. In *Common Sense* he attacked both the monarchy, referring to William the Conqueror as a bastard, and hereditary succession, which Paine claimed 'opens a door to the *foolish*, the *wicked*, and the *improper*'. Paine asserted 'Of more worth is one honest man to society, and in the sight of God, than all the crowned ruffians that ever lived'.[19]

Such sentiments would find a receptive audience on the waterfront. But Jack Tar did not need an enlightened philosophe to learn anti-authoritarianism and egalitarianism. In the eighteenth and nineteenth centuries Anglo-American maritime culture had a long tradition of opposing authority and asserting some equality extraneous to the Enlightenment. Lest this argument be misunderstood, it is not advocating the red Atlantic of Marcus Rediker and Peter Linebaugh. The Atlantic was blue, sometimes blue grey, but never red. While Rediker and Linebaugh's discussion of a many-headed hydra makes fascinating reading, they push a few strands of evidence too hard and too far. They argue for a consistent tradition of liberty and equality in opposition to developing capitalism among commoners, African slaves, and sailors that permeated the revolutionary Atlantic.[20] Would that they were right. But the sailors that emerge from their pages bear little resemblance to the sailors found in the sources. Instead of a proletariat in the making, sailors were a diverse group of individuals who adhered to a culture that included both a rejection of authority and on-going adherence to authority. These people may have supported equality, but they recognised and accepted that they lived and worked in a world dominated by

---

17   Porter, *Enlightenment,* p. 400.

18   Quoted in *Ibid.*, p. 398.

19   Thomas Paine, *Common Sense*, ed. Isaac Kramnick (New York, 1976), 71–81. Quotations pp. 79, 81.

20   Peter Linebaugh and Marcus Rediker, *The Many-Headed Hydra: Sailors, Slaves, Commoners, and the Hidden History of the Revolutionary Atlantic* (Boston, 2000).

hierarchy. Expressions of anti-authoritarianism and equality occasionally surfaced at sea, but most often appeared in port. A sailor flouted authority by playing the gentleman while his money lasted, drinking and carousing. Oddly, this bout with a sailor's liberty left him in a state of poverty so that he was compelled to sign aboard ship again in a state akin to debt peonage, if not slavery.[21]

When looking for evidence of the Enlightenment aboard the ships that traversed the Atlantic, we must therefore be careful not to jump to any quick conclusions. Robert Darnton argues that the *libelles* of the literary underground 'communicated a revolutionary point of view: they showed that social rot was consuming French society, eating its way downward from the top'. From this perspective, social criticism, even 'pornographic details got the point across to a public that could not assimilate the *Social Contract*'.[22] Given the fact that some elements of the 'revolutionary point of view' were inherent in Anglo-American maritime culture we must move beyond a cause and effect relationship. The common seamen might have responded to the trickling down of enlightened ideals because they gave form and substance to fundamental values that were already present.

Roy Porter argues that the literature of the later Enlightenment often pitted the corruption of the rich and well born against the virtue of common folk as a way to illuminate social criticism. Two popular plays from the late-eighteenth century that appeared on both sides of the Atlantic demonstrate this theme centred on the unscrupulous aristocrat and the honest tar. In J. C. Cross's *The Purse; or Benevolent Tar*, a sailor's wife finds herself besieged by a member of the local gentry. He promises to save her from her abject poverty only if she succumbs to his carnal desires. The temptation was great, especially because her surrender would alleviate the virtual bondage of her son under the harsh hand of the evil intentioned suitor. She resists, and her sailor husband returns to save both his wife and his child.[23] Isaac Bickerstaff's *Thomas and Sally: Or, The Sailor's Return* has a similar plot. Sally, who is first seen sitting by a spinning wheel, denoting her virtue, industry and domesticity, pledges her love to Thomas before he goes off to sea. Before he can return, however, she, too, is importuned by a rich squire. She resists. In the final scene, Sally is carrying a milk pail—again the agrarian female virtue is portrayed without subtlety—when the squire approaches. He offers her money, clothes, and all kinds of promises. She refuses and he attacks her, attempting to have his way with her. Of course, just at this moment Thomas returns, saves Sally from a fate worse than death, and they live happily ever after.[24]

---

21   This argument is elaborated in Gilje, *Liberty on the Waterfront.*

22   Darnton, *Literary Underground,* p. 35.

23   J. C. Cross, *The Purse; or, Benevolent Tar. A Musical Drama in One Act as Performed at the Boston Theatre, Federal Street* (Boston, 1797). For the English edition see Cross, *The Purse; Or, Benevolent Tar: a Musical Drama, in One Act, as Performed at the Theatre Royal in the Hay-market. By J. C. Cross. (The Music by Mr. Reeve.)* Fourth edition (London, 1794).

24   [Isaac Bickerstaffe], *Thomas and Sally; or, The Sailor's Return. A Musical Entertainment ...* (Philadelphia, 1791). Originally published in London. Bickerstaff, *Thomas and Sally: Or, the Sailor's Return a Musical Entertainment. As it Is Performed at the Theatre Royal in Covent-garden* (London, 1761).

Both plays were very popular and had an obvious appeal to the waterfront community. According to Porter and Darnton these otherwise innocuous melodramas should represent a political radicalism striking at the core of aristocratic pretension. Perhaps. But Jack Tar did not need the Enlightenment, nor playwrights Bickerstaff and Cross, to tell him that he was virtuous and that the aristocracy was venal. Nor did he need to be reminded of the sexual vulnerability of women—and the sexual temptations faced by women—while he was at sea. In other words, this popular literature might have reflected some of the ideas of the Enlightenment, but it did not necessarily indicate a popular espousal of those ideas. Social resentment pre-existed the Enlightenment, even if it was the Enlightenment that gave it a form and substance through publication that we as historians can see.

As shown in his attack on monarchy and hereditary distinctions, Thomas Paine understood that resentment and capitalised upon it. He also took the ideas of the Enlightenment and made them comprehensible for the common man. Paine simplified social contract theory, distinguishing between society and government. He wrote: 'Society is produced by our wants, and government by our wickedness; the former promotes our happiness *positively* by uniting affections, the latter *negatively* by restraining our vices. The one encourages intercourse, the other creates distinctions. The first is a patron, the last a punisher.'[25] The clarity of this prose is striking. *Common Sense* sold hundreds of thousands of copies and established Paine as the one enlightened writer that we know reached the forecastle. Melville claimed that the merchant Stephen Girard of Philadelphia named some of his ships after European philosophers like Voltaire and Diderot.[26] If he did so, few of the tars aboard these vessels would have known who these men were. Tom Paine was another thing. His influence went beyond his famous call for independence in 1776. Many of his writings found their way into the hands of common seamen. Paine was read and talked about in the taverns and aboard ships throughout the Atlantic. The evidence is scarce, but Paine pops up in the most unexpected places. Charles Herbert, an American held as prisoner of war in Great Britain, was able to purchase a copy of Paine's *American Crisis* as a book in Mill Prison in December 1777. Although poorly fed and clothed, Herbert thought it worthwhile to use his limited resources in the dead of winter not only to buy the book, but to give it to a friend.[27] Even Paine's most controversial ideas espousing deism and attacking organised religion were known to sailors. Simeon Crowell, who had worked his way from serving as a boy on fishing schooners on the Grand Banks to commanding coastal vessels, described how he and his first mate 'earnestly contended' over 'the Blasphemous writings of Tom Paine' in 1802.[28] Ned Myers ran into a deist steward at a naval hospital in the

---

25   Paine, *Common Sense*, p. 64.

26   Melville, pp. 326–7.

27   Charles Herbert, *A Relic of the Revolution, Containing a Full and Particular Account of the Sufferings and Privations of All the American Prisoners Captured on the High Seas …* (Boston, 1847), p. 78.

28   Simeon Crowell, 'Commonplace Book of Simeon Crowell', MS, dated 1801, with additions after that date, pp. 59–60, Massachusetts Historical Society.

early nineteenth century who introduced him to Tom Paine's works, making him 'indifferent to my bible and prayerbook, as well as careless of the future'.[29] More important than Paine in spreading the ideas of the Enlightenment, was the experience of living through the age of revolution. Sailors are a difficult group to study and understand. I have argued elsewhere that the commitment of many Jack Tars to the American Revolution was ambiguous—men switched sides and pursued the main chance with aplomb. Often common seamen were more concerned with surviving the moment than with any higher ideal.[30] But that does not mean that those ideals were entirely absent. Throughout the war, sailors seized upon the symbols of the revolution, especially connected to the word liberty, and made them their own. Even cabin boy Christopher Hawkins sported buttons on his jacket with 'liberty and property' etched upon them.[31] After the Revolutionary War, memory took over and further transformed the experience of the revolution. Along the American waterfront, the idea that so many sailors had sacrificed for liberty became deeply imbedded into the popular consciousness. The American maritime community pointed to the ordeal of the prison ship *Jersey* in New York harbour, where thousands had died of disease and malnutrition, as being emblematic of that sacrifice.[32] Somehow the words of Jefferson and Paine became folded into one another, compressed into the ideal of liberty. Common seamen may not have spoken of these ideals on every day of their lives, but they became a part of their common heritage, shared with others in yarns, brought to life through song. Following the erratic path of maritime commerce, men crisscrossed the Atlantic and served under many flags. Ideas, however inarticulately expressed, spread.

Then came the French Revolution. Ideas churned more turbulently throughout the Atlantic, inspiring would-be constitutional reformers in Great Britain, breaking out in slave insurrection in the West Indies, contributing to the movement for Irish separatism, sweeping across Europe, kindling independence movements in Latin America, and arousing political passions in the United States. We will never fully understand the role of the common seamen in this ideological ferment, but since commerce brought these men into direct contact with each region of upheaval, they experienced at first hand what others could only read about. The waterfront became the filter through which much of the passion of the age of revolution must have

---

29   J. Fenimore Cooper, ed., *Ned Myers; or, A Life Before the Mast* (Annapolis,1989; orig. pub. Philadelphia, 1843), p. 241.

30   Gilje, *Liberty on the Waterfront*, 97–129; Gilje, 'Liberty and Loyalty: The Ambiguous Patriotism of Jack Tar in the American Revolution', *Pennsylvania History*, 67/2 (2000): 165–93.

31   Christopher Hawkins, *The Adventures of Christopher Hawkins, Containing Details of His Captivity, A First and Second Time on the High Seas by the British ...* (New York, 1864), pp. 62–3.

32   On the memory of the American Revolution see Sarah J. Purcell, *Sealed With Blood: War, Sacrifice, and Memory in Revolutionary America* (Philadelphia, 2002); Michael Kammen, *A Season of Youth: The American Revolution and the Historical Imagination* (New York, 1978), esp. pp. 41–9; Alfred F. Young, *The Shoemaker and the Tea Party: Memory and the American Revolution* (Boston, 1999), esp., pp. 132–42. See also Robert E. Cray, Jr., 'Commemorating the Prison Ship Dead: Revolutionary Memory and the Politics of Sepulture in the Early Republic, 1776–1808', *William and Mary Quarterly*, 3rd ser. 55/3 (1999): 565–90.

passed.[33] Two examples from the United States suggest how potent the revolutionary experience had become. In January 1793 the Boston waterfront erupted in excitement over the French victory at Valmy. To mark this republican triumph Bostonians held a celebration at Oliver's Dock, the site of a great Stamp Act demonstration 28 years before. The people of Boston understood the symbolism of this location: they erected a liberty pole, a ritual borrowed from the American Revolution and resuscitated during the French Revolution, and renamed the place 'Liberty Square'. At another republican celebration a month later, Bostonians directly connected earlier events at Oliver's Dock to the universal movement for revolution sweeping the Atlantic by offering a toast that declared: 'May the citizens of the spot which in 1765 witnessed the destruction of an infamous Stamp Office be ever famous for celebrating events propitious to the Equal Liberty to all Mankind.'[34] The trans-Atlantic nature of this appeal appeared in Philadelphia when the French ship *L'Embuscade* arrived on May 2, 1793. The French ship, which had brought Citizen Edmond Genêt to the United States, sported banners from each masthead that proclaimed: 'enemies of equality, reform or tremble!'; 'Freemen, behold we are your friends and brothers!'; and 'we are armed for the defense of the rights of man!' As the French sailors disgorged on shore they filled the waterfront taverns with news of their revolution and of how they had earned prize money while fighting for liberty.[35]

Fuelled by the age of revolution, Jack Tar combined his own interest, a long standing egalitarianism, and the Enlightenment clarion for the rights of man in at least three areas. On the most fundamental level some common seamen used the idea that all men had inherent rights to denounce the often inhuman treatment they experienced at sea. Second, a few sailors extended the general assertion of the rights of mankind to attacks on slavery—although such attacks were often disguised. And third, in an odd twist of rhetoric, many American sailors rallied around the slogan 'free trade and sailors' rights' as the United States entered the War of 1812, to assert not only the fact that mariners shared rights with other men, but also to proclaim support for an unfettered commerce that would fulfil the antimercantilist dream of Adam Smith.

A few American seamen began to articulate ideas connected to the Enlightenment in the first decade of the nineteenth century. William Ray, a marine who served against the Barbary pirates, was captured on the *Philadelphia* off Tripoli in 1803. Before describing his ordeal he stated that he revered the American constitution as the 'conservator of liberty' because it 'expressly declares that her invaluable blessings are the equal and unalienable right of mankind'.[36] Ray also used his narrative to decry the treatment of common men in the navy where 'petty despotism' held sway and

---

33   Gilje, *Liberty on the Waterfront*, pp. 130–62.

34   Simon P. Newman, *Parades and the Politics of the Street: Festive Culture in the Early Republic* (Philadelphia, 1997), pp. 65–6, 150. Quoted on ibid., p. 66.

35   Meade Minnigerode, *Jefferson Friend of France, 1793: The Career of Edmond Charles Genêt* (New York, 1928), pp. 184–97; Stanley Elkins and Eric McKitrick, *The Age of Federalism: The Early American Republic, 1788–1800* (New York, 1993), pp. 330–54; Philadelphia *General Advertiser*, 17, 18 May 1793.

36   William Ray, *Horrors of Slavery: or the American Tars in Tripoli* (Troy, 1808), pp. 18–19.

'an insolent tyrant [can] inflict tortures for petty offences'. James Durand, who also served in the Mediterranean with the American fleet in the early nineteenth century, echoed these sentiments. He described floggings for minor crimes as 'outrages on human nature' and believed that they 'ought not to be permitted by a government which boasts of liberty'.[37]

These same ideas appeared in subsequent decades as other mariners demanded their rights at sea. William McNally in the 1830s conflated the founding documents of the United States in a revealing manner, suggesting the power of the idea of equality. He accused Commodore Isaac Chauncy of forgetting 'the principle feature in the declaration of independence and constitution of our country: "All men are born equal"'.[38] Solomon Sanborn began his 1841 expose on the United States Navy with a quote from Thomas Jefferson: 'I have sworn upon the altar of God, eternal hostility to every invasion of the rights of man.'[39] He put the same concept into his own words by asserting 'If the Rights of Man for which our fathers bared their breasts to the bayonets of the oppressor be worth preserving, they are worth preserving well; and every citizen, from the proudest to the most humble is *equally* entitled to the protection of the laws of mankind'. And Samuel Leech, whose career bridged both the British and American navy's during the War of 1812, proclaimed 'A man should be secured the rights of a citizen, as well on the planks as the soil of his country'.[40]

Concern with the rights of humanity expanded among some Anglo-American sailors to include slavery. This sentiment was not widespread and many seamen retained racist ideas even when they shared living space and worked with blacks. Yet there was a fine line between racism and a critique of the peculiar institution when a sailor compared his lot at sea with the plight of the slave. Tiphys Aegyptus—a name that itself suggest an African affinity that must be a pseudonym—wrote in the 1840s that using the lash against sailors was treating them as 'worse then the slave on a plantation'.[41] Whaler John Ross Browne proclaimed that he 'would gladly have exchanged my place with that of the most abject slave in Mississippi', and said that the men in the navy and in the whale fishery were 'white slaves'.[42] In the 1830s William McNally criticised the hypocrisy of abolitionist ship owners by stating 'Those who rail at negro slavery should take care that none of their own servants [the men who serve aboard their ships] are receiving the treatment of slaves'.[43]

---

37 James Durand, *James Durand: An Able Seaman of 1812: His Adventures on 'Old Ironsides' and as an Impressed Sailor in the British Navy*, ed. George S. Brooks (New Haven, 1926; orig. pub. 1820), pp. 18–19.

38 Willaim McNally, *Evils and Abuses in the Naval and Merchant Service, Exposed; With Proposals For Their Remedy and Redress* (Boston, 1839), p. 95.

39 Solomon H. Sanborn, *An Exposition of Official Tyranny in the United States Navy* (New York, 1841), p. 16.

40 Samuel Leech, *A Voice from the Main Deck: Being a Record of the Thirty Years' Adventures of Samuel Leech*, ed. Michael J. Crawford (Annapolis, 1999; orig. pub., Boston, 1843), pp. 237–8.

41 Tiphys Aegypytus, *The Navy's Friend, or Reminiscences of the Navy, Containing Memoirs of a Cruise in the U S. Enterprise* (Baltimore, 1843), p. 12.

42 Browne, pp. 315, 356.

43 McNally, p. 129.

Lest we think that this sort of commentary was limited to the antebellum period, after the age of Jefferson and the high water of the Enlightenment, we can turn to the 1790s and early 1800s to find other comparisons between slavery and the common sailor. During this period the plight of hundreds of American seamen captured by Barbary Pirates and desert ruffians in Africa elicited great public sympathy and a peculiar brand of early abolitionist literature centred on the irony of the enslavement of white Americans by dark skinned Africans. Matthew Carey, a trans-Atlantic political economist and printer, published his *A Short Account of Algiers* in 1794 detailing the treatment of American maritime captives on the Barbary Coast and drawing explicit comparisons to American slavery and implicitly attacking the treatment of any human being as chattel.[44] Susanna Rowson, who was born in North America, raised in England, and re-immigrated to the United States, wrote her play *Slaves in Algiers* also in 1794. It contrasted liberty loving Americans and despotic Algerians.[45] Royall Tyler, a Jeffersonian politician who almost married John Adams's daughter, published *The Algerine Captive* in 1797 in which Updike Underhill signs aboard a slaver as the ship's doctor. This son of New England sails to England, where he meets and argues with Tom Paine, and is then captured by Algerians off the coast of Africa. Tyler's message becomes all too clear in this twist of fate, the white slave trader himself becomes the slave of Africans.[46]

More significant, however, are the writings of sailors themselves. John Foss provided his own narrative of his ordeal at the hands of Algiers in 1798. Captured in 1793, he was held in 'the most inhuman slavery; loaded with almost an insupportable weight of chains' for three years.[47] Thomas Nicholson was captured by Barbary Pirates in 1809 and spent six years in slavery.[48] It is within this context that William Ray wrote his book, *Horrors of Slavery* in which he contrasted the treatment of seamen in the navy with their treatment as prisoners in Tripoli, labelling both akin to slavery. The most influential book in this genre was James Riley's *Authentic Narrative of the Loss of the American Brig Commerce*, which described a shipwreck off the coast of Africa, the incredible sacrifices of the captain to save the crew, his dehumanisation through slavery, and his ultimate redemption. With its antislavery subtext, the book became one of the best sellers of the first half of the nineteenth century. As editor of the *North American Review*, Jared Sparks praised its

---

44　Matthew Carey, *A Short Account of Algiers and of Its Several Wars* ..., 2nd ed. (Philadelphia, 1794). See also James Wilson Stevens, *An Historical and Geographical Account of Algiers* ... (Philadelphia, 1797); John Willcock, *The Voyages and Adventures of John Willcock, Mariner* ... (Philadelphia, 1798); *Humanity in Algiers: Or the Slave of Azem, By an American, Late a Slave of Algiers* (Troy, 1801); and Robert J. Allison, *The Crescent Obscured: The United States and the Muslim World, 1776–1815* (New York, 1995).

45　Susanna Rowson, *Slaves in Algiers, or, Struggle for Freedom* (Philadelphia, 1794).

46　[Royall Tyler], *The Algerine Captive; or the Life and Adventures of Doctor Updike Underhill* ... (Walpole, N.H., 1797).

47　John Foss, *A Journal of the Captivity and Sufferings of John Foss* ... (Newburyport, [1798]), 64–5.

48　Thomas Nicholson, *An Affecting Narrative of the Captivity and Sufferings of Thomas Nicholson [A Native of New Jersey] Who Has Been Six Years a Prisoner among the Algerines* ... (Boston, 1816).

'good faith and sailor-like frankness'. Henry David Thoreau thought of Riley's book as he ambled along the Cape Cod shore. And Abraham Lincoln listed it as one of the six books that had most influenced his life.[49]

The common seamen responded to the ideas of the Enlightenment when those ideas seem to speak to their own lives. Concepts like the universal rights of man and equality pulled on some basic chords that were deeply imbedded in Anglo-American maritime culture and that reflected the experience of living through the age of revolution. American sailors came to support the idea of free trade for the same reasons. Few seamen, if any, read or ever heard of Adam Smith. Yet, starting in the 1790s, and into the early 1800s, the American tar rallied around the concept of free trade and identified it with sailors' rights. The wars between Great Britain and France that began in 1793 presented a tremendous opportunity for American commerce. Neutral and free trade would allow American merchants to reap huge profits and American sailors high wages. Interest and ideology intersected. Seamen Charles Clinton must have recognised this fact when he wrote the words of the patriotic song 'Adams and Liberty' in his personal journal of 1802–1806:

> In a Clime whose rich vales feed the marts of the world
> Whose shores are unshaken by Europe's Commotion
> The Trident of Commerce Should Never be hurled
> To incense the Legitimate Powers of the Ocean
> But should Pirates [in this case the French] invade
> Though in thunder arrayed
> Let your Cannon Declare a free charter of Trade.[50]

Impressment of American sailors only intensified this sentiment. American sailors opposed impressment because it threatened their livelihoods and independence. When politicians trumpeted the issue, Jack Tar eagerly supported them. Impressment and free trade thus became increasingly identified with each other and at the outbreak of the War of 1812 became merged into the political slogan 'Free Trade and Sailors' Rights' which became an important battle cry during the conflict with Great Britain, and remained a potent catch-word for the common man for decades thereafter.[51]

While we can see some elements of the Enlightenment among common sailors, we must recognise that other components of the Age of Reason were consciously rejected when they seemed to conflict with Anglo-American maritime culture. In particular, Jack Tar often renounced the refinement and taste that became the hallmark of the emerging middle class. William Ray argued that most sailors were 'not a Franklin in economy' and rejected his parsimony. Ray goes on to explain the extremes of the sailor's behaviour on shore. Ray said that seamen's 'minds, actions and passions being long under restraint, like water, obstructed by a mound, when let

---

49 James Riley, *An Authentic Narrative of the Loss of the Brig 'Commerce'* (Hartford, 1817); Henry David Thoreau, *Cape Cod*, intro by Paul Theroux (New York, 1987), p. 234; Allison, *Crescent Obscured*, pp. 207–25.

50 Charles P. Clinton, 'His Journal Book', 1802–1806, Western Americana Collection, Beinecke Rare Book and Manuscript Library, Yale University, New Haven, Conn.

51 Gilje, *Liberty on the Waterfront*, pp. 167, 170, 180, 183–4, 218–19, 258.

loose overflows its channels, they lose themselves in the torrent of dissipation and lasciviousness'.[52]

Before offering a final answer to the question we began with—would sailors have gotten Melville's joke—we need to turn again to the story of Billy Budd. Melville recited briefly the history of the great mutinies at Spithead and the Nore in 1797 when British seamen refused their duty in an effort to gain a redress of grievances. Melville used these references to help explain Captain Vere's unflinching rigidity in punishing Billy after the inarticulate tar stammered and murdered a false accuser. Examination of the petitions and documents coming from the mutiny helps us to further understand the Enlightenment at sea. Most of the petitions dealt with fundamental issues like pay, treatment, and liberty ashore. Only occasionally did they refer to a larger ideological context. The more radical mutiny occurred at the Nore, where the sailors set up their own floating republic with an elaborate committee network. In one explanation for their rebellion intended for the popular press, the seamen proclaimed 'the age of reason has at length revolved. Long have we been endeavouring to find ourselves men. We now find ourselves so. We will be treated as such.' Richard Parker, who was elected president of the delegates of the fleet, confessed after he was sentenced to be executed that he was 'to die a Martyr to the cause of humanity'.[53] Provided with this context, and admitting that sailors often came to the ideas of the Enlightenment for their own reasons, we can conclude that the wry smiles of the oarsmen and the frowns of the officers as Billy bade farewell to the *Rights-of-Man* were not far fetched, and that Jack Tar would have gotten the joke.

---

52   Ray *Horrors of Slavery*, pp. 19–20, 36.

53   Job Sibly, *The Trial of Richard Parker, Complete; President of the Delegates, for Mutiny, &c* ... (Boston, 1797), pp. 275, 49. See also James Dugan, *The Great Mutiny* (New York, 1965); Dudley Pope, *The Black Ship* (New York, 1998; orig. pub. 1963); Joseph P. Moore, III, '"The Greatest Enormity that Prevails:" Direct Democracies and Workers' Self-Management in the British Naval Mutinies of 1797', in eds., Colin Howell and Richard J. Twomey, *Jack Tar in History: Essays in the History of Maritime Life and Labour* (Fredericton, New Brunswick, 1991), pp. 11–36, 76–104.

Works Cited

Manuscript Sources

Beinecke Rare Book Library,	Charles P. Clinton, His Journal Book, 1802– Yale University, New Haven 1806.
British Library, London	David Hume, Notebook, Add. Mss. 36638, pp. 8r, 8v, 9r, 13v, 14r, 18v.
Library of Congress, Washington	Thomas Jefferson Papers Series I, General Correspondence. 1651–1827, Digital Archives.
Massachusetts Historical Society, Boston	Simeon Crowell, Commonplace Book, 1801, with additions after that date.
National Library of Scotland, Edinburgh	Letter from D'Alembert to David Hume, MS 23153, no. 2, f. 365.
Royal College of Physicians, Edinburgh	John Walker's Natural History Syllabus

Printed Primary Sources

Aegyptus, Tiphys, *The Navy's Friend, or Reminiscences of the Navy, Containing Memoirs of a Cruise in the U. S. Enterprise* (Baltimore, 1843).

American Whig Review 1 (1845).

American Whig Review 6 (1850).

Barlow, Joel, *The Works of Joel Barlow*, William K. Bottorff and Arthur L. Ford (eds) (2 vols., Gainesville, FL: Scholars' Facsimiles & Reprints, 1970).

Beattie, James, *An Essay on the Nature and Immutability of Truth; in Opposition to Sophistry and Scepticism* (Edinburgh, 1770).

'The Beauties of the Power of Sympathy', *Massachusetts Magazine*, 1 (1789): 50–53.

Bellin, J. N., *Recueil des Memoires qui ont été publiés avec les Cartes* Hydrographiques (Paris, 1751).

Bellin, J. N., *Hydrographie Francaise* (2 vols, Paris, 1792).

[Bickerstaffe, Isaac], *Thomas and Sally; or, The Sailor's Return. A Musical Entertainment* (Philadelphia, 1791).

Blagden, C., 'On the Heat of the Water in the Gulf-Stream', *Philosophical Transactions of the Royal Society of London*, 71 (1781): 334–44.

Boston Society for the Religious and Moral Improvement of Seamen, *Address to Masters of Vessels on the Objects of the Boston Society for the Religious Improvement of Seamen* (Boston, 1812).

Boston Society for the Religious and Moral Improvement of Seamen, *The First Annual Report of the Executive Committee of the Boston Society for the Religious and Moral Improvement of Seamen* (Boston, 1813).

Boswell, James, *The Life of Johnson* (1791), Christopher Hibbert (ed.) (Harmondsworth: Penguin, 1979).

Boswell, James, *The Journal of a Tour to the Hebrides* (1775), Peter Levi (ed.) (London: Penguin, 1984).

Brooke, Henry, *The Fool of Quality; or, The History of Henry Earl of Moreland* (5 vols, London, 1766–1770; repr. New York and London: Garland, 1979).

Brown, William Hill, *The Power of Sympathy* (1789) (New York: Penguin, 1996).

Bülow, D. von, *Der Freistaat von Nord-Amerika in seinem neuesten Zustand* (Berlin: Unger, 1797).

Burke, Edmund, *The Correspondence of Edmund Burke*, Thomas W. Copeland (ed.) (Cambridge, 1958).

Burke, Edmund, *Reflections on the French Revolution* (1790), intro. A. J. Grieve (London: Dent; New York: Dutton, 1953).

Burton, John Hill, *Life and Correspondence of David Hume* (2 vols, Edinburgh, 1846).

Butterfield, L. H. *et al.* (eds), *The Adams Family Correspondence* (7 vols to date, Cambridge, Mass.: Harvard University Press, 1963–).

Butterfield, L. H., *John Witherspoon Comes to America: A Documentary Account* (Princeton: Princeton University Press, 1953).

Brackenridge, Hugh Henry, *Modern Chivalry* (1792–1797), Claude M. Newlin (ed.) (New York and London: Hafner, 1968).

Browne, John Ross, *Etchings of a Whaling Cruise* (1846), John Seelye (ed.) (Cambridge, Mass., 1968).

Carey, Henry C., *The Past, the Present, and the Future* (Philadelphia, 1848).

Carey, Henry C., *The Prospect: Agricultural, Manufacturing, Commercial, and Financial. At the Opening of the Year 1851* (Philadelphia, 1851).

Carey, Henry C., *The Slave Trade: Domestic and Foreign: Why It Exists, and How It May Be Extinguished* (London and Philadelphia, 1853).

Carey, Matthew, *A Short Account of Algiers and of Its Several Wars*, 2nd ed. (Philadelphia, 1794).

Cervantes Saavedra, Miguel de, *The Adventures of Don Quixote de la Mancha*, trans. Tobias Smollett (1755) (London: Deutsch, 1986).

Christian Examiner (Boston), 7 (1829).

[Clarke, Richard], *The Nabob, or Asiatic Plunderers* (London, 1773).

Colton, Calvin *Public Economy of the United States* (New York, 1848).

Cooper, James Fenimore (ed.), *Ned Myers; or, A Life Before the Mast* (1843) (Annapolis Naval Institute,1989).

Cooper, Thomas, *Lectures on the Elements of Political Economy*, 2nd ed. (1830) (New York, 1971).

Correspondance inédite de Condorcet et de Turgot 1770–1779, Charles Henry (ed.) (Paris, 1883).

Cowper, William, *The Poems of William Cowper,* John D. Baird and Charles Ryskamp (eds) (3 vols, Oxford: Oxford University Press, 1980–1995).

Cross, J. C., *The Purse; or, Benevolent Tar. A Musical Drama in One Act as Performed at the Boston Theatre, Federal Street* (Boston, 1797).

Decisions of the Court of Sessions, from November 1769 to January 1772, collected by Hamilton (Edinburgh, 1803).

Dew, Thomas Roderick, *Lectures on the Restrictive System Delivered to the Senior Political Class of William and Mary College* (Richmond, 1829).

Durand, James, *James Durand: An Able Seaman of 1812: His Adventures on 'Old Ironsides' and as an Impressed Sailor in the British Navy* (1820), George S. Brooks (ed.) (New Haven: Yale University Press, 1926).

Edwards, B., *The History, Civil and Commercial, of the British Colonies in the West Indies* (London, 1793).

Ein grosser Sieg welche die Braunschweig- u, Hessischen Truppen in Amerika bey Neu-York den 31. August gegen die Amerikanischen Truppen durch ihre Tapferkeit erhalten haben (s.l., 1776).

Estwick, Samuel, *Considerations on the Negroe Cause*, 2nd edition (London, 1773).

The Federalist (1787–88), Jacob E. Cooke (ed.) (Middletown, Conn.: Wesleyan University Press, 1961).

Fielding, Henry, *Don Quixote in England*, in *The Complete Works of Henry Fielding* (16 vols, London: Heinemann, 1903), vol. 11.

Fielding, Henry, *The History of the Adventures of Joseph Andrews, and of his Friend, Mr. Abraham Adams* (2 vols, London, 1742).

Fitzhugh, George, *Sociology for the South: or, The Failure of Free Society* (1854) (New York: B. Franklin, 1965).

Foss, John, *A Journal of the Captivity and Sufferings of John Foss* (Newburyport, 1798).

Fourth Report of the Royal Commission on Historical Manuscripts (London, 1874).

Franklin, Benjamin, *Information to Those who would Remove to America* (London: [n.p.], 1794).

[Franklin, B.], 'A Letter from Dr. Benjamin Franklin, to Mr. Alphonsus le Roy, Member of several Academies, at Paris. Containing sundry Maritime Observations', *Transactions of the American Philosophical Society*, 2 (1786): 294–324.

Freehling, William W. (ed.) *The Nullification Era: A Documentary Record* (New York, 1967).

Fuller, John, M.D., *The History of Berwick Upon Tweed, including a Short Account of the Villages of Tweedmouth and Spittal, &c.* (Edinburgh, 1799).

Gedanken über den Aufstand der englischen Colonien in dem nördlichen Amerika (Göttingen, 1776).

General Advertiser (Philadelphia), 17, 18 May 1793.

Gentz, Friedrich von, 'Ueber den Einfluß der Entdeckung von Amerika auf den Wohlstand und die Cultur des menschlichen Geschlechts', *Neue deutsche Monatsschrift* 2 (1795): 269–319.

Gentz, Frederick, *The French and American Revolutions Compared*, trans. J. Q. Adams, with an introduction by Russell Kirk (New York: Scholars' Facsimiles, 1955).

Hawkins, Christopher, *The Adventures of Christopher Hawkins, Containing Details of His Captivity, A First and Second Time on the High Seas by the British* (New York, 1864).

Hays, Mary, *Memoirs of Emma Courtney* (1796), Eleanor Ty (ed.) (Oxford: Oxford University Press, 2000).

Hegel, G. W. F., *The Phenomenology of Mind*, trans. J. B. Baillie, 2nd ed. (London: Allen and Unwin, 1931).

Herbert, Charles, *A Relic of the Revolution, Containing a Full and Particular Account of the Sufferings and Privations of All the American Prisoners Captured on the High Seas* (Boston, 1847).

Historisches Journal, von Mitgliedern des königlichen historischen Instituts zu Göttingen, herausgegeben von Joh. Christoph Gatterer. Neunter Theil (Göttingen, 1777).

The History of Sir George Warrington; or, The Political Quixote (3 vols, London, 1797).

Humanity in Algiers: Or the Slave of Azem, By an American, Late a Slave of Algiers (Troy, 1801).

Hume, David, *Dialogues concerning Natural Religion* (1779) (London, 1990).

Hume, David, *Essays: Moral, Political, and Literary* (1742–1752), Eugene Miller (ed.) (Indianapolis: Liberty Fund, 1987).

Hume, David, *Essays and Treatises on Several Subjects* (London, 1777).

Hume, David, *The History of England* (1754–1762) (6 vols, Indianapolis: Liberty Fund, 1983).

Hume, David, *The Letters of David Hume,*. J. Y. T.Greig (ed.) (2 vols, Oxford, 1969).

Hume, David, *New Letters of David Hume*, Raymond Klibansky and Ernest C. Mossner (eds), (Oxford, 1969).

Hume, David, *Political Discourses* (Edinburgh, 1752).

Hume, David, *A Treatise of Human Nature* (1739) (Oxford, 1978).

Irving, Washington, *A History of New York From the Beginning of the World to the End of the Dutch Dynasty* (1809) in *History, Tales and Sketches*, James W. Tuttleton (ed.) (Cambridge: Cambridge University Press, 1983), pp. 363–720.

J. W. [John Witherspoon,] 'Remarks on an Essay on Human Liberty', *Scots Magazine* 15 (April 1753): 165–70.

Jarvis, Charles, 'The Translator's Preface', in *The Life and Exploits of the Ingenious Gentleman Don Quixote de la Mancha*, Miguel de Cervantes Saavedra, trans. Charles Jarvis (2 vols, London, 1742), iii–xxiii.

Jefferson, Thomas, *Jefferson in Love: The Love Letters Between Thomas Jefferson & Maria Cosway*, John P. Kaminski (ed.) (Madison, WI: Madison House, 1999).

Jefferson, Thomas, *Literary Commonplace Book*, Douglas L. Wilson (ed.) (Princeton: Princeton University Press 1989).

Jefferson, Thomas, *Notes on the State of Virginia*, William H. Peden (ed.) (Chapel Hill: University of North Carolina Press, 1955).

Jefferson, Thomas, *The Papers of Thomas Jefferson*, Julian P. Boyd *et al.* (eds) (33 vols to date, Princeton: Princeton University Press, 1950–).

Jefferson, Thomas, *Writings*, Merrill D. Peterson (ed.) (New York: Library of America, 1984).

Johnson, Samuel, *A Journey to the Western Islands of Scotland*, Mary Lascelles (ed.) (New Haven: Yale University Press, 1971).

Johnson, Samuel, *Political Writings*, Donald J. Greene (ed.) (New Haven: Yale University Press, 1977).

Johnson, Samuel, *Rasselas and Other Tales*, Gwin J. Kolb (ed.) (New Haven: Yale University Press, 1990).

Johnson, Samuel, *Taxation no Tyranny* (London, 1775).

Kant, Immanuel, 'What is Enlightenment?' in *The Enlightenment: A Sourcebook and Reader*, Paul Hyland (ed.) (London and New York: Routledge, 2003), pp. 54–8.

Korn, C. H., *Geschichte der Kriege in und ausser Europa vom Anfange des Aufstandes der Brittischen Kolonien in Nordamerika an. Erster Theil* (Nürnberg, 1776).

Korn, C. H., *Geschichte der Kriege in und ausser Europa vom Anfange des Aufstandes der Brittischen Kolonien in Nordamerika an Dritter Theil* (Nürnberg, 1777).

Leech, Samuel, *A Voice from the Main Deck: Being a Record of the Thirty Years' Adventures of Samuel Leech* (1843), Michael J. Crawford (ed.) (Annapolis: Naval Institute Press, 1999).

Letters of Eminent Persons addressed to David Hume, John Hill Burton (ed.) (Edinburgh, 1849).

Lidner, Bengt *Samlade Skrifter av Bengt Lidner*, H. Elovson (ed.) (Stockholm: Albert Bonniers, 1932).

Lincoln, Abraham, *The Collected Works of Abraham Lincoln*, Roy Basler (ed.) (9 vols, New Brunswick, N.J.: Rutgers University Press, 1953–55).

List, Friedrich *National System of Political Economy*, trans. G. A. Matile, including the Notes of the French Translation by Henri Richelot, with a Preliminary Essay and Notes by Stephen Colwell (1841) (New York, 1974).

Long, E., *The History of Jamaica* (London, 1773).

Lucas, Charles, *The Infernal Quixote: A Tale of the Day* (1801), M. O. Grenby (ed.) (Peterborough, Ont.: Broadview, 2004).

Mayáns I Siscár, Gregorio, 'The Life of Michael de Cervantes Saavedra', trans. Mr. Ozell, in *Don Quixote*, trans. Charles Jarvis (2 vols, London, 1742), pp. 1–90.

McNally, William, *Evils and Abuses in the Naval and Merchant Service, Exposed; With Proposals For Their Remedy and Redress* (Boston, 1839).

Melville, Herman, *Billy Budd and Other Stories*, Harold Beaver (ed.) (New York, 1967).

Miller, Perry (ed.), *The American Puritans: Their Prose and Poetry* (New York: Doubleday-Anchor, 1956).

Montesquieu, Charles de Secondat, baron de, *The Spirit of the Laws*, Anne M. Cohler, Basia C. Miller and Harold S. Stone (eds) (Cambridge; Cambridge University Press, 1989).

Moser, J. J., *Nord-America nach den Friedenschlüssen vom Jahr 1783. Erster Band* (Leipzig, 1784).

The Naval Chaplain, Exhibiting A View of American Efforts to Benefit Seamen (Boston, 1831).

Nicholson, Thomas, *An Affecting Narrative of the Captivity and Sufferings of Thomas Nicholson [A Native of New Jersey] Who Has Been Six Years a Prisoner among the Algerines* (Boston, 1816).

Niles Weekly Register, 33 (1827).

North American Review 32 (1831).

Paine, Thomas *Common Sense* (1776), Isaac Kramnick (ed.), (New York: Penguin, 1976).

Paine, Thomas, *Rights of Man* (1791) and *Common Sense* (1776), intro. Michael Foot (London: Everyman, 1994).

Penny, Joshua, *The Life and Adventures of Joshua Penny* (New York, 1815).

Pfoeter, A. J., *Betracht über die Quellen und Folgen der merkwürdigsten Revolutionen unseres Jahrhunderts* (Vienna, 1794).

Pownall, T., *Hydraulic and Nautical Observations on the Currents in the Atlantic Ocean* (London, 1787).

Price, Richard, *Political Writings*, D. O. Thomas (ed.) (Cambridge: Cambridge University Press, 1991).

Ray, William, *Horrors of Slavery: or the American Tars in Tripoli* (Troy, 1808).

Raynal, G.-T.-F. [Abbé], *Histoire Philosophique et Politiques des Etablissements et du Commerce des Européen dans les Deux Indes* (Amsterdam, 1770).

Reid, Thomas, *Practical Ethics: Being Lectures and Papers on Natural Religion, Self-Government, Natural Jurisprudence, and the Law of Nations*, Knud Haakonssen (ed.) (Princeton: Princeton University Press, 1990).

Reid, Thomas, *Works*, Sir William Hamilton (ed.) (2 vols. Edinburgh, 1863).

Remer, Julius August, *Amerikanisches Archiv*, Dritter Band (Brunswick, 1778).

Riley, James, *An Authentic Narrative of the Loss of the Brig "Commerce"* (Hartford, 1817).

Rowson, Susanna, *Slaves in Algiers, or, Struggle for Freedom* (Philadelphia, 1794).

Sanborn, Solomon H., *An Exposition of Official Tyranny in the United States Navy* (New York, 1841).

Scott, Sir Walter, *The Letters of Sir Walter Scott*, H. J. C. Grierson (ed.) (12 vols., London, 1932–33).

Scott, Sir Walter, *Quentin Durward* (1823), Susan Manning (ed.) (Oxford and New York: Oxford University Press, 1992).

Schlözer, August, *Briefwechsel, meist historischen und politischen Inhalts* (Göttingen: 1779).

Schmohl, J. C., *Über Nordamerika und Demokratie. Ein Brief aus England*, (1782) ed. Rainer Wild, *Kleines Archiv des achtzehnten Jahrhunderts 14* (St. Ingbert: Werner J. Röhrig Verlag, 1992).

Selections from the Family Papers preserved at Caldwell (2 vols., Glasgow, 1874).

Sibly, Job, *The Trial of Richard Parker, Complete; President of the Delegates, for Mutiny, &c.* (Boston, 1797).

Sharp, Granville, *The Just Limitation of Slavery* (London, 1776).

Smith, Adam, *An Inquiry into the Nature and Causes of the Wealth of Nations* (1776), R. H. Campbell and A. S. Skinner (eds) (2 vols, Oxford: Oxford University Press, 1976).

Smith, Adam, *Theory of Moral Sentiments* (1759) (Indianapolis: Liberty Fund, 1976).

Smollett, Tobias, *The Life and Adventures of Sir Launcelot Greaves* (1760), David Evans (ed.) (New York and London: Oxford University Press, 1973).

Sprengel, M. C., *Briefe den gegenwärtigen Zustand von Amerika betreffend. Erste Sammlung* (Göttingen, 1777).

Sterne, Laurence, *Tristram Shandy* (1759), James Aiken Work (ed.) (New York: Odyssey Press, 1940).

Stevens, James Wilson, *An Historical and Geographical Account of Algiers* (Philadelphia, 1797).

Stevenson, Robert Louis, *The Scottish Stories and Essays*, Kenneth Gelder (ed.) (Edinburgh, 1989).

Taube, F. W., *Geschichte der Engländischen Handelschaft, Manufacturen, Colonien und Schiffarth in den alten, mittlern und neuen Zeiten, bis auf das laufende Jahr 1776. Mit einer zuverlässigen Nachricht von den wahren Ursachen des jetzigen Krieges in Nordamerika, und andern dergleichen Dingen* (Leipzig, 1776).

Thoreau, Henry David, *Cape Cod* (1865), intro by Paul Theroux (New York, 1987).

Twain, Mark, *Life on the Mississippi* (1883), James M. Cox (ed.) (Harmondsworth: Penguin Books, 1986).

Tyler, Royall, *The Algerine Captive; or, The Life and Adventures of Doctor Updike Underhill, Six Years a Prisoner Among the Algerines* (1797), Jack B. Moore (ed.) (2 vols, Gainesville, FL: Scholars' Facsimiles & Reprints, 1967).

Vattel, E. de, *The Law of Nations or Principles of the Law of Nature; applied to the Conduct and Affairs of Nations and Sovereigns* (London: J. Newbury *et al.*, 1760).

Vethake, Henry, *The Principles of Political Economy*, 2nd ed (1844) (New York: A. M. Kelly, 1971).

Washington, George, *The Writings of George Washington*, John C. Fitzpatrick (ed.) (38 vols, Washington, D.C.: Government Printing Office, 1931–44).

Webster, George Sidney, *The Seaman's Friend: A Sketch of the American Seaman's Friend Society, By Its Secretary* (New York, 1932).

Willcock, John, *The Voyages and Adventures of John Willcock, Mariner* (Philadelphia, 1798).

[Williams, Jonathan], 'Memoir of Jonathan Williams, on the Use of the Thermometer in Discovering Banks, Soundings, &c', *Transactions of the American Philosophical Society*, 3 (1793): 82–99.

[Williams, Jonathan], 'A Thermometrical Journal of the Temperature of the Atmosphere and Sea, on a Voyage to and from Oporto, with Explanatory Observations thereon', *Transactions of the American Philosophical Society*, 3 (1793): 194–202.

Witherspoon, John, *An Annotated Edition of Lectures on Moral Philosophy by John Witherspoon*, Jack Scott (ed.) (Newark: University of Delaware Press, 1982).

Witherspoon, John, *The Selected Writings of John Witherspoon*, Thomas Miller (ed.) (Carbondale: Southern Illinois University Press, 1990).

Witherspoon, John, *A Serious Inquiry into the Nature and Effects of the Stage* (Glasgow, 1757; reprinted in New York, 1812).

Witherspoon, John, *Works* (9 vols., Edinburgh, 1804–5).

Zimmermann, E. A. W., *Frankreich und die Freistaaten von Nordamerika. 1. Band* (Berlin, 1795).

Zimmermann, E. A. W., *Frankreich und die Freistaaten von Nordamerika. 2. Band* (Brunswick, 1800).

Secondary Sources

Ahlstrom, Sydney, 'Scottish Philosophy and American Theology', *Church History*, 24 (1955): 257–72.

Albanese, Catherine L., *Sons of the Fathers: The Civil Religion of the American Revolution* (Philadelphia: Temple University Press, 1976).

Allison, Robert J., *The Crescent Obscured: The United States and the Muslim World, 1776–1815* (New York, 1995).

[Anon.], (Review of) 'A Topographical Description of the Dominions of the United States of America', *Pennsylvania Magazine of History and Biography*, 74 (1950): 410–12.

Appleby, Joyce, *Capitalism and the New Social Order: The Republican Vision of the 1790s* (New York: New York University Press, 1984).

Armitage, David, *Ideological Origins of the British Empire* (Cambridge: Cambridge University Press, 2000).

Armitage, David, 'Three Concepts of Atlantic History', in David Armitage and Michael J. Braddick (eds), *The British Atlantic World, 1500–1800* (Basingstoke: Palgrave, 2002), pp. 11–27.

Arner, Robert D. 'Sentiment and Sensibility: The Role of Emotion and William Hill Brown's *The Power of Sympathy*', *Studies in American Fiction* 1 (1973): 125, 131.

Bailyn, Bernard, *Atlantic History: Concept and Contours* (Cambridge Mass.: Harvard University Press, 2005).

Bailyn, Bernard, *From Protestant Peasants to Jewish Intellectuals: the Germans in the Peopling of America* (Oxford: Berg [for the German Historical Institute], 1988).

Bailyn, Bernard, 'The Idea of Atlantic History', *Itinerario*, 20 (1996): 19–44.

Bailyn, Bernard, *The Ideological Origins of the American Revolution* (Cambridge, Mass.: Harvard University Press, 1967).

Bailyn, Bernard, *Voyagers to the West* (New York: Alfred A. Knopf, 1986).

Barnes, Elizabeth. 'Affecting Relations: Pedagogy, Patriarchy, and the Politics of Sympathy', *American Literary History* (Winter, 1996): 8:597–614.

Barnes, Timothy M. and Robert M. Calhoun, 'Moral Allegiance: John Witherspoon and Loyalist Recantation', *American Presbyterians* 63 (1985): 273–83.

Baucom, Ian, *Out of Place: Englishness, Empire, and the Locations of Identity* (Princeton: Princeton University Press, 1999).

Beasley, Jerry C., 'Charlotte Lennox', *DLB*, 39 (Ann Arbor, Michigan, 1985), pp. 306–12.

Bennett, Jim, 'The Travels and Trails of Mr Harrison's Timekeeper', in Marie-Nöelle Bourguet, Christian Licoppe and H. Otto Sibum (eds), *Instruments, Travel and Science: Itineraries of Precision from the Seventeenth to the Twentieth Centuries* (London: Routledge, 2002).

Bentley, Jerry H., 'Sea and Ocean Basins as Frameworks of Historical Analysis', *Geographical Review*, 89 (1999): 215–24.

Blank, Paul W., 'The Pacific: A Mediterranean in the Making?', *Geographical Review*, 89 (1999): 276–7.

Bloch, Ruth H., *Visionary Republic: Millennial Themes in American Thought, 1756–1800* (Cambridge: Cambridge University Press, 1985).

Boorstin, Daniel J., *The Americans: The Colonial Experience* (New York: Random House, 1958).

Bourguet, Marie-Noëlle, 'The Explorer', in Michel Vovelle (ed.), *Enlightenment Portraits* (Chicago: University of Chicago Press, 1997).

Bödeker, Hans-Erich, 'Prozesse und Strukturen politischer Bewußtseinsbildung der deutschen Aufklärung', in Hans-Erich Bödeker and Ulrich Hermann (eds), *Aufklärung als Politisierung—Politisierung der Aufklärung* (Hamburg: F. Meiner, 1987), pp. 10–31.

Bödeker, Hans-Erich, 'The Concept of the Republic in Eighteenth-Century German Thought', Jürgen Heideking and James A. Henretta (eds), *Republicanism and Liberalism in America and the German states, 1750–1850* (Cambridge: Cambridge University Press, 2002), pp. 35–52.

Bradbury, Malcolm, *Dangerous Pilgrimages: Trans-Atlantic Mythologies and the Novel* (London: Secker & Warburg, 1995).

Bravo, Michael, 'Ethnographic Navigation and the Geographical Gift,' in David N. Livingstone and Charles W. J. Withers (eds), *Geography and Enlightenment* Chicago: University of Chicago Press, 1999).

Brewer, Daniel, 'Lights in Space', *Eighteenth-Century Studies*, 37 (2004): 171–86.

Brodhead, Richard, *Hawthorne, Melville and the Novel* (Chicago: University of Chicago Press, 1976).

Brown, Gillian, *The Consent of the Governed: The Lockean Legacy in Early American Culture* (Cambridge, Mass.: Harvard University Press, 2001).

Brown, Laura, 'Oceans and Floods: Fables of Global Perspective', in Felicity A. Nussbaum (ed.), *The Global Eighteenth Century* (Baltimore: Johns Hopkins University Press, 2003).

Brown, Richard D., *Knowledge is Power: The Diffusion of Information in Early America, 1700–1865* (Oxford: Oxford University Press, 1989).

Bruckner, Martin, 'Lessons in Geography: Maps, Spellers, and Other Grammars of Nationalism in the Early Republic', *American Quarterly*, 51 (1999): 311–43.

Bruckner, Martin, *The Geographic Revolution in Early America: Maps, Literacy, & National Identity* (Chapel Hill: University of North Carolina Press, 2006).

Bryson, Gladys, *Man and Society: The Scottish Inquiry of the Eighteenth Century* (Princeton: Princeton University Press, 1945).

Bushman, Richard, *The Refinement of America: Persons, Houses, Cities* (New York: Alfred Knopf, 1992).

Butel, Paul, *The Atlantic*, trans. Iain Hamilton Grant (London: Routledge, 1999).

Calvert, Albert F., *The Life of Cervantes* (London: J. Lane, 1905).

Cañizares-Esguerra, Jorge, *How to Write the History of the New World: History, Epistemologies, and Identities in the Eighteenth-Century Atlantic World* (Stanford: Stanford University Press, 2001), 266–345.

Canny, Nicholas, 'Atlantic History: What and Why?', *European Review*, 9 (2001): 399–411.

Canny, Nicholas, 'Writing Atlantic History, or, Reconfiguring the History of Colonial British America', *Journal of American History*, 86 (1999): 1093–1114.

Carpenter, Jesse T., *The South as a Conscious Minority, 1789–1861: A Study in Political Thought*, with a new introduction by John McCardell (New York: New York University Press, 1930; Columbia, S.C.: University of South Carolina Press, 1990).

Cassirer, Ernst, *The Philosophy of the Enlightenment*, trans. Fritz C. A. Koelln and James P. Pettegrove (Boston: Beacon Press, 1955).

Chaplin, Joyce E., *An Anxious Pursuit: Agricultural Innovation and Modernity in the Lower South* (Chapel Hill: University of North Carolina Press, 1993).

Chapman, Mary and Glenn Hendler (eds), *Sentimental Men: Masculinity and the Politics of Affect in American Culture* (Berkeley and Los Angeles: University of California Press, 1999).

Christophersen, Bill, *The Apparition in the Glass: Charles Brockden Brown's American Gothic* (London: The University of Georgia Press, 1993).

Clark, J. C. D., *The Language of Liberty, 1660–1832: Political Discourse and Social Dynamism in the Anglo-American World* (Cambridge: Cambridge University Press, 1994).

Clive, John and Bernard Bailyn, 'England's Cultural Provinces: Scotland and America', *William and Mary Quarterly* 11 (April 1954): 200–213.

Close, Anthony, *The Romantic Approach to 'Don Quixote': A Critical History of the Romantic Tradition in 'Quixote' Criticism* (Cambridge: Cambridge University Press, 1978).

Cobban, Alfred (ed.), *The Eighteenth Century: Europe in the Age of Enlightenment* (London: Thames & Hudson, 1969).

Coclanis, Peter A., '*Drang nach Osten*: Bernard Bailyn, the World-Island, and the Idea of Atlantic History', *Journal of World History*, 13 (2002): 169–182.

Cogliano, Francis D., *Revolutionary America, 1763–1815: A Political History* (London: Routledge, 2000).

Cogliano, Francis D., *Thomas Jefferson: Reputation and Legacy* (Edinburgh: Edinburgh University Press, 2006).

Colley, Linda, *Britons: Forging the Nation, 1707–1837* (New Haven: Yale University Press, 1992).

Colley, Linda, 'The Sea Around Us,' *The New York Review of Books*, 53:11, June 22, 2006.

Collins, Varnum Lansing, *President Witherspoon* (2 vols, Princeton: Princeton University Press, 1925).

Commager, Henry S., *The Empire of Reason: How Europe Imagined and America Realized the Enlightenment* (Garden City: Doubleday, 1978).

Conkin, Paul *Prophets of Prosperity: America's First Political Economists* (Bloomington, IN: Indiana University Press, 1980).

Cordingly, David, *Women Sailors and Sailors' Women: An Untold Maritime History* (New York: Random House, 2001).

Crain, Caleb, *American Sympathy: Men, Friendship, and Literature in the New Nation* (New Haven: Yale University Press, 2001).

Crane, Elaine Forman, *Ebb Tide in New England: Women, Seaports and Social Change, 1630–1800* (Boston: Northeastern University Press, 1998).

Crawford, Robert, *Devolving English Literature* (Oxford: Oxford University Press, 1992).

Cray, Robert E., Jr., 'Commemorating the Prison Ship Dead: Revolutionary Memory and the Politics of Sepulture in the Early Republic, 1776–1808', *William and Mary Quarterly*, 55 (1999): 565–90.

Creighton, Margaret S. and Lisa Norling (eds), *Iron Men, Wooden Women: Gender and Seafaring in the Atlantic World, 1700–1920* (Baltimore: Johns Hopkins University Press, 1996).

Crowley, John E., *The Privileges of Independence: Neomercantilism and the American Revolution* (Baltimore: Johns Hopkins University Press, 1993).

Curtin, Philip D., *The Rise and Fall of the Plantation Complex: Essays in Atlantic History* (Cambridge: Cambridge University Press, 1990).

Darnton, Robert, *The Literary Underground of the Old Regime* (Cambridge, Mass.: Harvard University Press, 1982).

Davidson, Cathy N., *Revolution and the Word: The Rise of the Novel in America* (New York: Oxford Univeristy Press, 1986).

Davis, David Brion, *The Problem of Slavery in the Age of Revolution* (Ithaca, N.Y.: Cornell University Press, 1975).

Davis, Ralph, *The Rise of the Atlantic Economies* (London: Weidenfeld and Nicolson, 1973).

Deacon, Margaret, *Scientists and the Sea 1650–1900: A Study of Marine Science* (London: Academic Press, 1971).

Dekker, George, *The American Historical Romance* (Cambridge: Cambridge University Press, 1987).

Dickinson, Harry T. 'Britain's Imperial Sovereignty: the Ideological Case against the American Colonists', Harry T. Dickinson (ed.), *Britain and the American Revolution* (London: Addison Wesley Longman, 1998), pp. 64–96.

Dippel, Horst, *Germany and the American Revolution, 1770–1800: A Sociohistorical Investigation of Late Eighteenth-Century Political Thinking*, trans. Bernhard A. Uhlendorf (Chapel Hill: University of North Carolina Press, 1977).

Dorfman, Joseph, *The Economic Mind in American Civilization* (5 vols, New York: Viking, 1946-1959).

Douglas, Ann, *The Feminization of American Culture* (New York: Farrar, Strauss and Giroux, 1977).

Douglas, Bronwen, 'Seaborne Ethnography and the Natural History of Man', *Journal of Pacific History*, 38 (2003): 3–27.

Dubois, Laurent, 'An Enslaved Enlightenment: Rethinking the Intellectual History of the French Atlantic', *Social History*, 31 (2006): 1–14.

Duff, David, *Romance and Revolution: Shelley and the Politics of a Genre* (Cambridge: Cambridge University Press, 1994).

Dugan, James, *The Great Mutiny* (New York: G. P. Putnam's Sons, 1965).

Dunmore, John, *French Explorers in the Pacific* (2 vols, Oxford: Clarendon Press, 1965–1969).

Dwyer, John, *The Age of the Passions: An Interpretation of Adam Smith and Scottish Enlightenment Culture* (Edinburgh: University of Edinburgh Press, 1998).

Dwyer, John 'Virtue and Improvement: The Civic World of Adam Smith,' in Peter Jones and Andrew S. Skinner (eds), *Adam Smith Reviewed* (Edinburgh: Edinburgh University Press, 1992), pp. 190–216.

Eagleton, Terry, *Heathcliff and the Great Hunger: Studies in Irish Culture* (London: Verso, 1995).

Earle, Edward Mead 'Adam Smith, Alexander Hamilton, Friedrich List: The Economic Foundations of Military Power,' in Edward Mead Earle (ed.), *Makers of Modern Strategy: Military Thought from Machiavelli to Hitler* (Princeton: Princeton University Press, 1943), pp. 117–54.

Echeverria, Durand, *Mirage in the West: A History of the French Image of American Society to 1815* (Princeton: Princeton University Press, 1957).

Edney, Matthew, 'Cartography: Disciplinary History', in Gregory A. Good (ed.), *Sciences of the Earth: An Encyclopedia of Events, People and Phenomena* (2 vols, New York: Garland, 1998).

Edwards, Phillip, *The Story of the Voyage: Sea-Narratives in Eighteenth-Century England* (Cambridge: Cambridge University Press, 1994).

Elkins, Stanley and Eric McKitrick, *The Age of Federalism: The Early American Republic, 1788–1800* (New York: Oxford University Press, 1993).

Elliott, J.H. 'Atlantic History: A Circumnavigation', in David Armitage and Michael J. Braddick (eds), *The British Atlantic World, 1500–1800* (Basingstoke: Palgrave, 2002), pp. 233–4.

Elliott, J. H., *Do the Americas have a Common History? An Address* (Providence: Associates of John Carter Brown Library, 1998).

Ellis, Milton 'The Author of the First American Novel', *American Literature* 4 (1933): 361.

Emerson, Roger L., and Paul Wood, 'Science and Enlightenment in Glasgow, 1690–1802', in Charles W. J. Withers and Paul Wood (eds), *Science and Medicine in the Scottish Enlightenment* (East Linton: Tuckwell Press, 2002).

Emmer, Pieter, 'The Myth of Early Globalization: the Atlantic Economy, 1500–1800', *European Review*. 11 (2003): 37–47.

Fechner, Roger, 'The Godly and Virtuous Republic of John Witherspoon', in *Ideas in America's Cultures*, Hamilton Cravens (ed.) (Ames: Iowa State University Press, 1982): 7–26.

Ferguson, Niall, (ed.), *Virtual History: Alternatives and Counterfactuals* (London: Picador, 1997).

Ferguson, Robert, *The American Enlightenment, 1750–1820* (Cambridge MA: Harvard University Press, 1997).

Fernandez-Armesto, Felipe, *The Americas: The History of a Hemisphere* (London: Weidenfeld and Nicolson, 2003).

Flower, Elizabeth and Murray G. Murphey, *A History of Philosophy in America* (New York: G. P. Putnam's Sons, 1977).

Foucault, Michel, *The Order of Things: An Archaeology of the Human Sciences* (London: Tavistock, 1970).

Freehling, William W., *Prelude to Civil War: The Nullification Controversy in South Carolina, 1816–1836* (New York: Harper and Row, 1965).

Frost, Alan, 'The Pacific Ocean: the Eighteenth Century's "New World"', *Studies on Voltaire and the Eighteenth Century* 152 (1976): 779–822.

Fuentes, Carlos, 'Foreword', in *The Adventures of Don Quixote de la Mancha*, Miguel de Cervantes Saavedra, trans. Tobias Smollett (London: Deutsch, 1986), xi–xiii.

Garrett, Aaron, 'Hume's Revised Racism Revised', *Hume Studies*, 26 (2000).

Gaspar, David Barry and David Patrick Geggus (eds), *A Turbulent Time: The French Revolution and the Greater Caribbean* (Bloomington, In.: Indiana University Press, 1997).

Gavroglu, Kostas (ed.), *The Sciences in the European Periphery during the Enlightenment* (Dordrecht: Kluwer Academic, 1999).

Gay, Peter, *The Enlightenment: An Interpretation. The Rise of Modern Paganism* (New York: Knopf, 1966).

Gay, Peter, *The Enlightenment: An Interpretation. The Science of Freedom* (New York: Knopf, 1969).

Gerbi, Antonello, *The Dispute of the New World. The History of a Polemic, 1750–1900*. Revised edition, translated by Jeremy Moyle (Pittsburgh: Pittsburgh University Press, 1973).

Gilje, Paul, 'Liberty and Loyalty: The Ambiguous Patriotism of Jack Tar in the American Revolution', *Pennsylvania History*, 67 (2000): 165–93.

Gilje, Paul A., *Liberty on the Waterfront: American Maritime Culture in the Age of Revolution* (Philadelphia: University of Pennsylvania Press, 2004).

Gilroy, Paul, *The Black Atlantic* (Cambridge, Mass.: Harvard University Press, 1995).

Gipson, Alice, *John Home: A Study of His Life and Works* (New Haven: Yale University Press, 1916).

Godechot, Jacques, *France and the Atlantic Revolutions of the Eighteenth Century, 1770–1799*, trans. Herbert H. Rowen (New York: Free Press, 1965).

Golinski, Jan, 'Science *in* the Enlightenment', *History of Science*, 24 (1986), 411–24.

Golinski, Jan, *Making Natural Knowledge: Constructivism and the History of Science* (Cambridge: Cambridge University Press, 1998).

Gould, Eliga H. and Peter S. Onuf (eds), *Empire and Nation: The American Revolution in the Atlantic World* (Baltimore: Johns Hopkins University Press, 2005).

Gould, Eliga H., *The Persistence of Empire: British Political Culture in the Age of the American Revolution* (Chapel Hill: University of North Carolina Press, 2000).

Grave, S. A., *The Scottish Philosophy of Common Sense* (Oxford: Oxford University Press, 1960).

Gray, Edward G., *New World Babel: Languages and Nations in Early America* (Princeton: Princeton University Press, 1999).

Green, Ashbel, *The Life of the Revd John Witherspoon, with a brief review of his writings and a summary estimate of his character and talents*, Henry Lyttleton Savage (ed.) (Princeton: Princeton University Press, 1973).

Greenblatt, Stephen, *Marvellous Possessions: The Wonder of the New World* (Oxford: Clarendon Press, 1991).

Greene, Jack P., 'Empire and Identity from the Glorious Revolution to the American Revolution', in P. J. Marshall (ed.), *The Oxford History of the British Empire, vol. II: The Eighteenth Century* (Oxford: Oxford University Press, 1998), pp. 208–30.

Grove, Richard, *Green Imperialism: Colonial Expansion, Tropical Island Edens and the Origins of Environmentalism, 1600–1860* (Cambridge: Cambridge University Press, 1995).

Gunn, Giles, *Thinking Across the American Grain: Ideology, Intellect, and the New Pragmatism* (Chicago: University of Chicago Press, 1992).

Hancock, David, *Citizens of the World: London Merchants and the Integration of the British Atlantic Community, 1735–1785* (Cambridge: Cambridge University Press, 1985).

Harris, Steven, 'Long Distance Corporations, Big Sciences, and the Geography of Knowledge', *Configurations*, 6 (1998): 269–305.

Harrison, Richard A., *Princetonians: 1769–1775* (Princeton: Princeton University Press, 1980).

Hartley, Lodwick, 'The Dying Soldier and the Love-lorn Virgin: Notes on Sterne's Early Reception in America' in *The Winged Skull: Papers from the Laurence Stern Bicentenary Conference*, Arthur H. Cash and John M. Stedmond (eds) (Kent, 1971) pp. 159–69.

Hawes, Clement, 'Johnson and Imperialism', in *The Cambridge Companion to Samuel Johnson*, Greg Clingham (ed.) (Cambridge: Cambridge University Press, 1997), pp. 114–15.

Hazard, Paul, *The European Mind: The Critical Years 1690–1715* (New Haven: Yale University Press, 1953).

Hazard, Paul, *European Thought in the Eighteenth Century* (New Haven: Yale University Press, 1954).

Headrick, Daniel R., *When Information Came of Age: Technologies of Knowledge in the Age of Reason and Revolution, 1700–1850* (Oxford: Oxford University Press, 2000).

Hellmuth, E. and N. Pieroth, 'Germany 1760–1815', Hannah Barker and Simon Burrows (eds), *Press, Politics and the Public Sphere* (Cambridge, 2002), pp. 69–92.

Hirschman, Albert O., *The Passions and the Interests: Political Arguments for Capitalism Before Its Triumph* (Princeton: Princeton University Press, 1977).

Holifield, E. Brooks, *The Gentlemen Theologians: American Theology in Southern Culture, 1795–1860* (Durham, NC: Duke University Press, 1978).

Holifield, E. Brooks, *Theology in America* (New Haven: Yale University Press, 2003).

Honour, Hugh, *The New Golden Land: European Images of America from the Discoveries to the Present Time* (New York: Pantheon, 1975).

Hont, Istvan, 'Free Trade and the Economic Limits to National Markets: Neo-Machiavellian Political Economy Reconsidered', in John Dunn (ed.), *The Economic Limits to Modern Politics* (Cambridge: Cambridge University Press, 1990), pp. 41–120.

Hood, Fred J., *Reformed America: The Middle and Southern States, 1783–1837* (University: University of Alabama Press, 1980).

Hook, Andrew, *From Goosecreek to Gandercleugh: Studies in Scottish-American Literary and Cultural History* (East Linton: Tuckwell, 1999).

Howe, Daniel W., 'Church, State, and Education in the Young American Republic', *Journal of the Early Republic* 22 (Spring 2002): 1–24.

Howe, Daniel Walker. 'European Sources of Political Ideas in Jeffersonian America', *Reviews in American History,* 10 (December 1982): 629–64.

Howe, Daniel W. *Making the American Self: Jonathan Edwards to Abraham Lincoln* (Cambridge, Mass.: Harvard University Press, 1997).

Howe, Daniel W., 'The Political Psychology of *The Federalist*', *William and Mary Quarterly*, 46 (1987): 485–509.

Howe, Daniel W., *The Unitarian Conscience: Harvard Moral Philosophy, 1805–1861* (Cambridge: Harvard University Press, 1970).

Howe, Daniel W. 'Why the Scottish Enlightenment was Useful to the Framers of the American Constitution', *Comparative Studies in Society and History* 31 (July 1989): 72–87.

Hulme, Peter and Ludmilla Jordanova (eds.), *The Enlightenment and Its Shadows* (London: Routledge, 1990).

Iliffe, Rob, 'Science and Voyages of Discovery', in Roy Porter (ed.), *The Cambridge History of Science. Volume 4: Eighteenth-Century Science* (Cambridge: Cambridge University Press, 2003).

Irwin, Douglas, *Against the Tide: An Intellectual History of Free Trade* (Princeton: Princeton University Press, 1996).

Jacques, T. Carlos, 'From Savages and Barbarians to Primitives: Africa, Social Typologies, and History in Eighteenth-Century French Philosophy', *History and Theory*, 36 (1997): 190–215.

Jaffee, David, 'The Village Enlightenment in New England, 1760–1820', *William and Mary Quarterly*, 47 (1990): 327–46.

Jehlen, Myra and Michael Warner (eds), *The English Literatures of America, 1500–1800* (New York: Routledge, 1997).

Jordan, Winthrop D., *White over Black: American Attitudes toward the Negro, 1550–1812* (Chapel Hill: University of North Carolina Press, 1968).

Kagan, Richard L. and Geoffrey Parker (eds), *Spain, Europe and the Atlantic World* (Cambridge: Cambridge University Press, 1995).

Kammen, Michael, *A Season of Youth: The American Revolution and the Historical Imagination* (New York: Knopf, 1978).

Kaufman, Allen, *Capitalism, Slavery, and Republican Values: Antebellum Political Economists, 1819–1848* (Austin: University of Texas Press, 1982).

Keane, John, *Tom Paine: A Political Life* (London: Bloomsbury, 1995).

Kidd, Colin, 'Ethnicity in the British Atlantic world, 1688–1830', in Kathleen Wilson (ed.), *A New Imperial History: Culture, Identity and Modernity in Britain and the Empire 1660–1840* (Cambridge: Cambridge University Press, 2004), pp. 260–77.

Kirkham, David M. '"Inflamed with Study": Eighteenth-century higher education and the formation of the American constitutional mind' (Ph.D. thesis, George Washington University, 1989).

Klauber, Martin I., 'Reformed Orthodoxy in Transition: Benedict Pictet (1655–1724) and Enlightened Orthodoxy in Post-Reformation Geneva', *Later Calvinism: International Perspectives*, W. Fred Graham (ed.) (Kirkville, Mo.: Sixteenth-Century Journal Publishers, 1994), 93–113.

Kloppenberg, James, 'The Virtues of Liberalism: Christianity, Republicanism, and Ethics in Early American Political Discourse', *Journal of American History* 74 (June 1987): 9–33.

Knupfer, Peter B., *The Union As It Is: Constitutional Unionism and Sectional Compromise, 1787–1861* (Chapel Hill: University of North Carolina Press, 1991).

Koerner, Lisbet, 'Daedalus Hyperboreus: Baltic Natural History and Mineralogy in the Enlightenment', in William Clark, Jan Golinski, and Simon Schaffer (eds), *The Sciences in Enlightened Europe* (Chicago: University of Chicago Press, 1999).

Korsgaard, Christine, *The Sources of Normativity* (Cambridge, Cambridge University Press, 1996).

Kverndal, Roald, *Seamen's Missions: Their Origin and Early Growth: A Contribution to the History of the Church Maritime* (Pasadena: William Carey Library, 1986).

Landsman, Ned, 'The Legacy of British Union for the North American Colonies', in John Robertson (ed.), *A Union for Empire: Political Thought and the British Union of 1707* (Cambridge: Cambridge University Press, 1995): 297–317.

Landsman, Ned C., ed., Nation and Province in the First British Empire: Scotland and the Americas, 1600–1800 (Lewisburg, Pa.: Bucknell University Press, 2001).

Landsman, Ned. 'Witherspoon and the Problem of Provincial Identity in Scottish Evangelical Culture', in *Scotland and America in the Age of the Enlightenment*, Richard B. Sher and Jeffrey R. Smitten (eds) (Edinburgh: Edinburgh University Press, 1990), 29–45.

Langford, Paul, *Englishness Identified: Manners and Character, 1650–1850* (Oxford: Oxford University Press, 2000).

Langford, Paul, *A Polite and Commercial People: England 1727–1783* (New York: Oxford University Press, 1989).

Langley, Harold D., *Social Reform in the United States Navy, 1798–1862* (Annapolis: Naval Institute Press, 1980).

Langley, Lester D., *The Americas in the Age of Revolution* (New Haven: Yale University Press, 1997).

Langley, Lester D., *The Americas in the Modern Age* (New Haven: Yale University Press, 2003).

Latimer, John, *The Annals of Bristol in the Eighteenth Century* (Bristol: W. & F. Morgan, 1893).

Leask, Nigel, *Curiosity and the Aesthetics of Travel Writing 1770–1840* (Oxford: Oxford University Press, 2002).

Leask, Nigel, 'The Ghost in Catapultepec: Fanny Calderón de la Barca, William Prescott and 19th Century Mexican Travel Accounts', in Jas Elsner and Joan-Pau Rubiés (eds), *Voyages and Visions* (London: Reaktion Books, 1999).

Lemisch, Jesse, 'Jack Tar in the Streets: Merchant Seamen in the Politics of Revolutionary America', *William and Mary Quarterly*, 25 (1968): 371–407.

Lenner, Andrew C., *The Federal Principle in American Politics* (Lanham, Md.: Madison House, 2000).

Levin, David, ed., *Jonathan Edwards: A Profile* (New York: Hill & Wang, 1969).

Lewis, James E., Jr., *The American Union and the Problem of Neighborhood: The United States and the Collapse of the Spanish Empire, 1783–1829* (Chapel Hill: University of North Carolina Press, 1998).

Lewis, James E., *John Quincy Adams: Policymaker for the Union* (Wilmington, Del.: SR Books, 2001).

Lewis, Martin W., 'Dividing the Ocean Sea', *Geographical Review*, 89 (1999): 188–214.

Linebaugh, Peter and Marcus Rediker, *The Many-Headed Hydra: Sailors, Slaves, Commoners, and the Hidden History of the Revolutionary Atlantic* (Boston: Beacon Press, 2000).

Livingstone, David, *Putting Science in its Place: Geographies of Scientific Knowledge* (Chicago: University of Chicago Press, 2003).

Lonsdale, Roger (ed.), *The New Oxford Book of Eighteenth-Century Verse* (Oxford: Oxford University Press, 1984).

Looby, Christopher, *Voicing America: Language, Literary Form, and the Origins of the United States* (Chicago: University of Chicago Press, 1996).

Mackay, David, *In the Wake of Cook: Exploration, Science and Empire, 1780–1801* (London: Croom Helm, 1985).

MacLeod, Roy and Rehbock, Philip (eds), *Nature in its Greatest Extent: Western Science in the Pacific* (Honolulu: University of Hawaii Press, 1998).

McAllister, James, 'John Witherspoon: Academic Advocate for American Freedom', in *A Miscellany of American Christianity*, Stuart C. Henry (ed.) (Durham, NC: Duke University Press, 1963): 183–224.

McDermott, John, 'The Enlightenment on the Mississippi Frontier, 1763–1804', *Studies on Voltaire and the Eighteenth Century*, 26 (1963): 1129–42.

McDonald, Forrest, *States' Rights and the Union: Imperium in Imperio, 1776–1876* (Lawrence, KS: University of Kansas Press, 2000).

McDougall, Warren, 'Charles Elliot's Medical Publication and the International Book Trade', in Charles W. J. Withers and Paul Wood (eds), *Science and Medicine in the Scottish Enlightenment* (East Linton: Tuckwell Press, 2002).

McLachlan, James, 'The *Choice of Hercules*: American Student Societies in the Early 19th Century', in *The University in Society*, Lawrence Stone (ed.) (2 vols, Princeton: Princeton University Press, 1974), vol. 2, pp. 449–94.

McLachlan, James, *Princetonians, 1748–1768* (Princeton: Princeton University Press, 1976).

Maier, Pauline, *American Scripture: Making the Declaration of Independence* (New York: Knopf, 1997).

Mancke, Elizabeth, 'Early Modern Expansion and the Politicization of Oceanic Space', *Geographical Review*, 89 (1999): 225–36.

Manning, Susan, 'Did Mark Twain bring down the temple on Scott's shoulders?' in Janet Beer and Bridget Bennett (eds.), *Special Relationships: Anglo-American Affinities and Antagonisms, 1854–1936* (Manchester: Manchester University Press, 2002), pp. 8–27.

Manning, Susan, *Fragments of Union: Making Connections in Scottish and American Writing* (Basingstoke: Palgrave MacMillan, 2002).

Manning, Susan, 'Scott and Hawthorne: The Making of a National Literary Tradition,' in David Hewitt and J. H. Alexander (eds), *Scott and His Influence* (Aberdeen: Association for Scottish Literary Studies, 1983).

Marshall, P. J., and Williams, Glyndwr, *The Great Map of Mankind: British Perceptions of the World in the Age of Enlightenment* (London: J. M. Dent, 1982).

Marshall, P. J., 'Presidential Address: Britain and the World in the Eighteenth Century: IV, The Turning Outwards of Britain', *Transactions of the Royal Historical Society*, 6th series, 11 (2001), 1–15.

Matson, Cathy D., and Peter S. Onuf, *A Union of Interests: Political and Economic Thought in Revolutionary America* (Lawrence, KS: University of Kansas Press, 1990).

May, Henry F., *The Enlightenment in America* (Oxford: Oxford University Press, 1976).

May, Henry F., 'The Problem of the American Enlightenment', *New Literary History*, 1 (1970): 201–14.

Meek, Ronald L., *Social Science and the Ignoble Savage* (Cambridge: Cambridge University Press, 1976).

Meinig, Donald, *The Shaping of America: A Geographical Perspective on 500 years of History* (4 vols, New Haven: Yale University Press,1996–1998).

Merlan, Philip, 'Parva Hamanniana (II) Hamann and Schmohl', *Journal of the History of Ideas*, 10 (1949): 567–574.

Meyer, Donald Harvey, *Democratic Enlightenment* (New York: G. P. Putnam's Sons, 1976).

Milanich, Jerald T. and Susan Milbrath (eds), *First Encounters: Spanish Explorations in the Caribbean and the United States, 1492–1570* (Gainesville, Fl.: University of Florida Press, 1989).

Miller, David and Reill, Peter Hanns (eds), *Visions of Empire: Voyages, Botany, and Representations of Nature* (Cambridge: Cambridge University Press, 1996).

Miller, Perry, *Jonathan Edwards* (New York: W. Sloane Associates, 1949).

Miller, Perry, 'The Romantic Dilemma in American Nationalism and the Concept of Nature', in Perry Miller (ed.), *Nature's Nation* (Cambridge, Mass.: Harvard University Press, 1967).

Miller, Thomas P., 'Witherspoon, Blair, and the rhetoric of Civic Humanism', in *Scotland and America in the Age of the Enlightenment*, Richard B. Sher and Jeffrey R. Smitten (eds) (Edinburgh: Edinburgh University Press, 1990), 100–114.

Minnigerode, Meade, *Jefferson Friend of France, 1793: The Career of Edmond Charles Genet* (New York: G. P. Putnam's Sons, 1928).

Moore, Joseph P., III, 'The Greatest Enormity that Prevails: Direct Democracies and Workers' Self-Management in the British Naval Mutinies of 1797', in Colin Howell and Richard J. Twomey (eds), *Jack Tar in History: Essays in the History of Maritime Life and Labour* (Fredericton, N. B.: Acadiensis, 1991), pp. 11–36.

Morgan, Edmund S., *The Gentle Puritan* (New Haven: Yale University Press, 1962).

Morgan, Kenneth, *Bristol and the Atlantic Trade in the Eighteenth Century* (Cambridge: Cambridge University Press, 1993).

Morgan, Philip D., 'The Caribbean Islands in Atlantic Context, circa 1500–1800', in Felicity A. Nussbaum (ed.), *The Global Eighteenth Century* (Baltimore: Johns Hopkins University Press, 2003).

Morrison, Jeffrey H., *John Witherspoon and the Founding of the American Republic* (Notre Dame, In., University of Notre Dame Press, 2005).

Morrison, M. A. and Melinda Zook, *Revolutionary Currents. Nation Building in the Transatlantic World* (Lanham: Rowman & Littlefield, 2004).

Mossner, Ernest Campbell, *The Life of David Hume* (Edinburgh, 1954).

Munck, Thomas, *The Enlightenment: A Comparative Social History, 1721–1794* (London: Arnold, 2000).

Namier, Sir Lewis, *England in the Age of the American Revolution*, 2nd ed. (London: Macmillan, 1961).

Namier, Sir Lewis and John Brooke, *The History of Parliament: The House of Commons, 1754–1790* (3 vols.., London: Oxford University Press, 1964).

Newman, Simon P., *Parades and the Politics of the Street: Festive Culture in the Early Republic* (Philadelphia: University of Pennsylvania Press, 1997).

Noll, Mark, *America's God: From Jonathan Edwards to Abraham Lincoln* (New York: Oxford University Press, 2002).

Noll, Mark, 'The Irony of the Enlightenment for Presbyterians in the Early Republic', *Journal of the Early Republic* 5 (1985): 149–75.

Noll, Mark, *Princeton and the Republic, 1768–1822: The Search for a Christian Enlightenment in the Era of Samuel Stanhope Smith* (Princeton: Princeton University Press, 1989).

Norling, Lisa, *Captain Ahab Had a Wife: New England Women and the Whalefishery, 1720–1870* (Chapel Hill: University of North Carolina Press, 2000).

O'Brien, Patrick, 'Inseparable Connections: Trade, Economy, Fiscal State, and the Expansion of Empire, 1688–1815', in Peter J. Marshall (ed.), *The Oxford History of the British Empire: Volume 2. The Eighteenth Century* (Oxford: Oxford University Press, 1998).

Ogborn, Miles, 'Editorial: Atlantic Geographies', *Social and Cultural Geography*, 6 (2005): 381–7.

Ogborn, Miles, and Withers, Charles W. J., 'Travel, Trade and Empire: Knowing Other Places, 1660–1800', in Cynthia Wall (ed.), *New Perspectives on Literature: The Restoration and the Eighteenth Century* (Oxford: Blackwell, 2005).

O'Gorman, Edmundo, *The Invention of America: an Inquiry Into the Historical Nature of the New World and the Meaning of Its History* (Bloomington, In.: Indiana University Press, 1961).

Onuf, Peter S., 'Federalism, Republicanism, and the Origins of American Sectionalism', in Edward L. Ayers *et al.* (eds), *All Over the Map: Rethinking American Regions* (Baltimore: Johns Hopkins University Press, 1996), pp. 11–37.

O'Reilly, William, 'Migration, Recruitment and the Law: Europe Responds to the Atlantic World', in Horst Pietschmann (ed.), *Atlantic History. History of the Atlantic System 1580–1830* (Göttingen: Vandehock & Ruprecht, 2002), pp. 119– 137.

Pagden, Anthony, *European Encounters with the New World: From Renaissance to Romanticism* (New Haven: Yale University Press, 1993).

Palmer, R. R., *The Age of Democratic Revolution: A Political History of Europe and America, 1760–1800*, (2 vols, Princeton: Princeton University Press, 1959–1964).

Paulson, Ronald, *Don Quixote in England: The Aesthetics of Laughter* (Baltimore: Johns Hopkins University Press, 1998).

Persky, Joseph J., *The Burden of Dependency: Colonial Themes in Southern Economic Thought* (Baltimore: Johns Hopkins University Press, 1992).

Peterson, Merrill D., *Adam and Jefferson: A Revolutionary Dialogue* (Athens, Ga.: University of Georgia Press, 1976).

Phelps, Matthew, 'John Witherspoon and the Transmission of Common Sense Philosophy from Scotland to America' (D.Phil. Thesis, Oxford University, 2002).

Phillipson, Nicholas 'Adam Smith as Civic Moralist,' in Istvan Hont and Michael Ignatieff (eds), *Wealth and Virtue: The Shaping of Political Economy in the Scottish Enlightenment* (Cambridge: Cambridge University Press, 1983), pp. 179–202.

Phillipson, Nicholas, *Hume* (New York: Saint Martins, 1989).

Pincus, J. J., 'Tariff Policies,' in Jack P. Greene (ed.), *Encyclopedia of American Political History* (3 vols, New York, 1984), vol. 3, pp. 1259–70.

Plumb, J. H., 'British Attitudes to the American Revolution', in *The American Experience: The Collected Essays* (2 vols, New York: Harvester Wheatsheaf, 1989).

Pocock, J. G. A., '1776: The Revolution Against Parliament', in J. G. A. Pocock (ed.), *Three British Revolutions: 1641, 1688, 1776* (Princeton: Princeton University Press, 1980).

Pocock, J. G. A., *Barbarism and Religion: Narratives of Civil Government* (Cambridge: Cambridge University Press, 1999).

Pocock, J. G. A., 'Enlightenment and Revolution: The Case of English-Speaking North America', *Studies on Voltaire and the Eighteenth Century*, 263 (1989): 249–61.

Pocock, J. G. A. *et al.*, 'Forum: The New British History in Atlantic Perspective', *American Historical Review*, 104 (1999), 426–500.

Pocock, J .G. A., 'Hume and the American Revolution: The dying thoughts of a North Briton', in J. G. A. Pocock (ed.), *Virtue, Commerce, and History* (Cambridge: Cambridge University Press, 1985), 125–41.

Pocock, J. G. A., *Machiavellian Moment: Florentine Political Thought and the Atlantic Republican Tradition* (Princeton: Princeton University Press, 1975).

Pocock, J. G. A., 'Political Thought in the English-speaking Atlantic, 1760–1790: (i) The imperial crisis', J. G. A. Pocock (ed.), *The Varieties of British Political Thought, 1500–1800* (Cambridge: Cambridge University Press, 1993), pp. 246–82.

Pole, J. R., 'Enlightenment and the Politics of American Nature', in Roy Porter and Mikuláš Teich (eds), *The Enlightenment in National Context* (Cambridge: Cambridge University Press, 1981).

Pope, Dudley, *The Black Ship* (New York: Henry Holt, 1998).

Porter, Roy, *Enlightenment: Britain and the Creation of the Modern World* (London: Penguin, 2000).

Porter, Roy and Teich, Mikuláš (eds), *The Enlightenment in National Context* (Cambridge: Cambridge University Press, 1981).

Purcell, Sarah J., *Sealed With Blood: War, Sacrifice, and Memory in Revolutionary America* (Philadelphia: University of Pennsylvania Press, 2002).

Raphael, D. Daiches, *The Moral Sense* (London: Oxford University Press, 1947).

Rediker, Marcus, *Between the Devil and the Deep Blue Sea: Merchant Seamen, Pirates, and the Anglo-American Maritime World* (Cambridge: Cambridge University Press, 1987).

Reid-Maroney, Nina, *Philadelphia's Enlightenment: Kingdom of Christ, Empire of Reason* (Westport, Ct.: Greenwood Press 2001).

Riley, Woodbridge, *American Philosophy, the Early Schools* (New York: Dodd Mead, 1907).

Robbins, Caroline, *The Eighteenth-Century Commonwealthman* (Cambridge, Mass.: Harvard University Press, 1959).

Robertson, John, 'The Enlightenment Above National Context: Political Economy in Eighteenth-Century Scotland and Naples', *Historical Journal*, 40 (1997): 667–97.

Robertson, John, *The Case for Enlightenment: Scotland and Naples 1680–1760* (Cambridge: Cambridge University Press, 2005).

Rothschild, Emma, *Economic Sentiments: Adam Smith, Condorcet, and the Enlightenment* (Cambridge, Mass.: Harvard University Press, 2001).

Rothschild, Emma, 'Global Commerce and the Question of Sovereignty in the Eighteenth-Century Provinces', *Modern Intellectual History*, vol. 1, (2004): 1–25.

Rowe, William, *Thomas Reid on Freedom and Morality* (Ithaca, NY: Cornell University Press, 1991).

Rubin, Louis D. Jr, 'Introduction: "The Great American Joke"', in *The Comic Imagination in American Literature*, Louis D. Rubin Jr (ed.) (Washington, DC: United States Information Agency, 1977), pp. 3–15.

Ryan, Tom, '"Le Président des Terres Australes": Charles de Brosses and the French Enlightenment Beginnings of Oceanic Anthropology', *Journal of Pacific History*, 37 (2002), 157–86.

Said, Edward, *Orientalism* (London: Routledge, 1978).

Sanford, Charles L. (ed.), *Benjamin Franklin and the American Character* (Boston, 1955).

Setser, Vernon G., *The Commercial Reciprocity Policy of the United States* (Philadelphia: University of Pennsylvania Press, 1937).

Schaffer, Simon, 'Golden Means: Assay Instruments and the Geography of Precision in the Guinea Trade', in Marie-Noëlle Bourguet, Christian Licoppe and H. Otto Sibum (eds), *Instruments, Travel and Science: Itineraries of Precision from the Seventeenth to the Twentieth Century* (London: Routledge, 2002).

Schneider, Herbert W., *A History of American Philosophy* (New York: Columbia University Press, 1946).

Schutz, John A., 'Pownall, Thomas', in John A. Garraty and Mark C. Carnes (eds), *American National Biography* (24 vols, New York and Oxford: Oxford University Press, 1999).

Schmidt, George, *The Old Time College President* (New York: Columbia University Press, 1930).

Schmidt, Leigh Eric, *Holy Fairs: Scottish Communions and American Revivals in the Early Modern Period* (Princeton: Princeton University Press, 1989).

Schoen, Brian, 'The Fragile Fabric of Union: The Cotton South, Federal Politics, and the Atlantic World, 1783–1861' (Ph.D. diss., Virginia, 2003).

Schui, F. 'Prussia's "Trans-oceanic Moment": the Creation of the Prussian Asiatic Trade Company in 1750', *Historical Journal* 49 (2006): 143–160.

Semmel, Bernard, *The Liberal Ideal and the Demons of Empire: Theories of Imperialism from Adam Smith to Lenin* (Baltimore: Johns Hopkins University Press, 1993).

Semmel, Bernard, *The Rise of Free Trade Imperialism; Classical Political Economy, The Empire of Free Trade and Imperialism 1750–1850* (Cambridge: Cambridge University Press, 1970).

Sher, Richard B. 'Witherspoon's *Dominion of Providence* and the Scottish Jeremiad Tradition', in *Scotland and America in the Age of the Enlightenment*, Richard B. Sher and Jeffrey R. Smitten (eds) (Edinburgh: Edinburgh University Press, 1990), 46–64.

Simpson, David, *Romanticism, Nationalism, and the Revolt against Theory* (Chicago: University of Chicago Press, 1993).

Skinner, Andrew S., *A System of Social Science: Papers Relating to Adam Smith*, 2nd ed. (Oxford: Oxford University Press, 1996).

Sloan, Douglas, *The Scottish Enlightenment and the American College Ideal* (New York: Teacher's College Press, 1971).

Smith, Bernard, *European Vision and the South Pacific, 1768–1850: A Study in the History of Art and Ideas* (Sydney: Harper and Row, 1985).

Smith, Bernard, *Imagining the Pacific: In the Wake of the Cook Voyages* (New Haven: Yale University Press, 1992).

Smith, Crosbie, and Agar, Jon (eds), *Making Space for Science: Territorial Themes in the Making of Knowledge* (London: Macmillan, 1998).

Smith, Diana C. F., 'The Progress of the *Orcades* Survey, with Biographical Notes on Murdoch Mackenzie Senior (1712–1790)', *Annals of Science*, 44 (1987): 277–88.

Smith, Neil, *American Empire. Roosevelt's Geographer and the Prelude to Globalization* (Berkeley: University of California Press, 2003).

Smith, Wilson, *Professors and Public Ethics: Studies of the Northern Moral Philosophers* (Ithaca, NY: Cornell University Press, 1956).

Sorrenson, Richard, 'The Ship as a Scientific Instrument in the Eighteenth Century', *Osiris*, 11 (1996): 221–36.

Stark, Suzanne J., *Women aboard Ship in the Age of Sail* (Annapolis: Naval Institute Press, 1996).

Stern, Julia A., *The Plight of Feeling: Sympathy and Dissent in the Early American Novel* (Chicago: University of Chicago Press, 1997).

Stewart, Larry, 'Global Pillage: Science, Commerce and Empire', in Roy Porter (ed.), *The Cambridge History of Science. Volume 4: Eighteenth-Century Science* (Cambridge: Cambridge University Press, 2003).

Stohlman, Martha Lou Lemmon, *John Witherspoon, Parson, Politician, Patriot* (Philadelphia: Westminster Press, 1974).

Strugnell, Anthony, 'Raynal, Guillaume-Thomas', in Alan Kors *et al*. (eds), *Encyclopedia of the Enlightenment* (4 vols, Oxford: Oxford University Press, 2003).

Tait, L. Gordon, *The Piety of John Witherspoon: Pew, Pulpit, and Public Forum* (Louisville, Ky: Geneva Press, 2001).

Taussig, F. W., *The Tariff History of the United States*, 7th ed. (New York: G. P. Putnam's Sons, 1923).

Tave, Stuart, *The Amiable Humorist: A Study in the Comic Theory and Criticism of the Eighteenth and Early Nineteenth Centuries* (Chicago: University of Chicago Press, 1960).

Tenney, Tabitha Gilman, *Female Quixotism*: *Exhibited in the Romantic Opinions and Extravagant Adventures of Dorcasina Sheldon*, Jean Nienkamp and Andrea Collins (eds); foreword Cathy N. Davidson (New York and Oxford: Oxford University Press, 1992).

Thompson, E. P., *The Making of the English Working Class* (New York: Pantheon, 1964).

Thornton, John K., *Africa and Africans and the Making of the Atlantic World, 1400– 1800* (Cambridge: Cambridge University Press, 1998).

Tompkins, Jane , *Sensational Designs: The Cultural Work of American Fiction, 1790–1860* (Oxford: Oxford University Press, 1985).

Tribe, Keith, *Strategies of Economic Order: German Economic Discourse* (Cambridge: Cambridge University Press, 1995).

Trilling, Lionel, *The Liberal Imagination: Essays on Literature and Society* (New York: Viking, 1950).

Trumpener, Katie, *Bardic Nationalism: The Romantic Novel and the British Empire* (Princeton: Princeton University Press, 1997).

Van Doren, Carl, *Benjamin Franklin* (New York: Viking, 1938).

Venturi, F., *The End of the Old Regime in Europe, 1768–1776. The First Crisis*. Translated R. Burr Litchfield (Princeton: Princeton University Press, 1989).

Ward, W. R., *The Protestant Evangelical Awakening* (Cambridge: Cambridge University Press, 1992).

Warner, Michael, *The Letters of the Republic: Publication and the Public Sphere in Eighteenth-Century America* (Cambridge, Mass.: Harvard University Press, 1990).

Watts, Edward, *Writing and Postcolonialism in the Early Republic* (Charlottesville and London: University Press of Virginia, 1998).

Weber, Klaus, *Deutsche Kaufleute im Atlantikhandel 1680–1830. Unternehmen und Familien in Hamburg, Cadiz und Bordeaux* (München: C. H. Beck, 2004).

Wells, Colin, *The Devil & Doctor Dwight: Satire and Theology in the Early American Republic* (Chapel Hill: University of North Carolina Press, 2002).

Wertenbaker, Thomas J., 'John Witherspoon, Father of American Presbyterianism', in *Lives of Eighteen from Princeton*, Willard Thorp (ed.) (Princeton: Princeton University Press, 1946), 68–85.

Wickwire, Franklin and Mary Wickwire, *Cornwallis: The Imperial Years* (Chapel Hill: University of North Carolina Press, 1980).

Williams, Glyndwr, 'The Pacific: Exploration and Exploitation', in Peter J. Marshall (ed.), *The Oxford History of the British Empire: Volume 2. The Eighteenth Century* (Oxford: Oxford University Press, 1998).

Williams, Raymond, 'Base and Superstructure in Marxist Cultural Theory', *New Left Review* 82 (Nov–Dec, 1973).

Williams, Stanley T., *The Spanish Background of American Literature* (2 vols, New Haven, CT: Yale University Press, 1955).

Wills, Garry, *Inventing America: Jefferson's Declaration of Independence* (New York: Random House, 1978).

Withers, Charles W. J., *Geography, Science and National Identity: Scotland since 1520* (Cambridge: Cambridge University Press, 2001).

Withers, Charles W. J., 'Toward a Historical Geography of Enlightenment in Scotland', in Paul Wood (ed.), *The Scottish Enlightenment: Essays in Reinterpretation* (Rochester: Rochester University Press, 2000).

Withers, Charles W. J., 'Mapping', in Alan Kors *et al.* (eds), *Encyclopedia of the Enlightenment* (4 vols, New York and Oxford: Oxford University Press, 2003).

Withers, Charles W. J., 'Science At Sea: Charting the Gulf Stream in the Late Enlightenment', *Interdisciplinary Science Reviews*, 31 (2006): 58–76.

Withers, Charles W. J., *Placing the Enlightenment: Thinking Geographically about The Age of Reason* (Chicago: University of Chicago Press, 2007).

Withington, Ann Fairfax, *Toward a More Perfect Union: Virtue and the Formation of American Republics* (New York: Oxford University Press, 1991).

Wood, Gordon S., *The Americanization of Benjamin Franklin* (New York: Penguin, 2004).

Wood, Gordon S., *The Creation of the American Republic, 1776–1787* (Chapel Hill: University of North Carolina Press, 1969).

Wood, Gordon S., *The Radicalism of the American Revolution* (New York: Knopf, 1992).

Young, Alfred F. *The Shoemaker and the Tea Party: Memory and the American Revolution* (Boston: Beacon Press, 1999).

Index